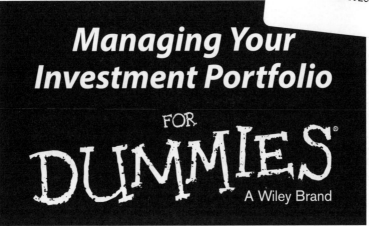

Managing Your Investment Portfolio

FOR DUMMIES®

A Wiley Brand

by David Stevenson

FOR DUMMIES®
A Wiley Brand

Managing Your Investment Portfolio For Dummies®

Published by: **John Wiley & Sons, Ltd.,** The Atrium, Southern Gate, Chichester, www.wiley.com

This edition first published 2013

© 2013 John Wiley & Sons, Ltd, Chichester, West Sussex.

Registered office

John Wiley & Sons Ltd, The Atrium, Southern Gate, Chichester, West Sussex, PO19 8SQ, United Kingdom

Contents at a Glance

Table of Contents

Part IV: Delving into More Specialist Techniques (with a Little Help) 229

Chapter 13: Advanced Investing in Commodities: Sharks and Rocket Scientists 231

Chapter 14: Investing in Emerging-Market Equities and Currencies 253

Introduction

・・・

*I*nvestment can be a scary business, with all those self-proclaimed masters of the universe wielding ultimate control over your pension and long-term savings pot. They're a worrying bunch and their ability to wreak havoc on the global financial markets and livelihoods worries more than just the Occupy Wall Street mob. Plus, the media doesn't help this sense of foreboding with (scaremongering) stories about unseen powers taking control of people's financial futures: global financial crises, big blowouts and meltdowns hog the headlines, scaring the wits out of even the smartest private investor.

But here's the good news: investing can be a rewarding pursuit . . . honest! As a humble private investor you can take control of your financial future, make profits and control the downside risks by leaving behind that fear of big scary markets. Smart, sophisticated investors like yourself can and do build successful and robust investment portfolios, full of ideas that help sustain year-on-year profits.

In this book I show you the route to becoming a more proficient, advanced investor, helping you figure out how to build a well-rounded, thought-through investment plan: in other words, a strong, diversified portfolio of financial assets. My central insight – a call to action if you like – is that private investors need to think a little bit more like the hedge funds of this world. Don't worry, I'm not implying that you sell the family hatchback and invest in a hedge-fund manager style Porsche. I mean that the hedge-fund community is full of smart people with useful information to pass on to you. Their ideas about obtaining absolute returns in all market conditions, controlling the downside, managing risks and understanding trends are simply good, old-fashioned commonsense.

I hope that this book acts as your guide to this advanced form of investing. It brazenly swipes ideas from the hedge-fund masters, acknowledges their failings and weaknesses, and attempts to put the best ideas in a practical context that you can use within your portfolio on a daily basis.

About This Book

Plenty of books about investing promise a magic formula. These get-rich-quick manuals offer some allegedly quick formula or special set of measures that instantly illuminates the darkest corners of the global investment world. Read those instant-promise books if you like, but you may as well just visit the horse races! Instead, I encourage you to be disciplined, careful, cautious and to think like a professional hedge-fund manager. This book doesn't promise to make you rich overnight, but it may help preserve some of your hard-earned wealth by helping you to think intelligently about the downsides of investing and the need to stay disciplined when looking for the upside.

This book may even encourage you to introduce new strategies that painstakingly produce relatively steady profits on a regular basis. After all, that's what some of the most successful investors in the world do – many of them hedge-fund managers. They concentrate on getting the small things right, on absolutely making sure that a simple investment insight works like clockwork on a regular basis. They grind out small, regular, steady profits by making sure that they don't have too much at risk in the frightening financial markets. Despite their reputations, hedge-fund managers are frequently cautious, careful types.

This book reveals some of their tried-and-trusted techniques and ideas. It talks about hedging your downside, using options to produce an income from volatile markets and working out which company or share constitutes 'good value'. In sum, this book is about preserving capital and having modest aspirations for making steady positive returns over the long term.

What You're Not to Read

I heard a rumour that not all readers read every page of every book that they buy. This shocking revelation doesn't leave me in despair, though. I realise that you're a busy person and that every once in a while a more entertaining activity may present itself while you're reading this book.

To help manage this painful neglect (!), this book is designed so that you can just dip in and out; I even highlight certain sections that you don't have to read. Sidebars (those grey boxes of text), for instance, give you a more in-depth look at a certain topic, but aren't essential to you understanding the rest of the book. Feel free to read or skip them. Similarly, you can a pass over the text that appears besides the Technical Stuff icons if you prefer. This technical material is interesting and may get you ahead of the pack, but you can still come away with everything you need without reading this text. Honestly, I won't be offended if you quietly skip over them and read the 'best' bits!

Conventions Used in This Book

I do my best to make this book as easy-to-read and pain-free as possible. For starters, I make use of the following conventions:

✔ Italic type indicates new terms that I define nearby.

✔ `Monofont` is used for web addresses. The Internet bring lots of facts and figures easily to hand, and so I direct you to many useful websites.

✔ The shaded grey boxes of text are filled with interesting but not essential information.

In general examples that require a gender, I use female in odd-numbered chapters and male in even-numbered chapters.

Foolish Assumptions

I assume a few things about you as follows (sorry for being presumptuous!):

✔ You're a relatively advanced, smart investor who has a portfolio with lots of different working aspects in it.

✔ You're already invested in shares and bonds and willing to experiment by looking at more adventurous investment ideas and *asset classes* (new investment categories).

✔ You're suspicious of the pointy-head types that you regularly see on TV pontificating about the secrets of their own success. Like all good cynical investors you sneakily concede that they may have some insights that you can learn from. But you want to check their ideas against the strategies outlined in this book and work out for yourself what's bravado and what's truly insightful.

✔ You're ready to think about investing in a new way that involves minimising your downside risk, riding the volatility of markets (to your advantage) and being modest about your investment aspirations. Gains of 4X5 per cent annually, year on year, without big losses, are more appealing to you than one fantastic year of amazing 50 per cent gains and then a following painful year of 70 per cent losses.

How This Book Is Organised

The information is laid out in a straightforward format. The six logical parts contain self-contained chapters that any investor interested in shares can follow easily.

Part I: It's All about Portfolios

The two chapters in this part are all about the basics. Chapter 1 explains why a diversified portfolio is so important and Chapter 2 shows you how your own attitude towards risk needs to influence the investments you plan to stuff in your portfolio. In particular, watch out for the idea of adjusting your mix of assets based on your long-term savings goals . . . and your age!

Part II: Picking the Strategies for You

Hedge funds contain some of the smartest people on the planet, who spend their time figuring out how the markets work and what investors have to do to maximise their upside and minimise their downside. This clutch of chapters digs deep into hedge-fund land, looking in Chapter 3 at core techniques and strategies and in Chapter 4 at how real world economies affect markets and why volatility matters. Chapter 5 covers the vital role that alternative assets, such as commodities and currencies, play in building a diversified portfolio, and Chapter 6 contains a warning that hedge funds can be expensive and not always rewarding to you. Buyer beware!

Part III: Thinking and Acting Like a Hedgie: Simple Strategies You Can Employ Yourself

Ask professional hedge-fund managers what exactly they do, and how, and you're likely to hear procrastination and general 'clouding of the air': 'it's far too difficult to explain to an outsider like you' is the common, general thrust of the response. But working out how hedge funds run their investment process isn't nightmarish or incredibly complicated, although the subject does have its more arcane and technical bits involving super computers that defy simple explanations.

But most hedge-fund investors don't rely on complex algorithms. They use fairly straightforward, easy-to-understand techniques that advanced investors can copy, as I describe in this part. Chapter 7 dishes the dirt on the longing to go short (as opposed to getting caught short trying to go long!), Chapter 8 discusses arbitrage (using price differences to profit) and Chapter 9 investigates the competing merits of value versus growth investing. In Chapter 10, I introduce you to using leverage (borrowing to invest) to increase your returns, in Chapter 11 to structured investments and in Chapter 12 to the mysterious art of shaking things up via shareholder activism.

Part IV: Delving Into More Specialist Techniques (with a Little Help)

In this part, I put some of the strategic thinking to the test in the real world of specialist investing.

Chapter 13 describes investing in commodities from gold to oil, Chapter 14 dips into the emerging markets of the developing world and Chapter 15 takes in the big economic picture with macro-investing.

Part V: Tools of the Trade: Useful Instruments

Hedge-fund investors are discerning about the instruments (the funds, options and betting products) they buy to make money on the markets. These sophisticated financial buyers have educated the marketplace and encouraged a huge wave of innovation, helping to fuel the rise of exchange-traded funds (the subject of Chapter 16) and spread betting on the direction of the markets, which I describe in Chapter 17.

In the right hands, backed up by sensible strategies, these innovative financial products and structures can make a huge difference, but you absolutely need to know when and how to use these products.

Part VI: The Part of Tens

This part is the *For Dummies* hallmark – the Part of Tens. These chapters give you a crash course in wealth preservation (Chapter 18) and a primer on strategies for making money that have withstood the test of time (Chapter 19).

Icons Used in This Book

To help you navigate your way around this book, I use the following icons to highlight certain types of text.

This icon flags a particular bit of practical advice that may give you an edge over other investors.

I use this icon to remind you to stash this information in your memory, whether you're new to investing or an old pro.

Pay special attention to this icon, because the advice can prevent headaches, heartbreaks and financial woes.

Throughout this book I aim to avoid technical text or jargon where possible, but sometimes such bits and pieces can help. This icon indicates more involved or complicated information, such as equations and background material, that you can skip if you want to without any harm coming to your investing!

I place this icon besides detailed descriptions of specific investment approaches. Often this text comprises a simple imagined scenario that walks you through a strategy easily and clearly.

Where to Go from Here

You can read this book in whatever way and in any order you like. If you want to get straight down to business, flip to the three top-ten chapters in Part V for immediate tips and follow the cross-references to whatever chapter grabs your fancy.

If you want the basics, be conventional and start with Parts I and II. They set out the ground rules for a more sophisticated kind of investing. Parts III and IV contain a wide variety of different strategies and not everything is going to light your particular fire, but if you read the first few chapters you're more likely to know what kind of investor you are and what's going to work for you.

After reading a few chapters, you'll feel a little more confident about testing out new ideas and advanced strategies and I hope become a smarter, more sophisticated investor who understands how to gear up your returns and minimise your downside.

Happy reading and I wish you a stable and profitable investment future.

Part I
It's All about Portfolios

getting started with Portfolios

In this part . . .

- ✔ Understand the value of creating a well-balanced investment portfolio and how to protect your money.

- ✔ Learn about university endowments and hedge-funds and assess whether these are good investment options for you.

- ✔ Examine your risk/return trade-off and select the investments that are right for you.

- ✔ Further develop your portfolio by considering more sophisticated investment strategies.

Chapter 1

Introducing Great Opportunities for Advanced Investors

Most investors follow a similar path when they start out: they invest, make mistakes and lose money, but they learn lessons from the process. With the passage of time, they develop a sensible, balanced style of investment that works for them, somewhere on the spectrum from ultra conservative to wildly adventurous.

In this introductory chapter on investment ideas for serious investors, I describe some techniques, stress the importance of creating a well-diversified portfolio, focus on university endowments in particular because of these investment funds' proven ability to deliver outstanding returns in difficult markets, and say briefly why you can learn from hedge-fund best practice.

Investing is all about building a diversified portfolio full of different ideas, strategies and *asset classes* (commodities, bonds, shares and so on).

Building a Balanced Portfolio

The basic building block for any investor is the humble *portfolio*, a long list of assets held within your stock-broking or investing account.

I hope that you're *not* invested in just one asset class to the exclusion of everything else, such as being invested in only one share or bond. If you are, I'm going to do everything in my power to convince you to do otherwise! The reason? Because you reduce risk when you diversify your portfolio.

Thinking about asset classes

Portfolio thinking starts with the idea of *diversification*, which means including different asset classes (bonds, stocks, commodities) within one portfolio.

An *asset class* is a broad grouping of investment opportunities that share a number of key characteristics. All government bonds, for instance, are largely similar in structure, as are stocks or shares – ditto for commodities. These asset classes represent broad buckets (groups) of opportunities available to you as an investor. Of course, thousands of different individual shares, bonds and investment products exist within each bucket, some of which are worth your consideration, but most of which you need to avoid with a lengthy barge pole.

Diving into a world of choice

The huge variety of asset classes and their contents means that investment life extends beyond a few big individual blue chip shares (names such as Apple or Google, BP or Exxon) or lending money to Uncle Sam through the massive US bond programme.

You have a world of choice available and I suggest that you make sure that your list of potential opportunities is long, even if your actual investment actions are relatively uncomplicated and succinct.

The key to investment success is to juggle these different buckets that comprise different asset classes in a sensible and intelligent fashion, which entails thinking long and hard about diversification. Luckily academics have done much of the heavy lifting for you and they've come up with some smart ideas about how you build a diversified portfolio of assets.

Dozens and dozens of different asset classes exist, but in essence you need to start with the three main groups:

- ✔ **Bonds:** Includes everything from lower-risk government securities to higher-risk corporate bonds issued by so-called risky companies.

- ✔ **Equities:** Includes stocks and shares. But within this simple definition is a world of different national markets (the US is the largest, followed by the UK, Europe and Japan), regional markets and even global markets (a composite of all the national markets). In addition, certain equity-based asset classes cut across these definitions to focus on particular sectors (energy companies, for instance) as well as themes such as value versus growth investing (the subject of Chapter 9).

- ✔ **Alternative assets:** Indicates the huge range of investment ideas that don't quite fit in the bonds and equity buckets, from hedge funds dabbling in esoteric commodity strategies (of the sort I discuss in Chapter 13) to forestry funds.

The sensible, diversified investor looks to invest in the full range of assets. No matter what your style, at the very least you need to consider investing in items from all three broad asset classes.

Diversifying Your Investments

Many investors intrinsically understand the concept of not putting all your eggs in one basket and probably practise a primitive form of diversification. Academic economists have taken this commonsense notion and turned it into the noble idea of *modern portfolio theory*.

I'm not going to bore you to death with a lengthy exposition of the ins and outs of this very specialised academic field. Suffice to say that most investors have three building blocks that comprise their total return:

- ✔ **Risk-free return:** Usually the rate of return you get from cash.

- ✔ **Return from *beta*:** The return you get above the risk-free rate of return from holding an asset class such as shares or a market. So if the risk-free rate of return is 2 per cent and you buy a tracker for the UK FTSE All Share index that gives you 8 per cent per year, your beta is 6 per cent.

- ✔ **Return from *alpha*:** The value added by a financial manager that's derived by the person moving away from the beta. Most managers aren't very good at adding this alpha, but they continue to charge you extra in terms of fees regardless!

Be careful with the distinction between beta and alpha, especially as regards fund managers. After a good year in which the market's overall value has greatly increased, you see many fund managers trumpeting their own individual success. This blatant mis-marketing frequently confuses the beta of a market (the overall return from investing in a market) with the alpha skills of the fund manager (that is, what special thing the person did that resulted in the higher return).

With alpha, look for consistent outperformance by a fund manager, not just one year's good result followed by endless average performances.

Mixing and matching different betas: Correlation

The concept of diversification means that lots of different kinds of markets and assets (bonds mixed with shares and, say, an alternative asset such as commodities) can give you lots of different betas, and if you're lucky those different betas don't move as one; that is, they aren't correlated as they jump up and down in value. Thus if equities go down bonds may rise in value along with, say, commodities such as gold. Mixing different betas therefore gives you added benefits and improves returns.

Correlation is a key term that you hear bandied about in the discussion on portfolios and it's connected to how two different asset classes move in relationship with each other:

- ✔ **Positive correlation:** If two different asset classes have a positive correlation of 1, they move as one. When one goes up, the other goes up as well. Similarly, when one goes down, so does the other.

- ✔ **Uncorrelated:** If two different asset classes are uncorrelated (have a correlation of zero), no relationship exists and they move independently of each other.

- ✔ **Negative correlation:** If the different asset classes have a negative correlation, one moves up as the other moves down.

In an ideal situation your diversified portfolio has some assets that are positively correlated with each other (perhaps emerging-market stocks and developed-world stocks, which I discuss in Chapter 14), some uncorrelated (commodities and bonds) and some negatively correlated (bonds and shares; I cover this relationship in the discussion on volatility and economic cycles in Chapters 4 and 15). The key is to mix asset classes with different correlations.

Be careful about putting in your portfolio lots of diversified assets that are very closely correlated with each other. For instance, watch out for lots of apparently diversified assets that all go up or down as one because they have the same sensitivity and therefore increase your risk.

Consider a portfolio made up of Chinese shares, mining company shares quoted on the London stock market and bonds issued by large Canadian banks. On paper, you seem to have a great deal of diversification within this portfolio, but in reality Chinese shares and UK-based mining shares tend to move in a similar way because in effect you're buying into the global business cycle and its effect on industrial production in China. And guess which country has a heavy exposure to mining and whose banks have lent substantial amounts of money to the mining sector? That's right . . . Canada and its banks. The bottom line is to think intelligently about diversification to ensure that your portfolio not only includes different asset classes but also includes a balance between positively, negatively and uncorrelated assets.

Combining assets and betas

Economists are so smitten with the idea of diversification – some call it the diversification *premium* – that they suggest it's the one free lunch left in investing. Although in recent years even that seems to come at a rather hefty price as markets begin to move as one during periods of stress.

The prime mover in the academic field of diversification analysis was economist Harry Markowitz, who showed how investors can combine different asset classes and betas *without increasing risk*.

Later economists and analysts have taken Markowitz's ideas and fleshed them out. The fund manager at Yale University's endowment fund David Swensen, for instance, spent decades running hugely diversified portfolios investing in everything from forests to private equity funds and hedge funds. I discuss some of his accumulated learning in the later section 'Investing in University Endowment Funds'.

Thinking like an asset allocator

In 1986, three leading academics looked at what really contributes towards the performance of a portfolio. These three wise men were called Brinson, Singer and Beebower, and in a seminal paper they looked at fund managers' market-timing skills, their ability to pick shares and their ability to diversify assets. They studied just under 100 of the largest pension plans in the US over a ten-year period, with portfolio sizes reaching to US$3 billion.

They discovered that a massive 91 per cent of investment return was explainable by careful use of diversification and the use of varying asset classes and markets over time. In fact, the study found that traditional and often much trumpeted active fund-management skills such as *timing* (making decisions to buy and sell based on predictions of future market prices) and *stock picking* (selecting stocks based on a set of criteria assumed to indicate the stock's growing value) produced *negative* returns over time after adjustments for risk.

The bottom line? Don't bother picking individual shares or trying to time the market, just allocate across different asset classes in an intelligent, diversified manner.

Including alternative assets in your portfolio

Including alternative assets, such as currencies and commodities, in a well-balanced portfolio can improve returns (flip to Chapter 5 for all about alternative-asset investing). A study by research firm Ibbotson Associates discovered that the average improvement in returns from these uncorrelated assets was worth 1.33 per cent per year. The company also found that asset allocation and active diversification accounted for 81.4 per cent of the monthly variation in balanced return funds.

Deciding how much diversification is enough

Accepting that diversification is a good thing is great, but then you need to apply this piece of wisdom within your portfolio.

Back in September 2005, US analysts Paul Merriman and Richard Buck attempted to resolve the question of how to go about building 'one portfolio for life'. Using the database of Dimensional Fund Advisers, the researchers looked at returns between 1955 and 2004, a 50-year period that included lots of *bear* (downwards), *bull* (upwards) and sideways tracking markets. They looked at three potential portfolios, each of which produced dramatically different results:

- ✔ **Option 1 – S&P 500 tracker:** Annual return of 10.9 per cent.

- ✔ **Option 2 – 60 per cent in the S&P 500 Index and 40 per cent in five-year Treasury notes:** Annual return of 9.6 per cent.

- ✔ **Option 3 – As option 2 but with the equity split four ways between US-based large-capitalised stocks, large-cap value stocks, small-cap stocks and small-cap value stocks:** Best annual return by far. 'Over the 50 years in our study,' Merriman and Buck report, 'this diversified 60/40 portfolio produced a return of 11.4 per cent, with a maximum *drawdown* (loss) of 25 per cent.'

Putting a figure on the benefits

Diversification can work wonders if done properly, especially if you're willing to stack up your portfolio with different types of asset classes. One US-based financial thinker called Geoff Considine has even gone so far as to put a number on the value of the diversification premium: 2–2.5 per cent per year.

No fixed rules apply to how many different asset classes to put in your portfolio, but certainly consider having some shares, some bonds and some alternative assets (especially hedge funds and hedge-fund strategies). If you're a cautious investor, focus on bonds; if you're more adventurous, put more money into shares.

Going global

Merriman and Bucks's original analysis (in the preceding section) looked only at US investments, but they suspected that benefits come from investing internationally as well.

Therefore, they looked at year-by-year returns from 1970 to 2004 for an investor using diversified option 3 but where the 60 per cent equity segment was split: 50 per cent into US-based stocks of varying sizes (large-cap stocks, large-cap value stocks, small-cap stocks and small-cap value stocks) and 50 per cent into international stocks (split five ways, to include large-cap stocks, large-cap value stocks, small-cap stocks, small-cap value stocks and stocks in emerging markets).

Returns increased by more than 40-fold! So the more you diversify internationally, the greater your potential returns.

Investing in University Endowment Funds

The research into diversification outlined in the earlier section 'Diversifying Your Investments' produces three simple but compelling recommendations:

- ✓ Think global.
- ✓ Think across different asset classes.
- ✓ Mix and match different options such as bonds and shares in varying combinations.

Seems simple enough, but in the real world you're faced with a massive and baffling array of options. What do you do when confronted by thousands of different investment strategies, ideas and products? Step forward the subject of this section – a rather unconventional source of wisdom for advanced investors called *university investment endowment funds*, which have an open-ended, long-term commitment to provide funding for institutions that are in many cases hundreds of years old.

Considering the university endowment model

Perhaps *the* single most successful investment model of the last decade, university-based investment funds have pioneered a raft of new strategies that continue to deliver exceptional returns in incredibly difficult markets. Leading institutions such as the Yale University endowment – managed by the charismatic US investor David Swenson – have developed a very distinctive approach that focuses on the extensive use of alternative assets as well as on the use of hard assets (think of oil and natural gas, gold and other precious metals, and real estate and farmland – assets that have intrinsic value) that may protect these august institutions against the ravages of future inflationary pressures.

The long-term focus of university endowments, however, doesn't mean that they don't also need to derive a generous income in the here and now – cost inflation at large US- and UK-based institutions (think institutions such as Oxford and Cambridge) is unrelenting and a limit applies to what governments or students can afford to pay through fees.

This focus on protection against inflation has made the large endowments keen to invest in hard assets that have inflationary protection – Yale, for instance, is a major investor in New Zealand forestry plantations while the large UK universities such as Cambridge own extensive agricultural land banks.

University endowments are also determined to keep costs to the minimum, running their own in-house investment advisory units and hiring expert, outside managers only at low rates for limited periods of time.

 I emphasise this powerful lesson throughout this book: keep costs to a minimum and don't let professional money managers rip you off with the promise of lots of extra returns!

Traditionally this focus on cost-effective, inflation-plus returns would have prompted these large institutions to focus on high-yielding mainstream shares. After all, shares are the only asset class in the last 100 years to consistently deliver real returns over a few per cent per year after net costs. Yet the endowments at Harvard and Yale have developed portfolios that look very different. Their portfolios are phenomenally diversified, with all manner of alternative assets including land, forestry, private equity and hedge funds, and a surprisingly small amount of direct equity exposure.

This explicit focus on a diversified portfolio of very differing asset classes delivered remarkable returns (see Table 1-1). The top five endowments in the US (with assets for each endowment of more than US$10 billion) returned 9.7 per cent per year for the last ten years to the end of June 2011. This is 5.1

per cent greater than the returns of a traditional US 60 per cent equity/40 per cent bond portfolio for a private investor, which returned just 4.6 per cent annually. (I describe these 60/40 portfolios in the earlier section 'Deciding how much diversification is enough'.)

Table 1-1	Ten-Year Returns by Endowment Fund Size to June 2011	
Portfolio	*10-year Annualised Return as Percentage*	*Alternative Assets as Percentage of Total*
Typical US equity (60%)/ bond (40%) portfolio	4.6	0
Average US endowment	5.6	53
Top-5 endowment funds with assets under management of more than US$10 billion	9.7	69
Harvard and Yale (the super-endowments)	9.8	69

Source: Frontier Investment Management – more details at http://www.frontierim.com/asset-allocation-driving-returns-research.aspx

Seeking alternatives

At the core of the endowment model is a relatively simple idea: diversifying your range of asset classes beyond the conventional shares and bonds. Many US endowment fund managers have devised a strategy that involves buying not only US stocks, but also a wide range of bonds, lots and lots of foreign stocks, plus a heavy dose of alternative assets that aren't highly correlated with the stock market (see Chapter 5 for details).

Whereas ordinary investors with a standard 60/40 split of assets (shares and bonds) have almost no exposure to alternatives, the big endowments invest a huge proportion of their funds in these alternative assets, which include everything from private equity to hedge funds. Table 1-2 shows the major asset classes in the largest university endowment funds. Notice the heavy exposure to hedge funds, private equity, real estate and commodities – most ordinary investors probably struggle to have more than a few per cent of their portfolio in each or all of these alternatives, but the endowments typically hold the *majority* of their assets in these alternatives.

Table 1-2	Top 20 US Endowment Funds by Assets
Asset Class	*Proportion of Fund (%)*
Private equity	20
Global equities	21
Hedge funds	22
Global bonds	10
Commodities	9
Real estate	10
Emerging equities	6

Source: Frontier Investment Management and various US University Annual Reports

Digging a bit deeper into the model's core investment ideas

These huge funds have adopted a number of core investing ideas:

- ✔ Diversify, diversify and diversify! The institutions have lots and lots of alternatives in their portfolios.

- ✔ Maintain an absolute global focus with a major shift away from local currency assets into developed-world markets. Not one of the major US or UK endowments invests more than 50 per cent of its assets in local currency assets (check out Chapter 5 for all about currencies).

- ✔ Keep bond investments (and especially gilts) to a very low level.

- ✔ Invest heavily in hard assets that provide protection against inflation – that means investing in land, residential and commercial property, and energy-based assets.

- ✔ Hold a diversified portfolio, avoid attempts at market timing and fine-tune allocations at extreme valuations.

- ✔ Use outside managers for all but the most routine or indexed investments. This outside manager must be expert in diversifying complex portfolios and using highly sophisticated investment strategies, areas of expertise that may be beyond the purview of in-house university staff cash managers.

University endowment funds use only those outside fund managers who add 'value' – called alpha in the trade, as I explain in the earlier section

'Diversifying Your Investments' – and make sure that you pick the very best.

✔ Hold relatively low levels of cash with a standard range between 5–10 per cent.

Remembering that the endowment model doesn't always work

The radical approach to investing embodied by the endowment model has been phenomenally successful but it doesn't make money in all markets, especially when absolutely everything, except perceived safe assets such as gilts, start tumbling in price.

In 2008, for instance, many of the large US endowments saw their funds crash in value. The median decline in return for all endowments to 30 June 2009 was 19 per cent, against a loss of 26.2 per cent for the S&P 500 over the same period. The super-big endowments lost even more money, with Harvard and Yale experiencing 27 per cent and 25 per cent respective declines. (***Note:*** Different from an average, a *median* is the middle value of a series of values arranged in an order of magnitude.)

The problem is the nature of *illiquid assets*; that is, assets that can't be easily or immediately sold, like property, collectibles and, in some cases, giant blocks of stock. Many alternative assets end up investing in strategies and ideas that are relatively illiquid. The big endowments are major investors in illiquid ideas because they can afford to be patient. Similarly, pension funds are willing to invest in more illiquid assets because they don't need to be able to access their funds in a matter of a few days. Private investors can also afford to be patient and invest in illiquid assets, especially if they have a very long-term plan and are willing to ignore day-to-day or month-to-month changes in price.

Illiquid assets can be very dangerous when investors are scared witless and want to keep their money safe in so-called liquid assets such as cash. During panics, illiquid assets are sometimes hit badly in price and then take many months to recover after confidence is restored.

Getting back in the game

The dark days of 2008 are now a relatively dim and distant memory for these large endowments – their recent performance has been exceptional, with Harvard and Yale notching up returns of more than 15 per cent in 2011. Table 1-3 shows that Harvard now has over US$30 billion in assets in its endowment compared to Yale with US$19 billion, although the University of Texas System produced the best results in 2011, with a gain of 22 per cent on its endowment.

Table 1-3	Top US Endowments in 2011		
Rank	*University*	*2011 Funds (US$ billions)*	*Percentage increase over 2010*
1	Harvard	31	15.1
2	Yale	19.3	16.3
3	University of Texas System	17	22
4	Princeton	17	18.95
5	Stanford	16.5	19

In addition, this return to superior performance didn't involve any particular change to what these large funds invest in. Table 1-4 shows that the largest and most successful funds (those over US$1 billion) continue to pump huge amounts of money into alternative assets including hedge funds and private equity funds. The smaller funds (those under US$25 million) tended to leave the largest allocation of their investment money in more traditional assets.

Table 1-4	US Endowment Asset Allocations for Fiscal Year 2011				
Size of Endow- ment	*Domestic Equities (%)*	*Fixed Income (%)*	*International Equities (%)*	*Alternative Strategies (%)*	*Cash or Equivalent (%)*
Large funds (over US$1 billion)	12	9	16	60	3
Smaller funds (under US$25 million)	41	25	14	10	10

Integrating endowment model principles in your own portfolio

The recent return to form for large endowment funds tells you an important fact – over the long term, the endowment model delivers exceptional returns in a relatively stable manner. They do so by using the following techniques:

- ✔ **Use alternatives:** Think out of the box and don't stick just to the standard 60/40 per cent equity/bond mix that I describe earlier in 'Deciding how much diversification is enough'.

- ✔ **Get the best managers:** Make sure that you hunt down the very best managers if you're going to pay for expert advice; otherwise keep things simple, cut costs and use index-tracking funds (including the exchange-traded funds that I cover in Chapter 16).

- ✔ **Be adventurous and think global:** For example, if you're based in the UK don't be overly focused on your home country and sterling.

- ✔ **Think real assets:** Ensure that you have some inflation proofing inside your portfolio by investing in hard assets, like metals, land, and energy sources – assets that tend to be negatively correlated to stocks and bonds (refer to the earlier section 'Mixing and matching different betas: Correlation'.

Although in theory you can apply these principles to any portfolio, no matter how big or small, the truth is that large endowments have huge advantages over mere mortals. For this reason many experts concede that the big endowment funds run strategies that average private investors can't easily copy.

For instance, many successful fund managers only accept money from outfits such as super-big endowments, because those funds are large, stable and for the long term. Some successful fund managers, especially in the private equity space, have also closed their offerings to new money, effectively locking out all but a tiny part of the market. But endowment enthusiasts don't think that you and I should give up, as the next three sections reveal.

David Swenson and Yale

David Swenson of Yale endowment fame (see the earlier section 'Considering the university endowment model') reckons that if you don't have access to his amazing panel of top return-producing fund managers, you shouldn't try to pick individual stocks or pay anyone to do it for you. He's a tireless critic of the mainstream for-profit mutual-fund industry.

Instead, he advocates that private investors should use low-cost index funds as one way of building a diversified portfolio. In his bestselling book

Unconventional Success: A Fundamental Approach to Personal Investment (and later revisions), Swenson maps out a 'well-diversified, equity-oriented portfolio' for private investors.

His current advice is that you create a single portfolio consisting of passive, index-tracking funds that invest in the following:

- ✔ **Domestic (US/UK) stock funds:** 30 per cent
- ✔ **Real estate investment trusts:** 15 per cent
- ✔ **US (or UK) Treasury bonds:** 15 per cent
- ✔ **US (or UK) Treasury inflation-protected securities:** 15 per cent
- ✔ **Foreign developed-market stock funds (such as the EU, Japan, Australia):** 15 per cent
- ✔ **Emerging-market stock funds (Brazil, Russia, India, China, Taiwan, South Korea and the rest of the developing world):** 10 per cent

Mike Azlen and Frontier

Other experts have their own endowment-based portfolio mixes. For instance, UK investor Mike Azlen, based at fund manager Frontier, runs low-cost multi-asset class portfolios that draw on the best ideas of university endowments (see Table 1-5). These varying-risk-based portfolios comprise passively managed funds at a cost of less than 1 per cent per year. In particular Azlen's funds mirror many of the same asset allocations used by Harvard and Yale universities.

Table 1-5	Endowment Index Portfolio: 2011 Asset Allocation
Asset Class	*Proportion of Fund (%)*
Private equity	27
Commodities	13
Global equities	13
Global bonds	10
Real estate	13
Hedge funds	8
Managed futures or CTA hedge funds	8
Emerging-markets equities	6
Emerging-markets bonds	Under 2

Source: Frontier Investment Management

Mebane Faber and Cambrian IM

US-based fund manager and investment writer Mebane Faber – chief investment officer at Cambrian IM – is a fan of the diversified endowment model.

In a recent book with Eric Richardson, *The Ivy Portfolio* (as in the Ivy League of top US universities), Faber outlines what he thinks a private investor's portfolio may look like, with all the building blocks comprised of cheap, low-cost passive tracking funds, such as ETFs (which I discuss in Chapter 16):

- ✔ **Domestic (US/UK) stocks:** 20 per cent
- ✔ **Foreign (non US or UK) stocks:** 20 per cent
- ✔ **Bonds:** 20 per cent
- ✔ **Real estate:** 20 per cent
- ✔ **Commodities:** 20 per cent

Loving Your Hedge-Fund Manager

Preserving your capital is a vital aspect of any investment strategy. Your accumulated long-term savings are the product of many years of hard work and yet they can be destroyed in a matter of weeks, by forces entirely beyond your control. You can always look to earn more or less, but your nest egg or pension fund has to last you for the rest of your life. If that money goes, you have to work a whole lot harder to rebuild your stash of capital, or accept that your twilight years may be blighted by poverty and low levels of income. (For immediate tips on protecting your wealth, visit Chapter 18.)

This gloomy way of thinking leads many investors to a central insight: preservation of capital is a primary consideration. Just as endowments (see the earlier section 'Investing in University Endowment Funds') have to keep funding lecturers' fees and maintaining grand libraries, so you have to keep paying out for your retirement costs.

The idea of capital preservation has found a willing audience within the hedge-fund community. Many of the best professional money managers have built successful careers around the idea of *absolute returns* (making money whether markets rise or fall; see Chapter 2 for more). Of course, cynical observers can easily denigrate successful hedge-fund managers as money vampires looking to impoverish investors through Ponzi schemes, excessive costs and duff trading strategies (I examine hedge-fund criticisms in Chapter 6).

Ponzi schemes are fraudulent investment schemes in which higher-than-average returns are promised to investors and then paid using the investors' own money. Named after Charles Ponzi who gained notoriety using the scheme in the 1920s, Ponzi schemes reemerge regularly. Recent schemes involve Nicholas Levene, who bilked investors of £32 million, and Bernie Madoff, whose massive Ponzi scheme cost investors billions of dollars.

But good hedge-fund managers are some of the best managers in existence today and many have concluded that private investors like you take too much risk with your accumulated savings. (Turn to Chapter 3 for a discussion on basic hedge-fund techniques and Chapter 2 for help deciding on the correct level of investment risk for you.) They suggest that you focus on preserving your capital and then look to grind out a steady, positive return no matter which direction the financial markets are going in.

These managers think that you should be aiming for a steady 4–10 per cent per year return, year in, year out. They believe that you need to be brave, sometimes adventurous, and look to all manner of different asset classes and investment strategies including controversial practices such as:

- **Shorting:** Selling what you don't own (see Chapter 7).
- **Arbitrage:** Buying and selling an asset at the same time to make a profit from the price difference (check out Chapter 8).
- **Leverage:** Borrowing other people's money to invest (if that sounds good, turn to Chapter 10).
- **Structured instruments:** Employing a simple risk/return trade-off that creates a series of options to increase your payout (mosey over to Chapter 11) for more.
- **Shareholder activism:** Pressuring a firm's managers and Board to increase the value of the company's shares (race to Chapter 12 when you're feeling 'active'!).
- **Spread betting:** Betting on the movements of financial markets (gamblers need to head to Chapter 17).

The core investment mantra of hedge-fund managers is: if you're willing to diversify ideas and strategies, you're better able to produce an absolute return in all markets. The big university endowments certainly believe this sales pitch and many of the world's wealthiest investors have also bought into this strategy – and so can you.

Chapter 2

Assessing Risk: Deciding What Kind of Investor You Are

*B*eing successful at anything in life involves knowing yourself well, and building an investment portfolio is no different. To invest wisely and profitably you need to assess your strengths and weaknesses and your current circumstances. Plus, having clear goals and strategies in mind as to what you're seeking from your portfolio now and in the future stands you in good stead, because investing requires understanding and balancing trade-offs, most obviously ones involving risk.

In this chapter I help you decide on the kind of investor you are by taking a look at two trade-offs that are central to building a successful portfolio, examining your investment priorities and tolerance for risk so that you can choose the investments that are right for you, and offering information about more-sophisticated investment strategies and principles you'll want to consider as you manage your portfolio.

A Tale of Two Trade-Offs

In the best of all possible worlds (apologies to Dickens and Voltaire fans for mixing literary references), there'd be no trade-offs, and you wouldn't have to compromise on one good thing to receive the benefits of another good thing. Alas, when portfolio planning in the real world, consider trade-offs you must. Specifically, you must think about the trade-off between risk and return and the trade-off between risk and your age.

Knowing how these two trade-offs work in reality is certainly crucial to investment success, but also your views on them helps you discover the sort of investor you are or want to become:

- ✔ **The trade-off between what returns you can expect versus the risks you're going to take:** Surprise, surprise, the more risk you're willing to take, the bigger the potential rewards! But this relationship isn't entirely straightforward and taking on extra risk doesn't necessarily mean that you make more money.

- ✔ **The trade-off between risk and your age:** By and large the older you are, the more risk averse you become. This change is partly driven by the fact that older investors tend to favour strategies that preserve their wealth and partly by a simple financial reality that after you retire your ability to earn extra money is massively depleted.

In the following sections, I explore how these trade-offs play out in portfolio terms and what they imply in terms of investment strategy.

Central to creating a successful investment portfolio is assessing your current circumstances with honesty, in particular the reality of your finances and how old you are (no point in succumbing to delusion or denial on either count!). This process boils down to understanding your risk/return trade-off and which investments and assets are right for you.

Balancing risk and return

Ask most investors what they think constitutes *returns* and you quickly get an answer: perhaps they say that their portfolio has risen by X per cent over the last year in terms of positive returns. In contrast, defining *risk* is a slightly more complex affair, involving not just the reverse of returns (that is, losses). The next sections give you the details.

The risk factor: Shares versus bonds

Risk comes in many shapes and sizes; some of these types can be measured very quickly while others are harder to define but easy to worry about – for instance, the fear of future inflationary trends is going to have an eventual real impact on returns but that fear is difficult to quantify in the short term. For more on risk, flip to the later section 'Delving Deeper into Risk'.

Usually risk is interpreted in the narrow sense of actual monetary losses – also referred to as *drawdowns*. In this sense, one essential fact stands above all else: shares (equities) are much riskier than their main alternative – bonds (check out the nearby sidebar 'Comparing shares and bonds').

> # Comparing shares and bonds
>
> Top quantitative analyst Andrew Lapthorne has expertly and succinctly compared the relative riskiness of shares and bonds. His key conclusion is that the fear of big drawdowns for shares is well-founded based on data from the recent past. He crunched a vast amount of historical data looking at the maximum drawdowns for a range of rolling five-year periods since 1950 for American shares and government bonds. His research clearly states that many times over the last 60 years US shares have lost 20 per cent or more in any one year whereas US government bonds have very rarely if ever lost this percentage via drawdowns at any time in this period.
>
> He notes that, 'The bond investor could have bought bonds 90% of the months since 1950 and avoided having a 20% drawdown or more, whilst the equity investor could have only invested in 40% of months to avoid such losses. Extreme drawdown of 40% or more, even on a real basis, is almost unheard of in the bond market, but seen 17% of the time in shares.'

Shares versus bonds, part 2: The return factor

The risk/return trade-off isn't just about risk, of course. You also need to understand where you can derive a positive return. In effect that means deciding which asset class has produced the greatest returns over the past few decades: shares, bonds or other alternative assets such as commodities? Most investment analysts say that shares should form an important part of a diversified portfolio because they produce higher returns than bonds. And the research evidence supports this view – shares are worth the extra risk because they produce extra returns over the very long term.

Part of the explanation for the stellar long-term returns is that shares are much, much riskier than other asset classes. Virtually every study of long-term returns from shares from as early as the 1870s (in the US) shows that, although shares have produced some amazing returns, it's been at the expense of very high volatility and therefore risk.

Balancing risk and age: Lifecycle investing

Your age impacts heavily on the type of investments you need to be making. For example, an ordinary investor in his twenties is much more able to withstand losses from an investment strategy because he can spend the next 40 years earning more money from his day job. In contrast, when an investor hits retirement he's much less able to use alternative cash flows to make up for rash investment decisions. Thus capital preservation becomes his priority. The same investment product can look completely different to investors of different ages.

The central insight of the trade-off between age and risk (known as *lifecycle investing*) is that age affects tolerance to risk.

Over the life of an average investor, the appetite for risk (and return) evolves. As their tolerance of risk changes, so too their choice of assets. They move from an interest in shares and no bonds, via a period shifting away from shares into some bonds, to a bias towards bonds in their later years, as the next sections explain.

As a young investor

Imagine that you're 20 years old and have just landed a great job working for a large multinational. You're earning enough money to put aside £100 a month in a fund that you plan to stick with for the next 40 years of your working life, but for now you want lots and lots of growth in your underlying investments.

Therefore you're willing to take on some risk now, and the long-term data on returns suggest that the riskiest, most rewarding of the major asset classes are shares. Bonds, by contrast, are a bit boring and safe; although you probably won't lose more than 20 per cent in any one year (called your *maximum drawdown*), equally you're never going to bag anything that makes your fortune. In summary, as a thrusting young buck you quite sensibly decide that your risk tolerance is high and that you want to stack up on equity exposure and 'go for it' in terms of risk.

As an investor nearing retirement

Flash forward 40 years. You're now a considerably older 60 year old. Retirement is only about five years away, and so you need to accumulate a large pot of savings capital to last you through to your twilight years (you may well live until you're 90 if current longevity studies are right). Therefore, capital preservation is all-important to you. You absolutely can't afford a capital loss or drawdown of something like 20 per cent in one year – and so you have a very negative view of shares and are a very big fan of bonds.

As a retired investor

Curiously, when the typical investor retires, the consensus on the 'correct' investment balance becomes a little muddier. On paper, retirees should be ultra cautious – they have to preserve their pension pot for a retirement that may last 30 or more years. But they also require an income to live on and the assets with the safest profile – bonds and government bonds or gilts – tend to pay the lowest yield.

Pensioners have to be cautious about the major risk of inflation. Sticking all your money in conventional bonds in high inflationary times may mean that you preserve your nominal (before inflation) returns, but the real value after inflation may be diminishing rapidly. Why? Because when you buy a government security that promises to pay £100 back in five years' time with annual interest of 4 per cent per annum, that's all you get even if inflation is romping ahead at

10 per cent per annum. In five years' time £100 may be worth as much as £160 (that's five years of 10 per cent inflation) but you still only get your £100 back.

Some academics and economists reckon that pensioners should be willing to take on extra risk, grow their income and increase the capital value of their investments. In this case, retired investors can consider taking on a little bit of extra risk via shares, and especially those shares that pay a dividend. Another good idea may be to reduce their bond exposure.

Changing investment strategies throughout life: The glidepath

The supposedly simple process of constructing a mix of assets that can be used as the building blocks of a single portfolio and can change over time, has evolved into a complex research literature at whose heart sits something called the glidepath.

A *glidepath* is an investment strategy that starts with high-risk assets, transitions through a balanced approach in mid-life and ends with a mixture of assets with a bias towards bonds later in life. The graph in Figure 2-1 shows a typical glidepath.

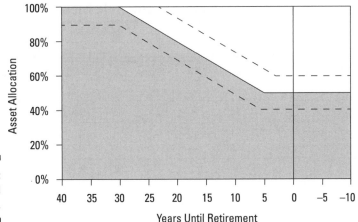

Figure 2-1: A typical glidepath.

Glidepaths are almost as common as 'amazing investment strategies' in the world of finance! Every adviser, wealth firm and private bank has their own version. Crucially providers and advisers have their own starting and ending points as well as different relative combinations, but they all feature exactly the same blended glidepath. The only real area of debate is whether a very young person needs some limited bond exposure and whether a retired person requires some equity exposure and at what level.

This simple analysis has evolved into a series of different permutations in the marketing-driven world of investment. Two popular glidepath structures are the target date fund and the target risk fund:

- ✔ **Target date fund:** One of the most popular structures. a *target date* fund involves you sitting down, working out your planned retirement age (which will nearly always be massively wide of the mark, given changing longevity patterns) and then finding a fund that has the closest equivalent to that year: your target date.

- ✔ Assume that the year is 2015, you're aged 50 and you intend to retire at the age of 70 (in 2035). You're going to be looking for a target date fund with the label 2035 stuck on it (I said it wasn't complicated!).

- ✔ **Target risk fund:** An alternative to the target date fund is the target risk fund, which doesn't use dates as such but risk tolerances. Because you have 20 years to go, you may be a typical middle-of-the-road risk-based investor, with a moderate or balanced risk/return profile (see the later section 'Choosing products for the middle-of-the-road investor').

Table 2-1 shows a range of target date funds from a US exchange-traded fund provider called XShares, who works closely with stockbroker TD Waterhouse. You can see exactly how the mixture of assets changes over time as the investor ages and (I hope) becomes wiser and more risk averse!

Table 2-1 **XShares TD Waterhouse Lifecycle Funds**

	Before Retirement							Retirement	After Retirement		
Years	35	30	25	20	15	10	5	0	5	10	15	20
Equity (%)	100	100	100	90	82.5	75	60	50	37.5	30	25	20
Fixed income (%)	0	0	0	4	8.5	14	29	40	63.75	62	67.5	73
Real estate (%)	0	0	0	6	9	11	11	10	8.75	8	7.5	7
Age	30	35	40	45	50	55	60	65	70	75	80	85
Portfolio	2040		2030	2025	2020	2015	2010	2005				

Be as careful about selecting a target date (or risk) fund as with any other fund. Examine the costs, the mixture of assets and the fund manager's record.

Delving Deeper into Risk

Intuitively everyone understands the simple concept of the risk/return trade-off. As your appetite for greater potential returns grows, so must your willingness to take on more risk. You don't get something for nothing in the world of finance and if you want 'sooper-dooper' returns, be prepared to take larger risks.

But as the earlier section 'Balancing risk and return' implies, the notion of risk is more complex than may at first appear and so I take a deeper look at it in this section.

Discovering the different risks

Risk is a fairly slippery customer and comes in lots of different types. Unfortunately many private investors look at risk in a very simplistic way – a typical query about risk may start with an investor asking, 'How much of my initial capital may I lose if I invest in an asset?' But risk involves much more than this narrow sense reveals.

As an investor, you need to think about risk in a much wider, more holistic sense. Risk can mean any or all of the following:

- ✔ **Credit risk:** If you buy a bond, what's the chance of the issuer defaulting on the final payment (or the regular interest payments)?

- ✔ **Currency risk:** Your investment in a foreign asset may increase in value but the currency in which it's denominated may move in the opposite direction.

- ✔ **Idiosyncratic risk:** If you employ a manager to manage your money, what risk are you taking if he makes a bad decision?

- ✔ **Legal risk:** Will regulators decide to change the rules governing your investment?

- ✔ **Leverage risk:** What happens if you borrow too much money and the cost of leverage starts to work against your investment (see Chapter 10 for all about leverage)?

- ✔ **Liquidity risk:** Your asset may increase in value but become increasingly difficult to sell; that is, it may become more illiquid, which is a risk if you need to access that investment immediately to raise some much needed cash!

- ✔ **Maximum drawdown:** The potential maximum loss over a period of time that may hit your financial asset. Many stock markets can easily lose 20 or even 30 per cent in a year, whereas most bonds rarely lose more than 10 per cent in any one year.

- ✔ **Systematic risk:** How an asset may respond to risks within the system; that is, how closely correlated the asset is with wider financial assets. If the US economy nosedives, is your asset going to crash in value as well?

- ✔ **Volatility:** How much the value of a share, bond or commodity varies on a daily basis. For many people, high volatility implies higher potential risk.

Assessing your preferred risk level

As I discuss in the earlier section 'Balancing risk and age: Lifecycle investing', age and risk are intimately connected. Generally older people are more cautious about risk and younger investors are better able to withstand risks that may deplete their wealth.

But attitude to risk isn't entirely straightforward. Some investors (young, middle-aged and old) are instinctively and fundamentally cautious and risk averse owing to their temperament and personality. These individuals are low-risk investors by nature, averse to buying too many assets that have the potential to collapse in value.

Other investors of all ages (though probably more often the younger) trade like dervishes and love a dash of risk! These higher-risk (or more adventurous) investors are absolutely willing to take on extra risks in order to have greater potential for returns. They're enthusiastic about investing in products that may be very volatile and yet may make mega-profits.

Sitting between these two archetype investors is the middle-of-the-road investor who's probably very balanced and pragmatic and wants a bit of the best of both worlds!

Many investors naturally think that they're middle-of-the-road, medium-risk investors with a penchant for terms such as 'balanced'. That may be true some of the time, but you need to also understand your retirement requirements, which could make your investment strategy more or less risk averse, regardless of your personal attitudes about risk. If you want to live a wonderful retirement with lots of cruises and trips around the world, you require lots of income and that means a large nest egg, which may force you to increase your level of risk and buy more adventurous funds. Equally you may have other forms of income coming in your retirement, which means that you can afford to take risks with your savings pot.

The reverse is also true. You may be in your thirties and willing to shoot the lights out in terms of risk but have no other assets to act as a cushion (second homes or soon-to-be-deceased aunts) and so you may take a more cautious attitude to risk. Also, many families save money in their forties for school or university tuition fees. Such investors may start off adventurous but end up very cautious.

Matching Horses for Courses: Choosing the Right Investment for You

After taking a look at your present circumstances, investment goals and risk attitude (as I describe in the earlier sections 'A Tale of Two Trade-Offs ' and 'Delving Deeper into Risk'), you want to ensure that you pick the appropriate financial products. Again, fully understanding the risk/return trade-off is central to these decisions.

Of course, pigeonholing individual investors is fraught with problems but experience shows that certain generalisations apply about how different people's risk/return trade-offs impact on investment strategies. Following on from the preceding section, and for convenience's sake only, I discuss the different types of investors in three rather crude but useful categories: low risk, middle of the road and adventurous.

Operating as a low-risk, cautious investor

Here are some strategies that characterise the average lower-risk investor:

- **Absolute returns:** Even low-risk investors like to think that they can make a positive return, which explains why so many are attracted to the idea of *absolute returns*; that is, making money in all markets, whether those markets are rising or falling in value. Check out the later section 'Thinking about absolute returns'.

- **Bonds:** Bonds are likely to be a favourite in terms of asset classes, simply because they tend to be less volatile and produce income. Crucially, the promise to repay that's implicit within a bond structure (at redemption) is likely to be very attractive.

✔ **Capital preservation:** Lower-risk investors hate losing accumulated capital, and so tend to want to preserve their capital no matter what. Alternative assets, such as gold, that speak to capital preservation may make a fleeting appearance in the cautious investor's portfolio.

✔ **Currency exposure:** Currency exposure probably becomes less of an issue for cautious investors. They usually want to limit their portfolio of investments to those denominated in the currency of their home base.

✔ **Equities:** Shares are likely to be much less attractive because they're regarded, rightly, as fairly risky (flip to the earlier section 'Balancing risk and return' for more). If an exposure to shares does exist within the portfolio they're likely to be blue chip stocks with strong balance sheets and sensible valuations.

No intrinsic reason exists as to why cautious investors shouldn't be interested in more sophisticated styles of investing that look to limit downside risk by hedging (see 'Encountering More Advanced Portfolio Thinking' later in this chapter).

✔ **Income:** This is critically important to many cautious investors largely because as they approach retirement they tend to turn their attention to eking out a monthly income from their accumulated savings.

More cautious investors need to think long and hard about their attitude towards three key issues:

✔ From where are they going to derive their future positive returns?

✔ Just how much bond exposure can they stomach?

✔ How important is capital preservation?

Choosing products for the middle-of-the-road investor

Unsurprisingly the world of investing is full of funds that are marketed for perceived middle-of-the-road investors. The names attached to these funds vary but they probably include a mention of being balanced. Here are the main strategies and so on of middle-of-the-road investors:

✔ The key is to balance growth potential and capital preservation, which usually means balancing shares and bonds in the portfolio mix:

– Shares provide a core enhanced level of income through dividends and also provide the main potential for capital growth.

– Bonds provide the core of any future 'guaranteed' capital return.

– Alternative assets provide occasional income, which isn't crucial unless investors have some specific needs such as funding their children's education.

Being an adventurous investor

Most professional advisers and investors probably prefer the ambitious adventurous investor, otherwise known as *growth-friendly* (after all, more investment activity tends to translate into more trading costs). These investors tend to be more optimistic about the future, more willing to take risks and more willing to be active in capitalising on opportunities.

In no particular order, adventurous investors are likely to have the following characteristics:

✔ A focus on capital growth.

✔ A willingness to make losses in the short term.

✔ Less concern about income.

✔ An interest in complex strategies that involve options, hedging and derivatives.

✔ A global focus, including in their currency exposure.

✔ A concentration on shares as their portfolio's core component.

✔ An emphasis within the share component of the portfolio on growth opportunities.

✔ A great interest in alternative assets.

For adventurous investors, three key concepts constantly lurk in the background:

✔ A willingness to be tactical, which means perhaps changing a core holding every few weeks or months, even if only by a small amount.

✔ The possibility of using *gearing*, using someone else's money to make an investment, to amplify returns (see the later section 'Considering gearing up' for more).

✔ A willingness to think outside the box, go for global assets and be alternative.

One challenge can be that you end up overtrading (so incurring extra costs) and believing too much in your own market-anticipation skills. You start thinking that you're an investing sage and can successfully divine the future twists and turns of the market.

Encountering More Advanced Portfolio Thinking

Investors don't have to believe blindly in the notion that shares and bonds always increase in value. They absolutely don't and in reality key asset classes can be a dreadful idea, not just for a few years but for decades. This fact should put you on your guard and make you think long and hard about conserving your wealth as well as where you can make future profits.

The quick skip through the general risk stereotypes in the preceding section makes clear that, whatever your attitude towards the risk/return and risk/age trade-offs, you need to think intelligently about how you use different investment strategies and asset classes to produce the returns you desire. For example:

- ✔ Adventurous types may well be much more open to new ideas such as emerging markets shares, but sticking with more tried-and-trusted techniques can often be wiser. Investing in so-called new ideas isn't always a guaranteed ticket to riches!

- ✔ Sitting tight on a few bonds or a mountain of cash, hoping that somehow everything's going to work out just fine. Advanced but cautious investors need to think long and hard about concepts such as absolute returns, hedging and going long/short and asset class.

In this section I look at some of the investment challenges in a little more detail, including absolute returns, hedging, outside-the-box assets and strategies and gearing. You can be sure of encountering many of these key aspects throughout this book.

Thinking about absolute returns

The term *absolute returns* is hugely popular with fund marketing types who love the promise of an absolute positive return (capital gain) in any kind of market. The problem, immediately apparent to anyone with a modicum of common sense, is that as an ideal it sounds a bit like modern alchemy. 'Make money all the time!' is a catchy advertising line but not terrifically easy to achieve in the grim, grey world of investing reality.

On balance you need to be cynical about the claims of absolute returns. Many fund managers fail to deliver on this ideal, with most offering a pale alternative – their investors don't lose quite so much money on the way down and don't make so much on the way up! In reality (too) many absolute returns funds should be marketed as 'Not quite so volatile', but that's obviously less catchy as a title.

But don't let my slightly trite remark about *volatility* (how much a share price moves up and down on a regular basis) obscure the fact that the idea of absolute returns is useful. If a fund manager can deliver most of the returns of the wider market but with much less volatility, that may be useful for investors looking to 'smooth' their returns. The ideal of investing in a fund with a high level of liquidity (cash) in order to conserve capital may also be very attractive to certain investors. Nothing's wrong with the aim of preserving your capital come what may.

Crucially, the idea of absolute returns forces managers to think creatively about investing. Instead of just expecting a market to keep on going up (where the fund is essentially long the market), an absolute returns fund manager explores alternative strategies, which may include new asset classes or making money from falling markets. In essence, when it works properly, absolute returns makes managers work harder to produce returns come what may. On balance that's a good idea and one that you can copy via your investing techniques. Just don't expect it to work all the time.

All that strenuous activity by the investment manager (the need to make money in falling markets, using alternative assets) to make sure that you conserve your capital introduces two specific risks:

- ✔ That the manager doesn't succeed! In other words, the person makes the wrong calls at the wrong time in the market. Too much activity doesn't necessarily equate to constant success.

- ✔ That constant trading and energetic fund management costs you extra money. Fees on absolute returns funds can hit the roof (with charges of 2 per cent or more standard in the sector) with the inevitable knock-on effect on your wealth.

  High fees are just about palatable if you're invested in a wunderkind manager, but they're a recipe for financial ruin if your manager undershoots the market. At that point you're hit with a double whammy of poor returns and high costs.

Deciding whether hedging or shorting are for you

Hedge-fund and absolute-return managers frequently get bad press from many investment commentators. The common charges centre on concerns about poor performance and high costs, plus a smattering of more systematic concerns, such as questions regarding the opportunistic nature of new managers in the market, the relative lack of regulatory oversight (at least until recently), and even whether the strategy itself works, given the overall poor performance of funds. But hedge-fund managers should be applauded for the noble objective (not always achieved) of trying to preserve your capital in any market. That aim forces them to be creative, which means that they're willing to consider strategies that include hedging their portfolio, shorting expensive assets and thinking unconventionally.

Hedging is a simple concept to comprehend. Imagine opening a very large position on the FTSE 100 benchmark UK equity index. You believe it will rise in the next year but you're also slightly worried that the local economy may suddenly slow down, hitting local share prices. *Hedging* involves working out the value of your main position and then opening up a counter-balancing position where you make a profit if your investing idea goes in the opposite direction: that is, the FTSE 100 goes down.

You may for instance look to invest in another asset that can be relied upon to *increase* in value while the FTSE 100 is *falling* in value (called *negative correlation* in finance jargon). Government bonds, for example, can usually be relied upon to do the exact opposite of local equity markets, and so may be a perfect hedge.

Shorting – where you make money from a financial asset falling in price – can be an essential part of a hedging strategy. In simple terms, you open a position with a broker where you sell an asset (that you probably don't own at that moment in time) and then wait for it to fall in price.

Imagine selling shares in ACME PLC for £100. You may be selling these shares in a *naked* fashion, which fortunately doesn't mean that you're sitting in the nude on the telephone but that you don't own shares in ACME PLC. Your plan is that in two months' time the price of ACME will be only £80 per share at which point you'd buy the shares (for £80) and then sell them, as agreed with your broker, for £100 each. Hey presto, a profit of £20 even though you don't own the asset!

Although shorting is widely used, it's the subject of much debate and controversy. Many central banks hate the idea of 'shorting' shares in vitally important institutions such as banks. They worry that short selling may bring down a bank, causing economic carnage. Also, shorting is risky: get it wrong and you can end up losing a vast amount of money very quickly, especially if the price of the underlying asset keeps going the wrong way.

You can also use alternative shorting strategies in hedging that involve using options. These essentially involve the same outcome but make use of derivatives-based options that increase in value as the index (or share) they're tracking goes down in price. These *puts*, as they're called, are widely used in financial markets and can be a brilliant way of hedging a portfolio.

Investigating alternative assets and strategies

Looking at asset classes that may move in a different way is another form of hedging – in other words, maintaining the value of your capital even in falling markets. One example is the idea I introduce in the preceding section, that of balancing an investment in the FTSE 100 equity market with an investment in government gilts (government gilts move in the opposite direction to local shares).

Another idea is to think unconventionally and look to invest in asset classes where the price isn't affected by the ebb and flow of local shares, such as investing in litigation funds or aircraft leasing structures or putting money into gold funds or agricultural commodities. Nothing much necessarily links these disparate ideas except that they may move up or down in value based on processes that have no impact on the FTSE 100 benchmark index. For instance, gold is a classic alternative hedge because its price is usually determined by factors that have little to do with UK interest rates. Equally, investing in forests in Latin America (a big new alternative asset) usually has almost nothing to do with the UK interest rate cycle or inflation rates.

Alternative assets are much in demand at the moment among a certain type of adventurous investor. In an ideal world they can provide extra diversification benefits and sometimes act as a hedge to mainstream shares. But alternative assets are by their nature alternative, which means that not everyone is into them. Therefore, their markets may be small and without a massive constant supply of sellers and buyers looking to set a price (unlike with shares and bonds where market liquidity is nearly always deep and global). This situation can produce relatively illiquid markets where the difference between the asking and selling price (called the *bid offer spread*) can be huge. Also, prices can collapse with a sudden surfeit of sellers looking to raise cash quickly and very few buyers.

Understanding the cycles

I'm not talking about the Mayor of London's chosen form of transport, but economic cycles. Alternative assets are useful because they move in different cycles to mainstream bond and equity markets. The weather may have an effect, for example, or the extent of government intervention, or the amount of gold jewellery in the second-hand market. The key is that different cycles affect different asset classes.

As you discover in Chapter 4, three rates hugely impact shares and bonds: interest rates, inflation and gross domestic product growth rates. These rates also impact a wider business cycle that ebbs and flows, waxes and wanes in a fairly defined way, with effects on the pricing of financial assets. For example, if you decide to invest in shares as an economy heads into a recession, you're likely to be on to a losing trade in the short to medium term. In a downturn most shares fall in price (whereas government bonds usually rally).

An understanding of the wider business and economic cycles can be hugely useful in avoiding big losses and so minimise your losses and preserve your capital. But this reading of cycles can have its own downside, which is that you can be encouraged to overtrade and believe that you can somehow 'time' the markets. Evidence suggests that most people are in fact fairly bad at spotting signals of a changing economic cycle. And even those who are brilliant at crystal-ball gazing tend to end up racking up huge trading costs, which eat into their total returns.

Considering gearing up

Gearing isn't a complex idea: you borrow money from someone else and then bet that money on a key trend. Gearing has the effect of leveraging your potential returns, which means that instead of making, say, a 1 per cent gain on every 1 per cent increase in the value of an underlying financial asset, you make 2 per cent or perhaps even 10 per cent (read Chapter 10 for much more on gearing and leverage).

A small but growing band of investors has taken a stand against the noise of the markets, deliberately eschewing their frenetic hyperactivity. These investors don't sit tight and ignore the markets, as many long-term buy-and-hold investors do, but choose instead to make big, leveraged moves on key trends. Most of the time these so-called macro-orientated investors retain a core of cash or very liquid investments, conserving their capital, not doing very much, because they don't have much conviction in any big trend.

But when they spot a key trend (such as an economy entering a recession) they spring to life and start using that mountain of cash. Instead of betting all that money on a key investment idea, however, they use gearing to increase their returns.

These investors cleverly invest only a small portion of their cash in any trade. For example, they may stay 95 per cent in cash and only invest 5 per cent in a big investment idea, but with leverage. If their gearing is, say, 10-fold, a small 10 per cent move in the underlying asset may produce a doubling in their investment. At this point the investors may sell their positions and bank the 5 per cent gain overall (the 5 per cent portfolio position has doubled in price to 10 per cent). If the trade goes wrong and the asset falls by 10 per cent, however, they've probably lost their entire investment, but remember that they bet only 5 per cent of their portfolio on the trade!

Many investors aren't quite as canny and insist on leveraging up their returns throughout their portfolios, turning into highly geared day-traders. Sadly most of these investors eventually come unstuck as leverage destroys their wealth; that is, all those costs from trading and borrowing eat away whatever gains have been made in the past, which is made worse by a run of poorly conceived trade ideas.

If you use some form of borrowing, or margin, to increase exponentially your returns from a more tactical strategy, you're also exponentially increasing your risk profile. Gearing can be useful if you have a strong conviction trade and can even be used by cautious investors who want to retain liquidity within their portfolio. But you need to use gearing with great care and only sparingly. (A *conviction trade* is a trade based on an investment principle your research has indicated will hold sway in the market. For example, if your research tells you that in the coming year a funding crisis will cause inflation to increase and the dollar to fall, your conviction trade may be to invest in gold and gold stocks.)

Knowing your own and other people's limitations

One risk to your investment is lurking in the background that you may not be aware of: you! Quite rightly you want to research new ideas and strategies but that extra effort needs to be accompanied with proper due diligence and research effort. It involves keeping an eye on the markets and the wider economy and sometimes going against the grain of the markets.

For many investors this task is impossible. They may not have the time to undertake the work and prefer to leave it all in the hands of their adviser. Unfortunately, others don't bother putting in the extra time and hard work and may even be ignorant of new ideas and strategies.

If you or your adviser can't devote the time to managing your money properly, I suggest you adopt a zen-like attitude towards the markets. Invest some money in a diversified series of cheap index-tracking funds, and then just sit back and get on with the rest of your life. Keep costs to the minimum, make sure that you're diversified and don't chase any new trends. Keep things simple and stick to long-term buy-and-hold investing.

If you do have the time and disposition to keep abreast of new ideas and strategies, remain aware of your own behavioural traits and weaknesses. Look at yourself in the mirror and understand where you may make mistakes; and then put in place rules to stop you from mucking up.

In addition, assess and understand the limitations of your professional advisers: many simply aren't knowledgeable enough or frankly that interested in investment. Annoyingly, many of the best advisers charge more money upfront for their expertise, which sadly puts off many investors. Be cynical too about the extravagant claims of many fund managers, especially hedge-fund types: the industry is full of marketing hype and mendacious claims and a lot of evidence suggests that overall the hedge-fund industry isn't very good at out-performing normal fund managers. Be wary, but also accept that you can learn from professional investors. Here's the ideal balance: cynical but always open to new ideas!

Part II
Picking the Strategies for You

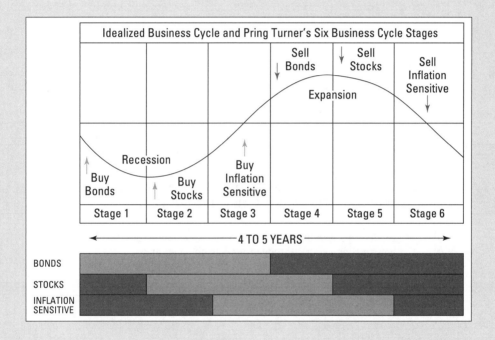

Idealized Business Cycle and Pring Turner's Six Business Cycle Stages

			Sell Bonds ↓	Sell Stocks ↓	Sell Inflation Sensitive ↓
				Expansion	
↑ Buy Bonds	Recession ↑ Buy Stocks	↑ Buy Inflation Sensitive			
Stage 1	Stage 2	Stage 3	Stage 4	Stage 5	Stage 6

←————————————— 4 TO 5 YEARS —————————————→

BONDS

STOCKS

INFLATION SENSITIVE

In this part . . .

- Got a hedge-fund headache? Learn about the pros and cons of hedge-funds and whether they are the right investment strategy for you.

- Use your knowledge of economic and financial cycles to develop your investment strategy and improve your returns.

- Get to grips with the market and reap the benefits from learning how to shape your strategy around its behavior and trends.

Chapter 3

Grasping Basic Hedge-Fund Strategies

*H*edge funds have been much in the news over the last few years, often for all the wrong reasons. But don't let the adverse headlines obscure the fact that they can be an effective investment strategy for the right canny investor who's willing to put in the work.

In essence, hedge funds involve taking long and short positions but use a variety of strategies. The most basic idea is the pairs trade (which involves finding two huge companies and making money from their relationship), but as you discover in this chapter hedge-fund approaches extend to covered call writing (profiting from premiums on options contracts), shareholder activism (kicking up a stink to get management to make profits for their shareholders), mergers and acquisitions arbitrage, and making hay from 'surprise' company earnings.

The great beauty of all the hedge-fund strategies that I highlight in this chapter is that they aren't enormously complicated, can be copied by ordinary investors (willing to take an active interest in investing) and involve liquid, large, multinational blue chip stocks (on paper the pricing of these mammoth corporate leviathans should be precise, rational and perfect . . . though isn't always). Yet hedge funds do involve lots of hard work, patient research (which you can carry out using free or cheap Internet sites) and an absolute willingness to learn from your mistakes.

Most hedge-fund investors make more than a living from these strategies because they deploy *leverage* (that is, they gear up returns). But this tactic is probably not a good one to follow if you're an ordinary investor who's afraid of losing money.

Introducing the Hedge-Fund Concept (and a Bit of Hedge-Fund History)

In 1949 Australian-born investor Alfred Winslow Jones created the world's first hedge fund. In many ways Jones was a fairly normal investor, who borrowed what were then fairly standard ideas about buying good, solid, cheap stocks with decent fundamental attributes such as a sound balance sheet or growing profits (I discuss these ideas in Chapter 9 on value investing).

In simple terms, he liked some stocks and – here's the important bit – disliked others. His radical idea was that he bought the stocks he liked (went *long* in the language of investing) while selling (or *shorting*) those he disliked. I describe the precise mechanism by which investors go short a stock in Chapter 7, but for now you just need to know that a revolutionary idea was born.

Winslow Jones used leverage (gearing via borrowing) to go long and short stocks in equal amounts to reduce significantly the market and sector risk while also delivering consistent profits. So in reality his strategy was a little more complicated than it first seems. In the late 1980s, Gerald Bamberger from Morgan Stanley popularised the concept and took the thinking one stage further, using complex mathematical ideas to spot opportunities through the mining of quantitative data (fundamental data consisting of profits estimates or balance sheet ratios).

Winslow Jones's radically new techniques proved highly successful and his funds significantly outperformed the market over the first few decades. In fact these ideas became so successful that before long hundreds of different so-called hedge funds were operating. Although an ill-defined and disparate group, these funds shared a common set of characteristics:

- ✔ The stocks targeted for trading tended to be fairly big, liquid stocks, such as those belonging to global multinationals.

- ✔ They were market neutral; that is, their aim was to make absolute returns (the technical term is *beta neutral*).

  Beta is the measurement of a stock's volatility relative to the market:

  – A stock with a beta of 1 moves historically in sync with the market.

  – A stock with a higher beta tends to be more volatile than the market.

  – A stock with a lower beta can be expected to rise and fall more slowly than the market.

- ✔ They used leverage.

- ✔ They were very active in taking a view on the merits (or otherwise) of a particular opportunity.

As with all profit-making opportunities, eventually hedge funds became mainstream and even big investment banks twigged that they could make money from these radical ideas. Many of today's large hedge funds from around the world continue to use this most basic form of hedge-fund activity through pairs trading as a means to deliver low-risk, high-reward returns to their investors and partners.

The key idea powering this huge industry is that markets are mostly right: that is, in general they don't offer up special opportunities every day. In layperson's terms, markets are fairly logical and efficient. Yet every once in a while these efficient markets make mistakes and create what economists call *an inefficiency*. After all, shares don't buy and sell themselves: people enter those orders and people are driven by emotions, which cause irrational decisions. This emotional decision-making characteristic is multiplied many times when it involves a crowd of people.

Economists call this strategy *statistical arbitrage*: that is, certain shares are correlated (related) in their day-to-day price movements and this offers profit-making opportunities.

Treating Companies as Couples: Pairs Trading

In pairs trading you find a pair of historically correlated stocks and, when the correlation weakens (when one stock goes up while the other stays the same or goes down), you go long on the stock that's fallen and go short on the stock that's risen on the assumption that the correlation will return. Your aim with this strategy is to make a profit regardless of the direction of the market: in simple terms you're *hedging* your market exposure (aiming to make money in all markets). Or you can look at the process as being that you're now suddenly *market neutral*: in other words, you make money regardless of the direction of the overall market.

The easiest way to explain pairs trading is to use the example of two of the world's most famous businesses.

Coca-Cola's great rival is Pepsi Cola and vice versa. In theory these companies are very similar: they operate in the same market, sell similar things and (most of the time) boast fairly similar operating margins. Yet their shares almost certainly don't behave in the same way.

This difference in behaviour is partly down to the fact that many different investors hold a big chunk of shares in these corporate giants, but also because many of those investors are nervous that those shares may be hit by company specifics. Equally, investors also have a relative view of the attractiveness of shares in each company; that is, one company's shares may be more attractive than those of the other.

For hedge funds the obvious way to proceed with these potential discrepancies is to treat the companies as a *pair* and go long (buy) one and short (sell) the other.

As a pairs hedge-fund trader, you monitor two similar stocks and aim to buy the oversold issue and simultaneously sell the overbought issue, exiting – that is selling both stocks – when the relationship returns to its norm.

By using this long/short pair, if the market generally goes up both your Coca-Cola and Pepsi Cola positions rise in price, though the stronger share should rise more provided that your analysis is correct and is ultimately recognised by other investors. Thus, the profit from your successful position more than offsets the loss from your short position in the weaker stock. As a bonus, you receive a rebate from your stockbroker on your short position (typically the risk-free rate of interest).

If you think that pairs trading is for you, do what many practitioners of market-neutral long/short share trading do and balance your longs and shorts in the same sector or industry. By being *sector neutral*, you avoid the risk of market swings heavily impacting a specific industry or sector. In addition, choose pairs that are in *deep* sectors: that is, with a large amount of liquidity (lots of shares on offer).

Here are two unique, important characteristics of pairs trading:

- ✔ **You're not trading the individual stocks based on their direction, but trading the difference between the two stock prices.** This approach is called *trading the differential* and makes this type of strategy very different from other trading methodologies.

- ✔ **You're moving away from a strategy that involves following the market's direction.** Instead you're focusing on trading the chart of the difference of the two correlated stocks.

Successful pairs-based hedge-fund managers are the ones with the greatest ability to select a basket of long stocks that perform better than the basket of shorts. If the longs don't outperform the shorts, then no matter how market-neutral your portfolio, it isn't going to generate meaningful returns.

Pairs trading seeks to achieve a consistent return by earning small, steady profits on lots and lots of positions, instead of trying for large gains that may end up becoming big losses. This tendency to earn small, steady gains characterises market-neutral long/short share funds in general, resulting in annual returns of about 10–12 per cent, without leverage in good years. To enhance returns, some funds do resort to leverage.

Putting pairs trading to work for you

Running a pairs-based strategy is remarkably straightforward – all you require is a flexible stockbroker willing to offer you the ability to go short a stock, some margin if necessary and access to decent technical charting software (check out the later section 'Step 2: Visually confirming correlation using charts'). In Chapter 4 I look in detail at technical indicators such as the moving average as a way of indicating potential opportunities.

Step 1: Choosing the stock pair

The first place to start is with an obvious set of parallel companies or markets. Competing companies in the same sector make natural potential pairs. Also certain companies have several classes of shares trading simultaneously (for example, common and preferred) that should move largely in unison. Many big companies are also simultaneously traded on multiple exchanges or have international subsidiaries (for example, Dutch and Royal Shell). Crucially, highly correlated pairs often (but not always) come from the same sector because they face similar systematic risks.

Both *common stocks*, the stocks most people think of when they hear the term 'stocks', and *preferred stocks* represent a percentage of ownership in a company. With common stocks, shareholders receive dividends, possess voting privileges and have limited liability in the event that the company goes bankrupt. In a bankruptcy, common stockholders are at the bottom of the 'who gets paid first' ladder and can receive company assets only after other creditors and preferred stockholders have been paid. With preferred stocks, shareholders receive a fixed dividend, have no voting rights and, in the event of liquidation, have a higher priority on the company's assets than do common stockholders.

Moving beyond these obvious candidates, the most basic method is to use some form of quantitative or statistical method. These techniques involve studying historical price patterns to project how well a stock is going to perform in the future. Most traditional hedge-fund managers use what's called *fundamental analysis* – systematically analysing industries and companies to find those on the brink of positive, or negative, change.

Step 2: Visually confirming correlation using charts

The Internet is full of great websites that offer state-of-the-art technical charting software, most of which allows you to put the recent share prices of two companies up against each other.

Try http://www.finance.yahoo.com/charts for some amazing real-time charting tools.

Figure 3-1 shows the share price of two peer companies – Pepsico (the thin-ner line) and Coca-Cola (the thicker line). As you can see, since 2007 these shares have moved largely in tandem with each other, indicating a potential pairs trade.

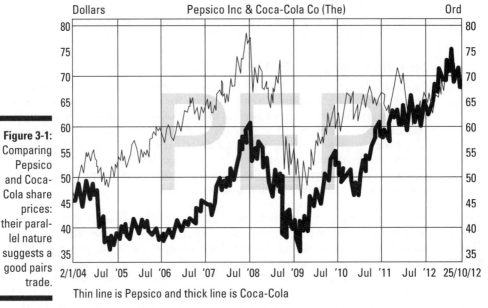

Figure 3-1:
Comparing Pepsico and Coca-Cola share prices: their paral-lel nature suggests a good pairs trade.

Thin line is Pepsico and thick line is Coca-Cola

Source: ShareScope

Step 3: Creating a chart showing the price ratio between the two stocks

A *price ratio* chart is a line chart of both stocks plotted together, which you calculate by dividing one stock price by the other. These charts measure devia-tion from the mean (or average spread) between the two stocks in the pair.

In Figure 3-1 (which isn't a price ratio chart) you can clearly see that since late 2007 these two shares have moved in a similar direction, but since 2011 the shares of Coca-Cola have notably diverged, with Coca-Cola moving ahead of Pepsico. In this example, therefore, a pairs strategy would involve going long (buying) shares in Coca-Cola and going short (selling) shares in Pepsico.

Many modern hedge-fund managers looking for potential pairs also use *neural networks*, which are a new generation of artificial intelligence that simulates the processes of the brain. In a way these technology-based brains are able to 'learn' from past experience. They identify the most likely outperformers and underperformers in a particular sector by looking at variables such as the relationship between the current price and the price in the recent past, and the interrelationship between prices of various shares.

Assessing the pros and cons of pairs trading

Pairs trading is a relatively simple-to-understand strategy – and one that ordinary investors can copy easily if they have access to online fundamentals-based data sources. (Fundamental-based data sources track information, such as the industry conditions, a company's current financial condition and potential for future growth and so on, to determine the company's intrinsic value.)

Pairs trading is hugely and rightly popular because it's self-funding (the short sale returns can be used to buy the long position) and the price of a share does follow certain key trends or processes. In particular, *the law of one price* is hugely relevant. This proposition states that two investments with the same payoff in every state of nature must have the same current value. A strong historical correlation suggests that they behave the same way in a large number of states, and so *should* be priced the same.

Simply put, the relationship between two correlated stocks is much more predictable and reliable than the outright prediction of the direction of a particular stock.

Pairs trading contains several potential challenges that you need to remember:

- ✔ **Immense popularity:** Perhaps the most obvious problem is that huge numbers of hedge funds and other institutional investors have now piled into pairs trading and evidence suggests that it's too popular for its own good. The original Morgan Stanley group, for instance, was initially extremely profitable but disbanded with losses only a few years later. Many other big investment institutions have also decided to abandon pairs-based trading operations and focus on more unconventional strategies.

- ✔ **Transaction costs:** Fees such as commissions and bid-ask spreads can eat up the theoretical returns in such an active strategy.

- ✔ **Spurious correlations:** This most deadly of problems is when an investor thinks that she's spotted shares that are closely correlated and yet in reality this relationship breaks down very quickly as outside forces intervene.

Comprehending Covered Call Writing

Many hedge-fund managers focus their interest on *blue chips*: that is, large, liquid stocks in well-known companies. These stocks are hugely attractive to hedge funds because so much is available to buy, sell, borrow and option in nearly endless quantities. In sum, blue chips can be cheaply and quickly traded. Plus, massive outfits such as BP, Exxon, GE and so on are very transparent to the market. As a result, hundreds of researchers and analysts are watching their every move, estimating every conceivable financial ratio (such as liquidity ratios, activity ratios, debt ratios and more, that allow comparisons between companies and between different time periods in one company) and closely watching all metrics (indicators, such as real revenue growth, operating expenses, return on assets and more, that give clues about a company's current financial health and potential future performance).

When most fund managers have these shares in their portfolios, they sit tight and wait for them to rise in value. But not hedge-fund managers. They can make extra money from stocks sitting in their portfolio by using what's called a *covered call options strategy*. They use their 'book' of *long assets* (shares they own) to write options that can make them extra money (from premiums) for frankly not doing very much at all!

Understanding options

Certainly stock markets can be volatile, scary places at times, but they can also go sideways for long periods. When that happens, making decent returns from just buying and holding shares can be a challenge. Covered call option writing is especially popular among share-based hedge-fund managers operating in relatively sideways-moving markets.

I look at the strange world of options trading in detail in Chapter 16, but for now you just need to know that *options* come in two basic forms:

- ✔ **Call option:** The right to buy a share at some point in the future (usually in three to six months).
- ✔ **Put option:** The right to sell a share in the future.

The idea behind covered call writing is simple – you hold a tight (concentrated and focused) portfolio of maybe 20 shares where you sell a series of in-the-money calls over a rolling three- or six-month period. Although the value of these futures-based options depends on loads of different variables, the crucial idea is whether the option is in-the-money or not.

To explain in-the-money, here's a practical example. Imagine buying a call option on stock with a strike price (at issue) of £22 while the price of the stock is £25. In this situation the call option is considered to be *in-the-money*, because the option gives you the right to buy the stock for £22 but you can immediately sell the stock for £25, a gain of £3.

All things being equal, an in-the-money option is more valuable than an out-of-the-money option (its reverse), although the potential for massive gains is much greater with the latter.

These calls effectively limit your upside – if the shares shoot way above the strike price, you have to deliver the underlying shares to the buyer at the agreed upon price. Yet they do provide you with a stream of options premiums that can be added to the returns from the underlying dividends paid out (assuming that the underlying shares produce a dividend, which you still receive even though you issued the option).

Any investor with a portfolio stuffed full of mainstream, liquid FTSE 100 stocks (particularly those generating a high yield) can use the covered call writing strategy. If you think that markets are unlikely to shoot up in value, you can write calls on your core shares and continue to collect dividends on your underlying investments.

Clearly, this strategy doesn't work if you sell too many calls in a booming market (you'd be selling away your upside) and it doesn't save you completely in a vicious bear (falling) market.

Discovering how covered calls work

Imagine that you have 10,000 BP shares worth 470 pence each. You think that they're unlikely to go up and that they may indeed fall slightly in the near future. However, you still want to hang on to them for the longer term. To boost your returns in the meantime, you grant ten call option contracts that expire next month: that is, you write out a contract that involves you 'selling' an option on those shares. These call options give the buyer the right to buy BP shares at a price of 480 pence. In return, you receive a premium of 15.75 pence per share.

Each call option contract represents 1,000 shares, and so for ten contracts you receive 10,000 × 15.75 pence = £1,575. Subtracting the 15.75 pence premium from today's share price of 470 pence means that you're protected from falls down to 454 pence. So 454 pence is your break-even point. After this, you make losses if the price falls any farther, albeit slightly offset by the premium income you received.

The options expiry date duly arrives. The share price is below the 480 pence strike price, which means that the option owner is clearly not going to exercise her right to buy, because she can buy BP shares more cheaply in the open market. Therefore you keep your shares, pocket the premium income from the dividend and also collect any dividends sent through over the time.

You're now free to repeat the operation by writing another set of calls with a new exercise price against your BP shares.

Combined with the dividends you receive on your holding of BP shares, a covered call writing strategy offers a nice way to supplement your income during quiet market times.

If you're going to write covered calls regularly, understanding the directional bias of the share in question is absolutely essential (that is, you want to know in which direction the stock is likely to move upon the release of anticipated financial reports and current events). You can generate steady returns if you find a share with a relatively stable price and a bias to the upside.

Weighing up trading strategies for writing calls

The really big problem with the strategy of writing covered calls is if the share price collapses, dropping below your break-even point in the process: at what point do you bail out?

Your alternatives when a share falls below its break-even point are:

- **Sell the shares, but keep the call option open, turning your covered call into a naked written call.** Now you're potentially on the hook for unlimited losses if the share unexpectedly sky-rockets and your options broker therefore requires you to lodge a deposit. Converting to naked call writing in this way isn't a recommended course of action for most people.

- **Exit the position in its entirety, selling the share and buying the option.** But this action is undesirable because you have to pay something to purchase the option, increasing the hit you've taken on the value of the share.

- **Take the risk of accepting the loss and writing calls on the share for the next month to help make up for any losses you make.** This choice can be successful if you manage to build up a small nest egg for those periods when the market moves against you.

Make sure that you remain aware of the dates when the shares you own go ex-dividend (the date at which the dividend goes to the person who bought the security rather than the person who sold the security). This event skews the premiums for call prices and you lose out if you don't hold the shares on the payment date. In a situation where the market is trending lower, you may want to think about reversing the strategy and look at trading covered *puts* – where you look to purchase the shares.

Following the Shareholder Activist Strategy

Like the other hedge-fund strategies that I describe in this chapter, the shareholder activist approach is also based on owning large-cap shares (shares in companies valued at US$10 billion or more). This time, however, it involves investors getting all muscular with the management of the company in which they own shares (I look at shareholder activism in much greater detail in Chapter 12).

Profiting from shareholder activism

Imagine a simple scenario. A hedge-fund manager owns shares in a large technology company where its competitors are slowly but steadily eating its lunch. As the competition chips away at the market edge this tech company previously commanded, its share price has done okay but is no star. The manager could profit from a pairs strategy (as I explain in the earlier section 'Treating Companies as Couples: Pairs Trading'), but can't make money from covered calls (see the earlier 'Comprehending Covered Call Writings' section) because the company doesn't issue dividends. She's generally dissatisfied but does think that value resides in the company and its shares (many shareholder activists are strongly influenced by the value investing ideas that I spell out in Chapter 9: see it as value investing on steroids!).

As a shareholder she decides that she's had enough. She writes to the management and demands change, especially as she owns a chunky block of shares amounting to a few per cent of the company. She wants the management to do something about the share price, ideally by changing the way it runs the company. She also expects the management to ignore her totally and so starts a campaign with other shareholders to create a fuss.

News articles appear and she corrals the group of investors ahead of the regular shareholder meetings. She puts up a rival bunch of directors and comes up with her own plan for change. Eventually the management caves in, makes changes, accepts her directors, starts selling businesses and reluctantly begins focusing on being nicer to the shareholders. The share price ticks up and the activist shareholder sells out having made a decent profit by being a bit difficult.

This is exactly what happened a few years back to a leading US technology company (Yahoo) that had the misfortune to be on the wrong end of a campaign by legendary hedge-fund manager and activist, Dan Loeb. Most importantly, dozens of managers around the world use this strategy, with varying degrees of success and noise.

As a private investor, make sure that you work out where the activists are going to pounce next and whether they have much chance of making the shareholders new profits.

Finding suitable 'at risk' candidates

Activist managers in the world of hedge funds have been around forever and value investors in the US have been turning up at the gates of the giant corporates since the end of the Second World War.

These buccaneers have been called various names over time, but one idea links all their battles: they like to target a decent company with solid fundamentals (characteristics making it a potentially strong company to invest in) that has lost its way and needs a new sense of direction, which the existing management probably can't provide.

This logic suggests a simple focus for you as an investor. Look for companies with decent fundamentals and sound business structures and see whether a shareholder activist is lurking on the share register. Crucially, make sure that room exists for some upside in the share price. Activists are unlikely to turn up at fabulously successful companies where the management are fab and the share price has already exploded. Apple for instance is unlikely to be a target for shareholder activists while its iPhones still rule the world, though that can all change after a few strategic mistakes!

Activists are more likely to emerge at companies with a mismatch between the share price and the total value of all the assets on the balance sheet. They also look to pick on companies with lots of cash swilling around but where that money is being badly spent by the managers (usually on executive pay and wasteful acquisitions). (In Chapter 9 I explore these key measures that shareholder activists use in more detail.)

Like all great investment strategies, the success of following the activist is largely about getting your timing right. When everyone joins in the merry game, the share price can move sharply and the opportunity for more profits begins to fade the higher the share price goes. The tactical and agile succeed at this strategy.

You also need to stay alert for two additional factors:

- **Managers can put up a very effective fight.** They may see off the activists and then slip back into their bad old ways – dragging down the share price yet again!

- **Activists' vitriol aimed at a board of directors can become corrosive to the company's future.** If investors start to think that matters have become dismal, the share price can keep on falling and attract the attention of vulture investors who sense a corporate crash. Short-sellers may emerge en masse, selling the shares to push the price down and make money – which spells disaster for your activist strategy.

Meeting Merger Arbitrage

Merger arbitrage is a strategy largely targeted at blue chip companies, which focuses on price discrepancies that open up during mergers and acquisitions (M&A) battles. Sometimes called *risk arbitrage*, it involves investment in *event-driven situations* such as leveraged buyouts, mergers and hostile takeovers. Merger arbitrage is based on the fact that share-price movements during a takeover tend to follow patterns.

The key insight with this strategy is that the price of the target usually rises, and the price of the acquirer usually falls, when a bid is announced (or even rumoured or otherwise anticipated). Because some degree of uncertainty usually applies as to whether an announced transaction ultimately happens – regulatory and financing hurdles, as well as shareholder approval, are among the potential obstacles to closing a deal – takeover targets often trade at a discount to the announced target price.

A typical approach may be to buy the target and short the acquirer, and profit from the price movements if the bid succeeds or the price is raised. An arbitrageur who expects the bid to fail would, similarly, short the target and buy the acquirer. Therefore, merger arbitrage is a market-neutral strategy (like pairs trading).

Observing the process in practice

Canada has lots of large, strategic oil companies that are frequently the target of international buyers. In July 2012, local oil and gas company Nexen became the target of a takeover bid from China National Offshore Oil Corp (CNOOC) for $27.50 per share. As you can see from the graphic in Figure 3-2, on the day of the offer the share price soared by 50 per cent to $26.

In the days and weeks following the announcement, you may have expected the share price to rise to a tad under $27.50 but in fact it declined in value to $25.60, 6.9 per cent below the agreed price by mid-October – before falling again to under $24 per share by the end of the month. This price differential tells you that in the weeks after the deal was announced the market was unsure about the deal going through: among other things, the Canadian government flagged it for review under the Investment Canada Act.

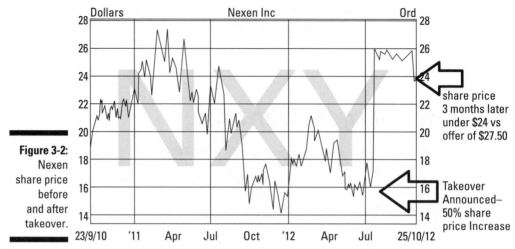

share price
3 months later
under $24 vs
offer of $27.50

Takeover
Announced–
50% share
price Increase

Figure 3-2:
Nexen
share price
before
and after
takeover.

Source: ShareScope

In such a situation, many hedge funds would be looking for the details of the offer, focusing in particular on the mix of shares and cash being offered. In an all-cash situation such as CNOOC's proposed acquisition of Nexen, the stock of the target company would be bought by the arbitrageur, whereas in the case of a largely stock-based offer the shares of the acquiring company are also sold short.

Your greatest opportunities are going to come from takeovers and not mergers, because the price movements are greater, and you're likely to make your biggest profits when the terms of the deal have to be improved. Hedge-fund managers look for circumstances where the acquiring company offers to buy for cash or exchange for its own stock all the outstanding shares of the target company and also where the acquirer doesn't already own substantially all the target's shares. Also, most merger-arbitrage funds hedge against market risk by purchasing S&P (Standard & Poor's) put options or put option spreads (a strategy, based on the expectation that the underlying asset will drop in price, in which the investor buys put options at one strike price while selling the same number of options at a lower strike price; if the price drops as anticipated, the investor's profit is the difference between the two strike prices; see the earlier section 'Understanding options'). Managers may also employ the use of share options as a low-risk alternative to the outright purchase or the sale of common stock.

Considering the risks of merger arbitrage

Here are a few issues to watch out for with merger arbitrage:

✔ **M&A deals don't always succeed.** If one falls through you can end up losing money unless you're adequately hedged.

✔ **The scope for arbitrage depends on the level of M&A activity.** This activity can vary enormously and merger arbitrage is also affected by how efficiently the market reacts to that activity.

✔ **M&A activity is hugely impacted by regulatory issues, which can negatively impact takeover *breakages* (when a deal falls apart).** Breakage rates vary enormously, with high levels back in 2006 when liquidity was high and companies were conducting mergers for financial rather than strategic reasons.

Some very useful US-based websites look closely at M&A activity, highlighting potential opportunities. Take a look at one of the best at `http://www.sinletter.com/merger-arbitrage`.

Encountering the Earnings Surprise Strategy

Hedge-fund managers sometimes use a blue chip share strategy that focuses on one of the most closely analysed aspects of corporate performance: profits, also known as *earnings*. In simple terms, many managers bet big on a company 'surprising' the market with profits that are in excess of the estimates suggested by the so-called consensus of market analysts and researchers.

The *earnings surprise factor* simply measures by how much a company's reported earnings differ from expectations, relative to the stock's price. The factor is quantified as follows, where EPS means earnings per share:

(Reported EPS – Expected EPS)

No set number constitutes an earnings surprise, other than the fact that it isn't within the expected consensus estimate. Often this surprise leads to a sharp reaction in the share price, which is also dependent on how closely the stock is followed by analysts and the public at large.

The market often under-reacts to meaningful changes in corporate fundamentals in the short run, leading to subsequent earnings surprises and price drifts in the direction of those surprises. In other words, the share price pretty much constantly rises over the months following an earnings surprise.

Locating earnings estimates

Most investors – hedge fund or otherwise – tend to rely on the profits estimates that stockbrokers or *sell-side analysts* (analysts who research and evaluate companies for potential earnings growth in order to make recommendations to the brokerage firms for which they work) and researchers provide. Yet these analysts don't produce their numbers in a vacuum – their estimates are influenced by the projections provided to them by company management. Corporate executives use these projections to provide a basis to explain to the analysts how they anticipate their company performing in the future. From there, the analysts layer in some of their own assumptions in order to create an independent earnings estimate.

Understanding the dynamics of this relationship and the vested interests is crucial:

- ✔ **Company executives:** It's not in the interests of the corporate executives to produce massively volatile earnings, especially because their bonuses are usually tied to those actual profits. They like to smooth out profits and generally show to analysts that their company is trending positively. Therefore these projections may be fairly conservative in their nature – a massive downturn doesn't earn a finance director any plaudits whereas a pleasant upside surprise can trigger a massive payment.

- ✔ **Analysts:** Clients act on a stockbroker analyst's recommendation only if they think that the advice is going to help them make money. The more money a firm's clients make from a particular analyst's recommendations, the more valuable the analyst is to that firm.

Crucially the number of *buy* notes vastly outnumbers the amount of *sell* notes (that is, analysts tend to write more positive, or bullish, reports than negative, or bearish, ones), resulting in a constant push to be positive and optimistic. Analysts at US research service www.zacks.com note that:

> *The incentive for issuing conservative earnings estimates is that the company has a better chance of reporting earnings that exceed forecasts. In turn, clients will be happy to see the stock's price rise. Conversely, there is no incentive to issue an earnings forecast that is overly optimistic.*

Equally, according to Zacks.com, missing a forecast estimate by analysts is 'the most dreaded outcome, since it suggests that a company is not performing as well as investors thought' and a 'stock's price will often tumble in response to an earnings miss'.

Finding the biggest opportunity

In 1979 Leonard Zack (of Zacks.com) looked at the slightly peculiar world of earnings surprises and disappointments and found that:

> *the stocks most likely to outperform are the ones whose earnings estimates are being raised. Similarly, the stocks most likely to underperform are the ones whose earnings estimates are being lowered.*

Analysts have since honed their understanding of what constitutes the perfect earnings surprise strategy. Here's the practical, no-nonsense advice from Zacks.com of what an investor should do:

- ✔ Start by looking for stocks with a minimum 100 per cent earnings surprise where the reported earnings are at least double the consensus (average) analyst forecast.

- ✔ Not focus on companies that routinely surprise but instead look for real surprises where the company hasn't reported consistent positive surprises in previous quarters.

- ✔ Disqualify stocks if the company's guidance for future growth isn't consistent with the just-reported results; that is, it has been fibbing about past failings and successes and has now moved the goalposts.

- ✔ Understand that the biggest opportunity is probably in smaller stocks because they're more likely to surprise and to be poorly researched by institutional analysts.

- ✔ Look for a big price move after an earnings surprise.

- ✔ Be sure that trading volume is up substantially following the positive news.

Seeking out surprise stocks

As an investor you can easily monitor quarterly earnings announcements, which for the most part happen when the markets are closed. US-based publications such as *Investor's Business Daily* (www.investors.com) and the *Wall Street Journal* (www.wsj.com) constantly follow these numbers, and online services such as Zacks also do a sterling job. You can find the Zacks service at www.zacks.com and alternative sources are the earnings section of www.streetinsider.com and the Market Pulse report at www.market watch.com.

Earnings surprise is a popular criterion for selecting stocks to trade because the market watches earnings reports closely, and positive (or negative) earnings relative to market expectations tend to send stocks higher (or lower). Focusing on companies that produce a big earnings surprise sounds elegantly simple, and it works. Analysis of the 3,000 largest US-listed names shows that those sporting an earnings surprise usually experience substantial share price increases over the subsequent month. The top-rated 20 per cent outperformed the bottom 20 per cent by 0.21 per cent per month, every month, from August 2000 to December 2011.

Many hedge funds make their investors a great deal of money by focusing on companies boasting an earnings surprise, but academic research reveals that much of the strategy's added value comes from the least liquid stocks. Therefore, running this strategy on a very large basis is difficult. The most positive returns are from the most illiquid shares, which are likely to be the most difficult and expensive to trade in; that is, they have the highest bid-ask spreads. If you pursue securities in order to take advantage of the price increase or decrease that typically follows an earnings surprise, be aware that the price may not go in the direction you anticipate and that, because of the often-illiquid nature of these stocks, you may put yourself at risk for extensive losses.

Chapter 4

Dealing with Volatility and Economic Cycles

*E*very profession has its tools of the trade; even clever boffins who run investment funds need the right equipment. For advanced investors the most important tools aren't chisels or hammers (though they can come in handy for taking out their frustrations) or even the humble computer and Internet-dealing account. No, the most powerful investment tools are based on understanding how economic cycles play out over time and how these dark, sometimes baffling, forces affect your portfolio.

These tools effectively operate like indicators or signals of two basic sorts:

✔ Powerful, clear signals can lead inexorably to hard and fast investment conclusions, for example 'definitely sell' or 'buy now!'. These signals tell an obvious story, such as of the onset of a recession in which shares are going to drop like a brick and bonds do very well.

✔ Subtler signals can be complicated and difficult to understand. You may need to interpret and align them with other discrete but inter-linked signals. This type of indicator is more common and works as an indeterminate suggestion that you need to keep an eye on the growing levels of risk.

No sensible, sophisticated investor can afford to ignore any of these signs, even if they choose to ascribe only a low level of importance to the contained message itself.

In this chapter I focus on four main categories of economic and financial cycle, each with its own distinct tools: the emergence of bubbles; the technical analysis tools focusing on the financial markets; the volatility of the markets; and wider economic cycles and how they impact markets.

Forever Blowing (Economic) Bubbles

Markets sometimes behave like frightened or excited animals, hence the widespread use of terms such as 'bull' and 'bear' to describe investors' attitudes towards buying and selling shares and bonds. This observation of the investment community behaving like a herd and so creating economic cycles is more than just an artful use of words. The insights built into it power technical analysis and its copious use of charts (see the later section 'Using Technical Analysis').

In this section I describe a simple economic cycle that every investor needs to understand – how *economic bubbles*, periods of madly trading assets whose market value far outpaces the assets' actual worth, emerge.

Bubbling up from trends

Key to the origin of an economic bubble is a *trend*, which when established (whether heading upwards or downwards) is difficult to buck as an investor. When investors get it into their heads that, say, markets are about to boom, and that companies are going to experience a rapid rise in profits, woe betide the solitary soul who stands in the middle of the herd shouting 'it's all a sham and is going to end in disaster!'. Not that the contrarians stop doing precisely that.

The bottom line is that perfectly harmless trends can quickly turn into something much uglier and more dangerous: bubbles with disastrous consequences. You may well remember the great growth sector of the 1990s – the technology dot.coms – and how the whole affair ended badly in an enormous bubble and then devastating bust.

Analysing the life of a bubble

Economists (or perhaps 'bubblanalysts') such as Hyman Minsky and Charles Kindleberger have identified five stages of an economic bubble:

1. **Displacement.** This term simply means that some external shock, surprise or new piece of technology arrives that creates a whole bundle of new profitable opportunities. The dot.com bubble of the 1990s was a displacement as the Internet opened people's eyes to the possibility of huge, global transformations in which entire industries may die and new business champions arise. From 2001 to 2008 the displacement involved a massive housing boom and the emergence of cheap, easy-to-access credit from large international banks.

2. **Credit creation.** The initial phase of displacement creates an enormous boom and large amounts of capital flood into the sector. As those profit-making opportunities become more common, banks and credit institutions sense that they can make money and they offer loan and credit facilities to all and sundry: from hedge funds (using gearing/leverage on their margin accounts – see Chapter 10) through syndicated loan facilities to huge private-equity houses that scramble to buy the best companies. Eventually demand for a particular asset outstrips supply, at which point all the money chasing a diminishing number of opportunities creates a massive increase in prices.

3. **Euphoria**. The technical term for euphoria is *momentum*. Eventually all this enthusiasm for a company, sector or theme gets out of hand and the prices of shares keep trending upwards, hitting new highs. Debts start to pile up among those feverishly optimistic investors, helped by the promise of ever-increasing underlying asset prices.

4. **Financial distress.** What follows is inevitable. Insiders cash in, sell shares and take profits. Banks start to worry about the risks and the share price of great growth stocks wobbles. Companies loaded to the gunnels with debt now find themselves in financial distress and the credit tap is firmly switched off. Frauds also become obvious as the tide turns against the sector: fictitious businesses suddenly find their cash flows dwindling to next to nothing. Mayhem breaks out and prices start to collapse.

5. **Revulsion.** After the event, everyone admits that of course they knew secretly the situation was a sham all along. Credit is stopped, and sellers are forced to sell their rapidly devaluing assets into a market that's choked with too much supply and barely any demand. Prices collapse and eventually everyone says that they'll never go near these kinds of assets again. A stage of revulsion is reached and the share price of what's now an 'ex' growth stock collapses. Eventually everyone moves on to the next big thing and prices flat line for many months if not years. Savvy investors say that everyone else has *capitulated* and then . . . quietly start buying again!

Anticipating bubbles

No hard and fast way exists of definitively spotting a bubble in the making. Some analysts suggest that whatever measure you use – whether fundamentals-based measures such as the PE (price–earnings) ratio or moving averages (see the later section 'Meeting moving averages') – look for an average value, work out a single standard deviation measure based on this 'average' and then start taking risk off the table as the price heads over that one standard deviation level.

Many clever investors stay well away from a sudden increase in asset values. One general response that you can emulate is to take profits slowly as the market eases into a bubble while tightening up your downside stop-losses. By placing an order to sell your shares when the price dips to a certain level, you can minimise your losses in the event the bubble bursts. Bubbles, however, are followed by busts and these busts can be fantastic hunting grounds if you're a contrarian investor who wants to buy a quality asset at a much reduced price. But most such contrarians only enter a market after everyone else has capitulated: that is, prices are low, volume is low and institutional investors have abandoned the asset.

Using Technical Analysis

Markets sometimes move like a swarm or herd, pushing prices up or down based on a trend. This insight has spawned a huge amount of interest in what's called *technical analysis*, involving carefully studying lots of charts and graphics to work out what the market trend or the price of your share is telling you.

As I discuss in the preceding section, trends are hugely important in the investment world. These great ebbs and flows in sentiment are quantifiable and so can be summed up clearly and easily in simple lines on a chart, using the constantly changing share price (or bond price, for that matter) as the basis of measurement.

In this section, I introduce you to a few popular tools for spotting and measuring trends. Note that the standard setting for most of these technical analysis software packages is 14-day long periods, but shorter ones are also popular.

Constantly staring at a price chart probably wouldn't mean very much if financial assets (shares, bonds) changed randomly every day, with no predictability. But that isn't true. Even academic economists who rave about supposedly efficient markets (which I cover in Chapter 6) accept that for some, if not most, of the time, markets move in broad trends that can last for a long time.

You can apply all these technical measures not only to individual shares but also to whole markets, as measured by an index such as the S&P 500 or FTSE 100. Simply call up the index chart (you can usually buy the index through an exchange-traded fund; more on ETFs in the later section 'Thinking about duration in volatility investing') and then put the technical measure to work.

Variability in the price of risky assets goes with the territory and since time immemorial shares and stocks have increased and decreased by substantial margins. Technical analysis simply puts that variance under the microscope, giving it shape and showing exactly how a market or share price is moving compared to its peers.

Spotting the trend

The vital analysis skill is to look at a chart and see whether you can spot the trends. In the chart in Figure 4-1 you can see a typical set of trend lines for a stock, with the support and resistance lines (as the lower and upper dotted lines, respectively) marked – when a lot of buying or selling happens at a certain price, these levels often become important barriers on the chart.

A barrier that stops a price from rising is called *resistance* and a barrier that prevents it from falling is called *support*. After you identify these levels on a chart, you can use them to plan your entry and exit into the market and also where to put your stop-loss.

To understand how this technical measure works in reality look at Figure 4-1, which uses a very popular piece of technical software called ShareScope (available at `www.sharescope.co.uk`). The chart highlights the popular media stock BSkyB (a major satellite TV network). You can see the trend lines for this stock since the beginning of 2010 through to August 2012 – the support moves from around 550 to 650 pence while the resistance increases from about 760 to 850 pence.

If a share breaches its trend lines in either direction, you need to be very careful. A breach of the lower support line may mean that the share's very cheap or that it's about to become much, much cheaper by falling sharply! Equally, a breach above (of the upper resistance line) may indicate that a share is over-priced or signal a sudden sharp move upwards. You need to treat shares pushing through trend lines with extra caution and deploy other technical and fundamental measures (such as looking for trend reversals, retracements or sideways movements; or focusing on financial reports and market fluctuations) to make a better informed guess about what may happen next.

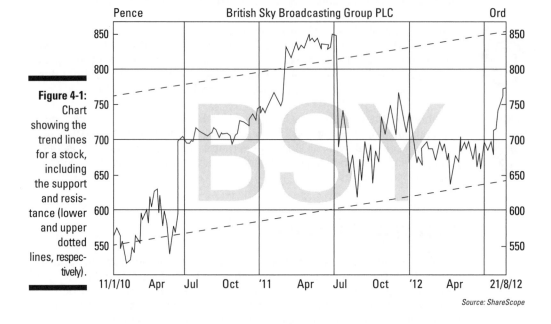

Figure 4-1: Chart showing the trend lines for a stock, including the support and resistance (lower and upper dotted lines, respectively).

Source: ShareScope

Trend lines and other technical indicators are just that: signals that command you to undertake further research. They don't tell you anything for certain about the future direction of the price of a financial asset. They are, however, a useful way of managing potential risk within a portfolio. If a share is constantly drawing attention to itself by breaching barriers or trends, it's either a great opportunity or a disaster waiting to happen!

Meeting moving averages

Moving averages (MAs) are one of the most popular and easy-to-use tools available to the investor. They help make a period of market data easier to read in terms of being able to spot trends, something especially helpful in volatile markets. MAs also form the foundation for many other technical indicators and theories.

The MA indicator is the arithmetic average of the prices of the selected range of days. It plots the moving average for the price and date range chosen. You can interpret a moving average in a number of ways, but generally prices above the moving average indicate a bullish trend and prices below the moving average indicate a bearish trend.

Moving averages are used to highlight the direction of a trend and smooth out price and volume fluctuations (so-called market noise). For example, an upward movement is confirmed when a short-term average (based on the last 15 or 20 days) crosses *above* a longer-term average (say, 50 days). This bullish signal is called a *golden cross*. A short-term MA crossing *below* a longer-term one is a bearish signal known as a *dead cross*.

You can apply all sorts of moving averages to technical charts but many experts believe that the 200-day MA is most useful: if a share trades consistently above that moving average it's in bullish territory (likely to carry on increasing), whereas if it trades consistently below that line it's widely regarded as a bearish signal. In the example in Figure 4-2 of BSkyB shares, about 760 pence is well above the 200-day moving average, indicating that the share price should stay relatively strong.

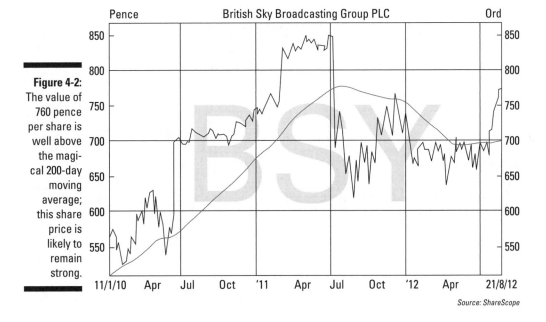

Figure 4-2: The value of 760 pence per share is well above the magical 200-day moving average; this share price is likely to remain strong.

Source: ShareScope

Beholding the Bollinger bands

Decades of careful market analysis suggests that financial markets move in trends (up and down) roughly two-thirds of the time and Bollinger bands aim to capture that core trading range of prices. In particular Bollinger bands remind you that however strongly a price is rising or falling, it usually strays only so far from a moving average before snapping back.

Bollinger bands aim to capture 95 per cent of price activity around the moving average. You calculate Bollinger bands as follows:

Middle band = Simple Moving Average of the closing price over n time periods

Upper band = Middle band + X

Lower band = Middle band – X

where $X = D \times$ SQRT (SUM(Closing Price – Middle band)$^2/n$) and n is the number of time periods, D is the number of standard deviations, SUM is the sum over n days of the moving average and SQRT is the square root.

In the chart in Figure 4-3 the thick lines indicate the Bollinger bands for BSkyB's share price, with its current share price of about 760 pence indicating that it's at the very top of its current band, with a possible short-term price drop on the cards. (Note that many charts, like this one, don't include the middle Bollinger band because doing so can become confusing.)

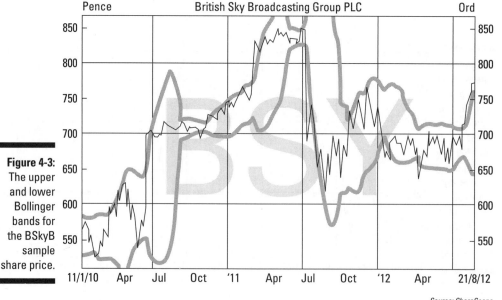

Figure 4-3: The upper and lower Bollinger bands for the BSkyB sample share price.

Bringing the Relative Strength Index into play

The Relative Strength Index (RSI) measures a share's performance against itself, and traders regard it as one of the most important indicators available to them. This indicator uses a formula to compare increases and decreases in the price of a share over a period of time. It can be used on weekly, daily or intraday charts and investors can change the settings using their own software or web-charting tools.

A low number indicates a more oversold market and a high value indicates a more overbought market. The indicator has a range of 0–100 (see Figure 4-4):

✔ Readings of 0–30 are considered *oversold*, meaning that the price may temporarily have gone down too much.

✔ Readings of 70–100 are considered *overbought*, meaning that a price may temporarily have gone up too much.

Here's a typical formula for RSI:

$$RSI = 100 - (100/(1 + (U/D)))$$

where U = average upwards price movement over the period and D = average downwards price movement over the period.

In Figure 4-4, for example, you can see the link between the price of the asset (top panel) with the asset's RSI (bottom panel). Notice how, for example, the RSI changes as the price fluctuates.

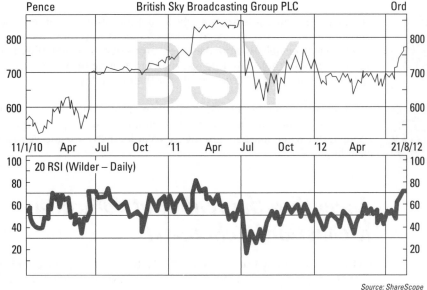

Figure 4-4: As the price of an asset fluctuates, so too does its RSI.

Source: ShareScope

Here are some important golden rules relating to the RSI indicator:

✔ Never use the RSI to justify going against a trend

✔ In an uptrend, use the RSI to find opportunities to join the trend when the indicator gives an oversold reading (0–30).

✔ In a downtrend, use the RSI to find opportunities to join the trend, when it gives an overbought reading (70–100).

Playing with Volatility

If we don't change direction soon, we'll end up where we're going.

Professor Irwin Corey, American vaudeville comic and actor

Investors are timid creatures, despite their protestations to the contrary. The language of financial markets may feature muscular terms such as rampaging bulls and ravenous bears, but in reality investors fight shy of too much change in the market measured by share-price *volatility* (that is, their movement up and down on a real-time and daily basis). This is despite the fact that investors can't possibly hope to make a super-sized return of, say, 20 or even 50 per cent by investing in shares unless they're willing to lose this much or even more on the downside.

But in recent years many mainstream investors decided that the potential for great losses is just too miserable to contemplate. Risk has been taken off the table globally and investors switched en masse from stocks and shares to supposedly less risky assets such as bonds or even cash.

The fact is that markets are volatile; sometimes more so, other times less so. And shares are inherently volatile, which means that they're risky. But that variance is precisely what makes them attractive. This volatility is in fact a major source of their superior return over the long term. Investors hope that upside days more than compensate for the down days.

Don't always be terrified of very volatile markets. Volatility can represent enormous opportunity if you're clever enough to work out where the markets go next. But when markets are highly volatile, take care and keep a buffer of cash in place.

Accepting the reality of volatility: It constantly changes!

Risk as measured by the term volatility is, by definition, constantly changing – investments based on an index that uses forward-looking options is never going to be a boring process and that change in pricing offers investors some specific opportunities. Most investors (correctly) think of volatility as inherently dangerous, but volatility as an asset class on its own can be profitable if you're willing to be tactical.

Although most investors rightly tend to steer away from volatile stocks, that doesn't mean that you can't make money as a trader from investing in volatility indices such as the VIX.

Volatility in the American S&P 500 market index is measured using the VIX options-based index and other instruments and is also trackable by all manner of financial instruments. These funds, notes and products can go up and down in value on a daily basis and investors can build a successful tactical strategy around these changes. Even longer-term investors can use volatility within their portfolios, through intelligent use of structured investments as part of a strategy that deliberately looks to diversify between different assets.

UK stocks have an equivalent volatility index (the VFTSE) and the European one is called the VSTXX. Through these different indices, you can in a sense 'invest' in volatility and look upon it as yet another asset class. In fact, it can be an excellent hedge for equity-focused investors. Many professional investors watch the VIX, VFTSE and VSTXX indices carefully.

Avoid volatility as a distinct asset class unless you're willing to understand it, examine how it's measured and tracked, and discover how you can use it tactically.

Measuring volatility

The daily increase or decrease in the price of an asset – bond or share – is measured through its *variance*, a statistical term that measures the underlying volatility of an asset.

Imagine two otherwise similar stocks over a month period in which both start and end at the same price – stock A moves up and down by an average of 2 per cent every day for a month, whereas Stock B changes by 10 per cent every day for a month. Both shares started and ended the period at the same price but Stock B is more volatile.

Investment analysis suggests that, if Stock B stays more volatile for extended periods of time, eventually its returns will probably be negative whereas Stock A's returns should prove positive, especially with dividends included. Yet volatility is rarely that predictable – many stocks move through phases when they're intensely volatile and then 'settle down', with a subsequent decline in volatility.

What's true for Stocks A and B in the example is also true for indices such as the S&P 500. These big, well-known indices go through periods of high volatility (usually inspired by fear) and then longer bouts of relative calm (where volatility on a daily basis ebbs away).

VIXing to invest in volatility

The VIX index was first developed in Chicago by the local futures exchange (the CBOE), which defines it as follows:

> The VIX measures 30-day implied volatility of the S&P 500 Index. The components of VIX are near- and next-term put and call options, usually in the first and second SPX contract months. 'Near-term' options must have at least one week to expiration; a requirement intended to minimise pricing anomalies that may occur close to expiration. When the near-term options have less than a week to expiration, VIX 'rolls' to the second and third SPX contract months. For example, on the second Friday in June, VIX would be calculated using SPX options expiring in June and July. On the following Monday, July would replace June as the 'near-term' and August would replace July as the 'next-term'.

Source: www.cboe.com/micro/vix/vixwhite.pdf

The VIX is an options-based index that features a spot price built on a series of rolling futures-based options. In other words, you can't buy the spot price as such but have to use options that range in duration from one day to many years (check out Chapters 3 and 16 for more about options).

The returns you can expect from investing in this spot price vary greatly from returns for an index; that is, the S&P 500 may go in a different direction to the VIX index. For some periods of time the correlation between the VIX and the S&P 500 can head in the opposite direction – in times of fear, the VIX shoots up whereas the S&P 500 falls and vice versa.

To view this relationship in action, take a look at the top chart in Figure 4-5. From 28 August 2008 through to a low point of 10 March 2009, the S&P 500 index declined from 1300 to 719, whereas over this same period the VIX index trebled in value.

By way of contrast, the top chart in Figure 4-6 shows returns from that last day (10 March 2009) through to April 2010. Over this period of time the S&P 500 (the thin line) surged from the low of 719 to a high of 1283 and the VIX (the thick line) collapsed by more than 60 per cent in value.

Figure 4-5:
Relationship
of the S&P
500 and VIX
indices. Top
chart: thin
line shows
the S&P 500
index falling
and thick line
shows the
VIX index
climbing
over the
same period.
Bottom
chart: The
correlation
between the
two during
the same
time period.

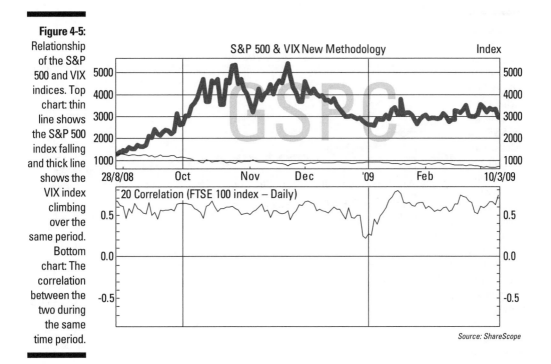

Source: ShareScope

Note: The volatility (or any measure of risk) leads to a fall in the stock prices if the index rises and is therefore bad for investment for the purpose of buying stocks. However, options become more valuable if the underlying asset (S&P 500, as is used in this example) is more volatile. Hence, the VIX is more for trading options but not stocks per se.

Volatility is usually negatively correlated with shares and so you can hope to see an increase in value for VIX trackers as share markets decline.

Volatility is one of the best ways of making money from sudden bouts of 'fear'; that is, you can view the VIX as the classic Fear Index!

Figure 4-6:
Relationship
of the S&P
500 and VIX
indices. Top
chart: thin
line shows
the S&P 500
index climb-
ing and
thick line
shows the
VIX index
falling over
the same
period.
Bottom
chart: The
correlation
between the
two during
the same
time period.

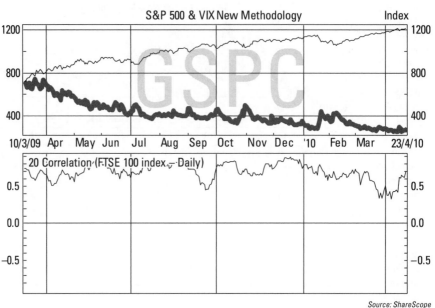

Source: ShareScope

Making (or losing!) money from volatility: Key trends and tactics

A small army of professional investors watch the volatility indices like hawks. These so-called vol traders have spent much of the last decade minutely examining volatility as its own asset class, constantly churning out key statistically derived observations.

If you look at these studies of volatility you soon discover that the average level for the VIX since 2004 (when the latest version of the index emerged) has been 21, while the standard deviation is about 10. These numbers imply that a move above 31 for the VIX index is a statistically significant increase in the spot price; that is, the increase is not caused by mere chance. The same studies also suggest that spikes in volatility aren't predictable and don't tend to cluster for fixed periods. For instance, the VIX climbed above that significant level of 31 over an extended period between 15 September 2008 and 24 May 2009, more than eight months in total. Yet more recent spikes (in May 2010 and August 2011) have lasted between one and three months.

Volatility as an asset class in its own right seems to experience *regime changes*. In other words, volatility remains at low levels for extended periods of time, followed by a pronounced regime change where it suddenly increases substantially for many weeks and months.

This regime change way of looking at volatility suggests that investors can make substantial profits as markets move from a regime of 'complacency' (when the VIX is low) to a regime of 'fear' (when volatility levels markedly rise).

A spot level of 30 is a significant trigger level for the VIX index, followed by a VIX spot level of 60. Also, if the VIX index pushes above 30 a good chance exists that volatility levels remain at these elevated levels for many days and possibly even many weeks.

If you're looking to make substantial profits from an increase in volatility (in a regime change) look at products such as geared *trackers* (index funds that attempt to match, or 'track', the performance of the index itself; in the US, 2 and 3 times leveraged trackers are popular), as well as covered *warrants* (derivatives giving holders the right to buy the underlying share at a certain price for a certain period of time) and *turbos* (options, specifically *barrier options*, in which the option is void if the price falls below the barrier level). With these products, returns from tracking an index are amplified or geared over short and very specific periods of time; that is, the leverage effect of the product structure increases the payoff that arises from an increase in VIX levels.

Volatility can be dangerous for your wealth

Volatility can be a killer and the most volatile stocks within a large index such as the FTSE 100 are usually the worst investments over the long term. Therefore, an index or portfolio where the most volatile stocks are excluded produces much better long-term returns than a standard 'all-in' index. In other words, the top 10 or 20 per cent most volatile stocks in an index destroy returns for the wider index.

Many investors believe that the most volatile stocks eventually destroy investor interest, causing a slow but remorseless fall in the share price as the long-term, buy-and-hold community of investors simply loses interest. If you're one of these investors, consider a *low* or *minimum* volatility index, where all highly volatile stocks are screened out or excluded. Doing so may be the best option over the very long term.

Volatility has increased in recent years

To illustrate the changing face of volatility over the last few years, take a look at the top chart in Figure 4-7. This shows the benchmark S&P 500 index (the thin line) and the VIX volatility index (the thick line). You can see that the S&P 500 has gently increased in value over the period from 2003 whereas its variance as measured by the VIX shot up in value to hit unprecedented peaks in recent years, before falling back since 2011.

In essence, Figure 4-7 reveals that recent years have seen a marked increase in volatility.

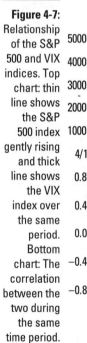

Figure 4-7: Relationship of the S&P 500 and VIX indices. Top chart: thin line shows the S&P 500 index gently rising and thick line shows the VIX index over the same period. Bottom chart: The correlation between the two during the same time period.

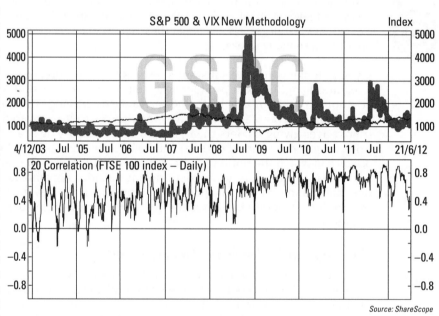

Source: ShareScope

Market volatility has increased on a day-to-day basis

The suggestion from the preceding section that volatility has increased over recent years is confirmed by Figure 4-8 from Chicago Board, the major US futures market. It shows historic volatility for the VIX index, revealing the huge change in daily price terms over the last six years.

Figure 4-8 suggests that daily price changes have become much more volatile, regardless of whether one uses the spot price of the VIX index or near-term futures that trade off this level. Markets have become more volatile and investors have come to expect substantial daily movements in share prices.

HIGH VOLATILITY OF VOLATILITY
Historic Volatility of Daily Returns

Figure 4-8:
Historic
volatility
for the VIX
index's daily
price terms
over the last
six years.

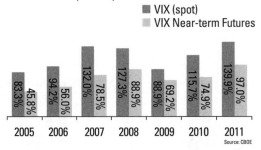

Source: CBOE volatility indices

In recent years big moves of 5 per cent aren't unusual. This increases risk within the market and spooks mainstream, institutional investors such as pension funds who have to constantly 'mark-to-market' the value of their now volatile share investments (*mark-to-market* means to represent the fair value of the asset, based on its current market price).

Thinking about duration in volatility investing

From what I write about volatility in this section, you may be thinking about using hedging in this area – if one part of your portfolio is aggressively long equities, you may think, why not hedge it by staying long VIX over many months? Although this sounds like a sensible hedging strategy, it doesn't always work in the real world of financial products because of the cost of rolling forward all those futures options.

Remember that the VIX index is composed of a series of rolling futures contracts and each time a contract is rolled forward, the seller has to write a new contract that includes the cost of funding that contract, plus a margin that compensates the buyer for taking on 'future' risk. The net effect is that over time on short-term futures (that is, a day to a few months) those returns from tracking the VIX decay because of this *carry*.

Figure 4-9 illustrates the problem of carry in practice. The top chart shows one of the first US-based exchange-traded funds (ETFs) that tracks the VIX short-term index. The ETF is from Barclays and has a ticker of VXX. Since its launch in early 2009, most investors may assume that volatility has stayed at pronounced and high levels, and yet the actual value of this tracker has mas-sively declined over time. The thick line shows returns from the VIX index and the thin line shows returns from the ETF. In reality the ETF has lost over 90 per cent of its value whereas the index has declined by only 50 per cent.

The difference can almost entirely be accounted for by the cost of carry; that is, rolling those one-month contracts every month for three years.

Figure 4-9:
Comparison of Barclay's ETF and the VIX index revealing the cost of carry. Top chart: thin line shows the ETF returns and thick line shows the VIX index returns over a 16-month period. Bottom chart: The correlation between the two during the same time period.

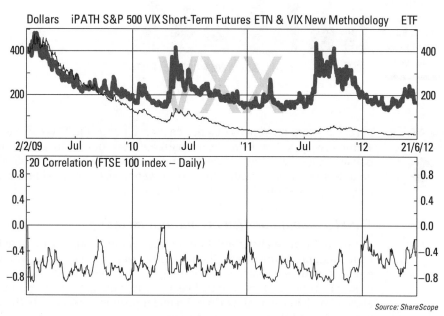

Source: ShareScope

But don't simply assume that the VXX tracker is a complete bust – volatility trackers can be extraordinarily useful *over short periods of time*. The top chart in Figure 4-10 shows returns for less than one month in 2010. The index and the tracker diverged a small amount, but by and large the ETF provided close to the expected returns.

If you intend to track volatility, do so only for short periods (a few days to a couple of months, at most) unless you can access a structure that minimises the medium-term effect of carrying forward futures contracts.

Figure 4-10:
Comparison
of Barclay's
ETF and
the VIX
index. Top
chart: thin
line shows
the ETF
returns and
thick line
shows the
VIX index
returns over
one month.
Bottom
chart: The
correlation
between the
two during
the same
time period.

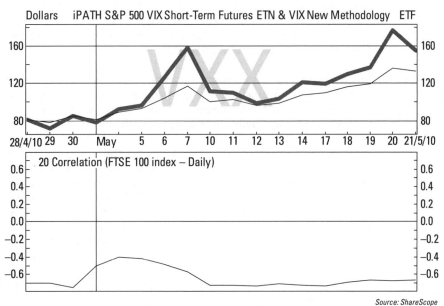

Source: ShareScope

Investors looking to hedge this downside can most easily run a hedging strategy in the short term; that is, over a matter of weeks or a small number of months. A successful hedging strategy for the short-term investor may be to go long (buy) a product that tracks the VIX index (based in turn on tracking the variability of the benchmark S&P 500 index) if you believe that markets are soon to become much more volatile . . . and fearful.

The moral of the story with any futures-based contract is not to use short-term volatility trackers over anything more than a few months at the very most. If you do, be willing to trade in and out of them at short notice.

Hedging over the medium term

Investors with a more strategic view of asset allocation are probably best advised to avoid short-term hedging strategies and focus instead on medium-term options-based structures (ideally, around the 3–6 months end of the range of maturities). In these structures, you look to invest in a futures contract that tracks, say, the VIX index, but with a 3–7 month duration. In these medium-term contracts the carry cost of the futures roll falls substantially to a level of 2–5 per cent per year. This lower cost allows you to stay invested for a period of months (probably no more than 6 months, at most) and still capture the main direction of volatility.

To understand this opportunity, assume that you believe that current levels of the VIX are abnormally low – and that risk is going to rise in the autumn as troubles in Europe start coming to the fore again. At this point you can invest in a medium-term product or tracker when the VIX is at 22.

Your working assumption is that you expect the VIX to jump to an index level of 45; that is, to double at some point before the end of November. Further imagine that over this four-month period, VIX does exactly as you think and share prices collapse in value, with the VIX hitting 45. The carry cost of rolling this medium-term contract probably amounts to 10–15 per cent of any gain, but your tracker has probably increased by just under 100 per cent. In net terms, you probably make a gain of somewhere near to 80 per cent from falling stock markets.

You need to invest only a relatively small amount of money in a product or tracker to get this exposure. Many portfolio-based investors invest at most 5 per cent of their total portfolio and only when they believe that markets are about to face substantial levels of stress, which can in turn involve losses of more than 10–20 per cent on the equity part of a portfolio.

Understanding the Importance of Economic Cycles

In this section I take a look at *macro trading*, the idea that economic cycles and the constant ebb and flow of businesses, economies, credit and spending have a massive impact on the *direction* of the pricing of certain key assets such as bonds and shares.

I examine this incredibly simple idea, which has turned into a hugely successful and fairly complex sub-sector of hedge-fund investing, in more detail in Chapter 15. Here I explore just the basics of the relationships. You can use the information in this section to adjust your investments to meet the challenges and opportunities that arise as a result of ever-changing economic factors.

Examining three economic rates that matter

Crucial to the subject of economic cycles are three simple rates and their impact on the wider economy and thus financial markets: the inflation rate, the interest rate and the currency exchange rate.

Inflation rate

The inflation rate, usually given by the retail prices or consumer prices indices, simply measures the change in prices of a basket of goods, services and, in some limited cases, assets. In simple terms, a sharp increase in inflation rates generally tends to indicate that an economy is operating near its current capacity.

That spike in prices is usually very bad news for investors in conventional bonds, including government securities. These have a fixed rate of interest and so any increase in inflation rates blunts that income, putting off potential buyers and generally lowering the real, inflation-adjusted price of the financial asset. For shares, the picture is slightly muddier because some equity sectors tend to benefit from rising prices (especially those based around resources) whereas most other sectors tend eventually to be hurt badly in terms of profits by rising inflation.

Interest and exchange rates

A sharp rise in inflation rates usually has two distinct knock-on effects on the interest rate and the currency rate. As central bankers become more worried about rising prices, they push up interest rates, forcing a slowdown in the economy and a sudden collapse in the price of shares. This sudden spike in interest rates is better news for bond investors because the result is a general scramble to move into safer government securities that pay a pre-determined interest rate.

Increasing inflation is also bad news for the currency exchange rates of a country. Increasing prices tend to deter outside investors who worry that they're invested in a veritable disaster of a country and currency. They start selling that currency, pushing down the exchange rate, increasing local inflation rates even more (although exports become cheaper) and trapping a country into a fast-deteriorating situation.

Reaching up for the growth cycle

The inflation, interest and exchange rates have a direct and sometimes immediate impact on a much longer-term cycle of economic activity: the ebb and flow of growth within an economy. The most commonly used way of measuring this cycle is to look at the growth rate of gross domestic product (GDP). This widely used measure tells you how fast an economy is growing in any one year. Crucially, this growth rate also fits into a longer-trend pattern, which indicates the long-term growth rate for an economy. Many developed world economies trend between 1 and 3 per cent GDP growth per year.

These trend GDP growth rates have a direct effect on two key financial variables – the earnings or profits of a company and the dividends it pays out. In simple terms, big companies within a broad index such as the S&P 500 tend to increase their profits at a rate that's roughly 1 to 2 per cent above trend GDP growth rates. Dividends also show a remarkably steady pattern, growing at a rate of about 1.4 per cent per year above and beyond the GDP growth rate and the annual inflation rate.

Recognising the importance of the business cycle

The longer-term GDP growth rate interacts with shorter-term interest and inflation rates with something called the *business cycle*. Basically, this cycle contains three distinct phases: the *expansion phase*, also called the *growth* phase, when the economy is growing; the *contraction*, or *slowdown*, phase, in which the economy slows down; and the *trough*, or *recession*, phase in which the economy hits bottom (this phase can sometimes result in a deep depression).

This phasing of growth and recession (accompanied sometimes by that less frequent depression) can be attributed to all manner of underlying causes:

- ✔ **The inflation, interest and exchange rates:** These can have a direct and immediate impact. For example, if interest rates increase sharply following a surge in inflation, you can expect to move from heightened economic growth to a sudden and sharp recession.

- ✔ **The ebb and flow of the credit cycle:** Many economists brought up on a particularly free market version of history (called the *Austrians* after their Austrian-born founding fathers) believe that the ebb and flow of the credit cycle (lending) has a massive impact. This group in particular pays close attention to the boom/bust cycle of bubbles that I discuss earlier in this chapter in the 'Forever Blowing (Economic) Bubbles' section.

- ✔ **The state of the housing market:** Another variant on the preceding business model approach looks at the housing market and how that affects the economic cycle and thus the business cycle. This group of economists tends to focus on economies such as the US and how the volume of new house starts, lending activity and local prices have an impact on the wider economy.

Whatever the exact cause of this ebb and flow within the economic cycle, a business cycle definitely exists and economists have minutely detailed every up and down of this cycle for the last 60 years. Table 4-1 shows the US business cycle as defined by its main national economic forecasting service.

As interesting as the historical data on business cycles can be, especially for investors, what you need to know is how to manage your portfolio to maximise your gains regardless of business cycle phase. For info on that, head to the 'Bringing cycles together: Asset allocation cycle' section, later in this chapter.

Table 4-1		The US Business Cycle (in months)			
Peak	**Trough**	**Contraction**	**Expansion**	**Cycle**	
		Peak to Trough	Previous Trough to Peak	Trough from Previous Peak	Peak from Previous Peak
Feb-45	Oct-45	8	80	88	93
Nov-48	Oct-49	11	37	48	45
Jul-53	May-54	10	45	55	56
Aug-57	Apr-58	8	39	47	49
Apr-60	Feb-61	10	24	34	32
Dec-69	Nov-70	11	106	117	116
Nov-73	Mar-75	16	36	52	47
Jan-80	Jul-80	6	58	64	74
Jul-81	Nov-82	16	12	28	18
Jul-90	Mar-91	8	92	100	108
Mar-01	Nov-01	8	120	128	128
Dec-07	Jun-09	18	73	91	81
Average, all cycles:					
1854–2009 (33 cycles)		16	42	56	55*
1854–1919 (16 cycles)		22	27	48	49**
1919–1945 (6 cycles)		18	35	53	53
1945–2009 (11 cycles)		11	59	73	66

*32 cycles; ** 15 cycles*

Source: National Bureau of Economic Research, Inc., 1050 Massachusetts Avenue, Cambridge MA 02138

The business cycle has a major impact on the pricing of financial assets. Put simply, a move into a recession is very bad news for shares and good news for government bond investors. A bottoming out of a recession offers a wonderful entry point for investors whereas a move into sustained growth (and possibly higher trend inflation) is bad news for bond investors.

Giving credit to the corporate credit default cycle

Bond investors pay particular attention to a derivation of the wider business cycles called the *corporate credit default cycle*. As the name suggests, this measures the rate of defaults by corporate creditors; that is, those companies that borrow money from investors using corporate bonds.

Figure 4-11 shows a chart from credit rating agency Moody's that covers the period between 1920 and 1999, pin-pointing the All Corporate Default Rate and US Industrial Production index. The latter index measures changes in US industrial output, while the default rates measure the percentage of outstanding loans to companies that fall into default.

No prizes for guessing the relationship between the two! As industrial output slows down, the number of companies defaulting on their loans (bonds) increases. An increase in default rates is clearly bad news for bond investors because it means that they don't get back their initial investment if they've invested in a defaulting bond. If default rates shoot up to, say, 0.10 (which means that 10 per cent of all loans default), any income received from a diversified portfolio of corporate bonds (anything between 5 and 10 per cent a year) is likely to be swamped by the flood of defaults.

Bond investors tend to anticipate these changes in the default rate and start selling off at least six months ahead of an industrial index slowdown.

Bringing cycles together: Asset allocation cycle

This section shows that investors are faced with a blizzard of different economic and technical cycles. They all sound very compelling, but to make sense of them you need to step back and think about how sudden switches in key measures can have an impact on your portfolio.

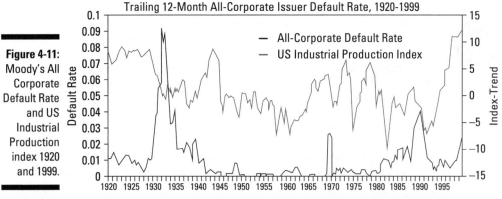

*Source:*http://ukmarkets.rbs.com/MediaLibrary/Document/
PDF/David%20Steven-son/TOTM_June_v4.pdf

Figure 4-11: Moody's All Corporate Default Rate and US Industrial Production index 1920 and 1999.

You also need to look at the net effect of change in key measures to see whether the economy is moving from one part of a cycle to the next. Help is at hand, however. US-based investment advisory firm Pring Turner has distilled all these cycles and processes into one, simple to understand, asset allocation framework. All the key shifts are well known, but the simple diagram in Figure 4-12 does show how the business cycle over 4–10 years impacts on individual investors.

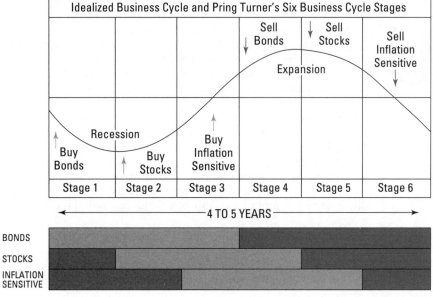

Figure 4-12: The Idealized Business Cycle and resulting Six Business Cycle Stages.

Source: Pring Turner at www.pring.com

The cycle and its stages in Figure 4-12 contain their own major asset class switch – as a recession deepens, you buy bonds but as that recession bottoms out you start to buy shares. Expansion is good news for shares but as an economy reaches capacity you move into inflation-sensitive bonds and then sell conventional bonds. At the height of the business upturn you sell shares and then start the slow retreat into conventional government bonds as the economy slows down.

Here are some general guidelines:

- **During a contraction:** When the business cycle begins to slow down, you'll want to move from riskier stuff like equities to less risky bonds.

- **During the trough:** As I note earlier, the trough represents the bottoming out of the cycle. Prices won't get lower, but you don't know how long it will take them to rebound and begin to rise again. In this case, you'll want to start moving out of 'safe' bonds and slowly into risky equities.

- **During the expansion:** A growing economy is a boon to everyone, especially investors. In this stage, keep investing in equities.

- **During a peak:** A peak, like a bubble, is a time of a lot of enthusiasm – but a contraction is just around the corner. During this period, you'll want to start building up cash and selling those profitable equity positions.

Choosing an approach to follow

If you don't have the time (or disposition) to keep track of these broad economic cycles, I suggest that you sit tight with a buy-and-hold strategy that's powered by the lifecycle approach I discuss in Chapter 2. Don't attempt to be clever and work out where you are in the business cycle. Instead, decide on your mix of asset classes and stop reading the papers!

If you're a speculative investor willing to indulge your trading habits, you can probably make most use of technical indicators (refer to the earlier section 'Using Technical Analysis'), but you need to be willing to move in and out of a position using signals based on price volatility. Whatever signal you use, speed is of the absolute essence! This approach requires much more trading activity and a willingness to use spread betting (in which you speculate on the price movement of a stock) and exchange-traded funds (ETFs).

If you fall somewhere between being a buy-and-hold and a speculative investor, set a timescale over which you're willing to make some tactical changes, but not every few days: perhaps a horizon between a few months and a few years. You don't want to make money from volatility or daily price changes but do want to avoid big losses from sudden switches in the business or credit cycle. In this case, analysis of the broader macro-economic cycle is the best approach for you.

Chapter 5

Digging Deeper into Alternative Assets: Commodities and Currencies

*F*or most people, investing is about shares (equities) and bonds (corporate or government). But many smart investors know that another more interesting game is also in town. *Alternative assets* is a term widely used by hedge funds, investment banks and pension funds to cover a range of underlying markets that don't fit into the mainstream categories and yet offer up opportunities for those in-the-know.

This alternate investment universe covers loads of different adventurous ideas, but for most people alternatives as an asset class boils down to two options: commodities and currencies. In this chapter you get under the skin of these two huge, global markets, discovering what makes them tick, examining why futures markets are so important to them and working out how these markets can sometimes be inefficient or predictable . . . or both.

Thinking about Alternative Investments

On paper at least, commodities and currencies *should* provide investors with the holy grail of modern finance: diversified returns that aren't closely correlated with shares or bonds. As you may expect, in practice things can be somewhat different.

Diversified returns (that is, returns from investments in different types of assets and asset classes) are hugely important because you don't want all the different portfolio investments to move as one if the share markets decide to crash in value. Ideally alternative assets should move in price (upwards and downwards) according to their own rhythm and cycles. In other words, they provide *non-correlated* returns, generated by investing in non-correlated assets. Non-correlated assets don't respond similarly to the same market trends; either no demonstrable relationship exists between their behaviour or the correlation is negative – that is, when one asset's value increases, the other's decreases. (Refer to Chapter 1 for more on diversification and correlation.)

Investing in alternative assets such as commodities and currencies can provide diversified, non-correlated returns, but that's not much use if they don't also provide the most important ingredient for a successful investment – a profit! Some debate exists about whether you can rely upon commodities and currencies to produce a positive return. As I explain in the next section, certain commodities have increased quite substantially in value over time, whereas others have decreased in value. And in the later section 'Keeping Current: Investing in Currencies', investing in currencies is, by definition, close to a *zero sum game* – that is, unlike shares, currencies as an aggregate don't increase in value over the long term.

Nevertheless, if you know what you're doing and pay attention to key principles and proven commodity and currency investment strategies, these asset classes can be advantageous additions to your portfolio.

Considering Commodities as an Investment

The global commodity business is absolutely enormous. It encompasses a huge assortment of individual commodities, ranging from stuff everyone knows about and despairs paying for (look at the recent price of oil and gold, for example) to more esoteric markets such as coffee beans or rare earth minerals used as components on electronic circuit boards.

Two aspects link all these diverse commodities:

- They trade internationally.
- Each one has a market price, that is, a *spot price*.

The market price varies greatly (as you discover a little later in this section) and isn't necessarily the same all over the world; the spot price of a barrel of oil in London for instance may not be the same as the price in Juno, Alaska.

To add to the confusion, the spot price is only one price among many. As I discuss in the later section 'Examining spot prices versus the futures index', the spot price only alludes to the price someone will pay for *actual physical delivery* at that specific point in time. Most participants in the global commodity markets (centred on London, New York and Chicago) don't want or even need that price. They need a price in the future (called the *future price*) when they can plan to deliver or transport their commodity.

Futures prices vary greatly and may bear only a passing resemblance to the spot price.

Consider commodities as a great *inflation hedge*. The significant number is the correlation between a key commodity index, the Commodity Research Bureau (CRB) index, which tracks the overall movement in commodity prices, and the US Consumer Prices Index (CPI), which measures how much the US dollar is worth, a key factor in determining inflation rates. A comparison reveals that the value of the US dollar and the overall movement of the commodities market is significantly and negatively correlated; that is, when one goes up the other goes down. If you look at the numbers, the correlation is –0.78 per cent for the broad index (a correlation value of –1.0 means that the assets demonstrate a perfect negative correlation); if you look at just the livestock sector of the commodities market, the correlation rises to –0.85 per cent). Thus commodities can work wonders in 'stagflationary' markets (when economic growth is slow, unemployment is high and prices are rising), with gold likely to do especially well.

Introducing the world of commodities

All the different commodity prices in varying places provide a potential profit-making opportunity for the smart investor, especially among the hedge-fund community. Financial institutions of all shapes and sizes have piled into the commodity markets in recent decades; according to some estimates, assets under management in commodity-related funds generally are approaching US$410 billion.

Investment-based traders are a major part of the commodity markets, in some cases dwarfing the original market participants – the producers of commodities (mines and energy producers) and their end users (large companies and governments). Table 5-1 shows the size of different global commodity markets and the financial size of turnover. Not unsurprisingly given their importance, oil and natural gas dominate with annual turnover of US$23 trillion (though that number also includes a huge amount of speculative transactions), whereas actual physical production accounts for just US$2.3 trillion. (***Note:*** 'Open interest' refers to the number of options and futures contracts that haven't been closed at the end of a particular trading day; some market watchers believe that a large number indicates more activity and liquidity for the contract.)

Table 5-1	Size of Global Commodity Markets: Physical and Financial Market Size of Major Commodities (2009/2010 US$ Billion)				
Commodity	Annual Production	Annual Exports	Inventories (End Period)	Annual Turnover Exchange-Traded Financial Market	Open Interest
Oil	2395	206	31.2	22843	193
Natural gas	584	67	NA	2084	29
Coal	844	124	NA	24	4
Iron ore	222	117	NA	NA	NA
Copper	143	44	6	10891	81
Gold	104	NA	NA	6249	76
Corn	130	16	23	1093	20
Soybeans	199	68	29	4775	41
Sugar	81	27	14	4425	27

Source: Federal Reserve of Australia – more details available at http://ideas.repec.org/a/rba/rbabul/jun2011-07.html

A few mind-blowing figures

The huge commodity markets have grown inexorably in the last few decades. Here are a few examples.

The financial market for (West Texas) based oil futures grew from US$30 billion in 1990 to US$120 billion in 2011, closely followed by futures trading in gold, which increased from about US$25 billion to just over US$60 billion.

Growth in some other commodity markets has been a tad subdued by contrast. Back in 1990, markets in natural gas, wheat, copper and sugar were all running at under US$10 billion per year whereas by 2011 that had increased to US$50 billion for copper and about US$15 billion for sugar and wheat.

As these global commodity markets grew in size (both physically in terms of output and financially in hard dollars), they also became volatile. Table 5-2 shows the volatility of daily returns from investing in a range of commodities (for comparison, I include data for shares). With just one exception these numbers suggest that the standard deviation (the measure of the asset's volatility) of daily returns has increased in all key markets since 2007, indicating that volatility has increased in all markets. (**Note:** A higher standard deviation implies more volatility; a lower standard deviation means less volatility.)

Table 5-2 Volatility in Commodity and Other Asset Prices: Standard Deviation of Daily Returns, Percentage Points

Commodity Indices or Individual Prices	Jan 1990 to June 2007	July 2007 to May 2011
Natural Gas	3.6	3.5
WTI Oil	2.3	2.9
Sugar	2.1	2.7
Wheat	1.6	2.6
Copper	1.4	2.2
Soybeans	1.3	1.9
Gold	0.9	1.4
Individual companies on S&P 500	2.4	2.8
S&P 500 Energy index	1.2	2.3
Goldman Sachs Commodity Index	1.2	1.9
S&P 500 Equity index	1	1.7
CRB Commodity Index	0.9	1.5

Source: Federal Reserve of Australia – more details available at http://ideas.repec.org/a/rba/rbabul/jun2011-07.html

Examining spot prices versus the futures index

Whenever you watch TV reports about increasing commodity prices, the spot price of the commodity usually gets a mention (sometimes followed by an off-the-cuff, grim warning about future riots and the collapse of global civilisation!). Although spot prices are certainly useful as a reference price, most commodity market participants (investors in mining companies, indus-trial buyers and hedge funds) focus on a very different set of numbers – the price of futures contracts with durations ranging from a few days or a month forward through to many years hence. These futures prices are absolutely essential when understanding the changing prices on the key commodity indices.

In the jargon of the commodity trade, these commodity indices measure the total return of something called a *non-leveraged* (no loans involved) *futures* port-folio. This term means that the full contract value of a futures contract – not just the margin requirement – nominally secures each position in the index. Talk of non-leveraged futures may sound confusing but in reality the key issue is that you're investing in a futures contract.

Imagine a futures index for gold where the spot price of each ounce is $1,900. You have two parties to a futures contract:

- **Producers** of gold want to make sure that they have a good idea of the price their future production of gold is going to fetch and may even sell the rights to future production now in order to lock-in prices.

- **Buyers** of gold such as Indian jewellers want to lock-in a decent price now for in three months' time.

These two sides agree a price for 3 or even 12 months in the future, or any-thing in-between. To secure the purchase, the gold buyer may pay an option price – after all, in this case the jeweller is simply buying a futures-based option on a commodity – and then deposit the rest of the final payment as a deposit in the form of Treasury bills. This way, the buyer locks-in the price and the producer receives payment. Add up all these non-leveraged futures contracts and you have a futures index.

Making money from commodities

The returns from futures-based commodities come in three different ways:

- **Interest** earned on the collateral deposited to secure the futures posi-tions (typically you pay an advance as a deposit, based on collateralised Treasury bills on which you earn income).

- **Return** obtained (if any) from holding and trading futures themselves (based on moves in the underlying spot price).

- **Roll yield**, which is buying cheaper short-term futures contracts and selling them as delivery approaches.

To discover more about this mysterious sounding roll yield, recall the example in the preceding section of gold with a spot price for delivery today of $1,900 per ounce. Assume that the supply of gold is low because stocks are down. Futures contracts may start trading at $1,895 a few weeks out and then fall to, say, $1,890 for two months. A smart investor like yourself can decide to buy these futures contracts and then sit around and wait for the due delivery date on the futures.

If nothing happens to the spot price, you'd expect the futures price to move towards the spot price as the delivery date approaches. Therefore you sell your fast-maturing futures contract (bought for $1,895) closer to $1,900 and then buy another futures contract for the $1,895 again. Over time, roll yield produces a handy profit.

The roll yield is a crucial part of total index returns. Futures indices capture the 'roll' from one contract to another, selling the expiring contract and buying the new one. The next month's/quarter's contract frequently changes in price – if it costs more the market is in *contango* and you lose out, while if it costs less the market is *backwardated* and you make more money. The existence of contango indicates, among other things, that adequate supplies exist to be carried into future months. This roll yield is hugely important long term and probably accounts for a large component of total long-term commodity index returns.

Futures prices are marked to the market, and this has important implications when you're buying or selling futures contracts. All open contracts are marked to the market at the close of trading every day, and the day's profits and losses are transferred in cash from losers' accounts to winners' accounts. These daily cash flows, generated by fluctuating futures prices, are known as the *variation margin*. If the cash position of a party dips below a specified level, the party has to deposit the difference to maintain the margin. When the cash position goes below the specified level, the losing party gets a *margin call*, also known as a *maintenance margin*. A rise in the futures price makes the seller of the futures a winner, and a fall in the futures price makes her a loser. The opposite is true for buyers.

Sifting through the different commodity indices

Investing in commodities is relatively straightforward after you get a grip on the issue of spot versus futures prices (refer to the earlier section 'Examining spot prices versus the futures index'). Instead of bravely towing an oil tanker out off the coast of Saudi Arabia and touting for physical deliveries, you sit quietly at home in front of a computer and invest in commodity markets tracked by major indices.

These commodity indices come in all shapes and sizes. The most popular choice is a bunch of major *composite* indices that include a wide series of individual commodities ranging from oil to pork bellies. But you can also drill down into even greater detail if you choose – some investors want to buy only hard commodities outside energy (say, metals) whereas others want to invest in agricultural commodities but not include wheat.

For many investors a broad composite index isn't quite good enough. They prefer a 'basket' of individual indices. These baskets tend to break down into four main sub-groups:

- ✔ Energy commodities
- ✔ Agriculturals broken into goods that are grown, such as coffee, sugar, pork and timber, goods that are mined or extracted, such as rubber, and livestock
- ✔ Industrial metals, including copper and nickel
- ✔ Precious metals

Beyond these baskets of commodities you're into individual indices that track a specific commodity. These indices are the territory of professional investors with specialist knowledge and are best avoided by most private investors.

Although the large variety and range of different index structures can complicate using an index to invest in commodities, here's my simple guide to the big commodity index providers:

- ✔ **S&P Goldman Sachs Commodity Index (GSCI):** Perhaps the most widely used index in the US and what's called a *production-weighted benchmark* of 24 commodities adjusted for liquidity. It's currently heavily weighted in energy products with 40 per cent of the index's weight comprising crude oil futures. Agricultural and softs, such as wheat and sugar, make up 11 per cent, metals 6 per cent and livestock 2.86 per cent. Because the GSCI index is based around the notion of 'world production', the constituents can vary widely – the dominant energy sector, for instance, has varied over time from 44 per cent through to 78 per cent, making it very volatile indeed. This makes the GSCI most susceptible to the effect of rotation between contango and backwardation in crude oil prices (aspects I cover in the earlier section 'Making money from commodities').

  This index is best for investors who want more exposure to energy assets, while at the same time (and because of the index's broad range of commodities), protecting their investment from events that could drag down a single commodity sector.

✔ **Dow Jones-AIG Commodity Index:** An equally popular series of indices that sits at the core of the exchange-traded funds (ETF) securities range of funds (see Chapter 16). It's made up of 19 commodities weighted primarily for trading volume and secondarily based on global production, with index rules 'designed to dampen volatility' by setting floors and caps on component weights. Crucially, the index has been set up so that no single commodity can comprise more than 15 per cent of the index and no single sector can make up more than one-third of the benchmark's weight. By sector, energy carries the biggest weight, at 33 per cent, followed by industrial metals at 20 per cent, precious metals at 10 per cent, softs at 8.7 per cent and grains at 18 per cent.

This index, like the GSCI, is best for investors who want greater exposure to the energy sector and lower volatility.

✔ **Deutsche Bank Liquid Commodity Index (DBLCI):** Consists of only six commodities, based around the most liquid (in trading terms) commodities in each sector: heating oil, light crude oil, wheat, aluminium, gold and corn. The index company claims that this narrow range of underlying commodities reduces the actual cost of roll and rebalancing. In practical terms, it means that energy makes up 55 per cent of the DBLCI; agriculturals and metals equally split the remaining 45 per cent. This index family contains no exposure to livestock or softs. Crucially, the designers – and the Powershares range of exchange-traded funds that tracks it – claim a unique 'roll strategy': rather than simply rolling expiring contracts to the next available month, the DBLCI looks out as far as 13 months for the contract with the highest roll yield. Theoretically, the index developers claim, this improves roll yields in backwardated and contango-ed markets.

Because the DBLCI chooses only the most representative commodities in each of the included sectors, it enables investors to buy fewer contracts (6, rather than the 19 or 24 of the other indices, for example) yet still track the index's performance).

✔ **CRB Commodity Index:** Started by the Commodity Research Bureau in 1981, this index comprises 22 futures contracts combined into an 'All Commodities' grouping, with two major sub-divisions: raw industrials and foodstuffs. Metals make up 20 per cent, energy carries a weight of 39 per cent and soft commodities 39 per cent.

This index, because of its reliance on agricultural commodities, has historically tended to produce lower annual returns than the more volatile, and hence, potentially profitable indices that rely on a preponderance of energy commodities. However, as agriculture heats up, this index may be attractive to investors building a more agriculture-centric portfolio.

✔ **Rogers International Commodity Index (RICI):** By far and away the broadest and most international of all the indices. Preferred by commodity purists, the RICI consists of 35 commodities, including such exotics as azuki beans, silk, rubber and wool. Energy comprises 44 per cent of the index, agriculturals and softs 32 per cent, metals 21 per cent and livestock 3 per cent.

A hallmark of this index is its stability (it's had relatively few changes since its creation in 1998) and it's best for investors who want exposure to international commodity exchanges.

Meeting a few methods for investing in commodities

A vast amount of opportunity exists in the world of commodities for advanced investors and traders. Hundreds of hedge funds focus on the commodity markets, using all sorts of strategies, some of which the more diligent, sophisticated private investor can copy.

The long and short of it: Treating commodity markets as just another asset

The most popular strategy is *go long and short key commodities, using key macro economic variables and index puts/calls.* This approach uses commodity markets as just another financial asset alongside bonds and shares but with the added insight that the broader economic business cycle has a huge role to play in determining the direction of markets.

In Chapters 14 and 15 I look in more detail at how this strategy works in practice, but here's a simple example.

Oil prices are heavily determined by the global economic and business cycle. If a country such as the US or China starts to slow down markedly, expecting demand for crude oil from industrial users and hard pressed consumers driving cars to diminish is reasonable. This reaction has a knock-on, cyclical effect on crude oil prices, which probably fall back. As an investor, you may take a 1–3-month *short* position on futures prices if you think that a recession is imminent.

As the price decline picks up speed you'd expect profits for large oil companies to start falling sharply and perhaps oil company share prices to fall as well, which again offers an opportunity for a short position.

Paradoxically, slowing growth or a recession may be good news for gold investors, because gold is traditionally seen as a safe asset in times of economic distress. This suggests a *long* position on gold.

Let's contango! Playing the roll yield

Another very popular strategy is to play the roll yield and the ebb and flow of backwardation and contango, which I discuss earlier in this chapter in the 'Making money from commodities' section. Commodity markets are very dynamic and can switch from contango to backwardation reasonably quickly, making savvy investors a great deal of money.

A simple trade may involve the oil markets (again) and contango, in a market where the price of a futures contract is trading above the spot price; that is, if the spot price of a barrel of oil is $100, the one-month futures contract may be at $105. In this circumstance a hedge fund may buy lots of physical oil on the spot markets (at $100) and then sit tight, holding vast amounts in rented storage depots. As long as the cost of that storage is less than the price difference between the futures contract (deliverable in one month's time at $105) and the spot price (the difference in this example is $5), the hedge fund makes a profit.

Commodity markets often exhibit the same characteristics as the mainstream share and bond markets, including having their own rhythms. For long periods of time, a market may trend higher as momentum builds. The strategy, popular with equity investors, of taking advantage of the swings between contango and backwardation can also be used in commodities and in fact has become so popular that a whole sub-species of hedge-fund managers has appeared called commodity trading advisors (CTAs). CTAs use sophisticated software programs to track and analyse all sorts of market- and commodity-specific information and to automate trading in order to take advantage of the changes in the asset's movement, either up or down. I explore this weird and wonderful world of rocket scientists and computing power in Chapter 13.

Using pricing inefficiencies

Price inefficiencies (in which the price of the asset doesn't accurately reflect the available information) also exist in commodity markets, especially if the flow of news information doesn't keep up with market prices. Natural disasters can have a major impact on commodity production, especially foodstuffs; the massive impact on potential future output from, say, a storm may not be immediately priced-in by the markets. This situation presents a hedge fund with an opportunity to exploit inefficiency through an aggressive trading strategy, called *arbitrage* in which you buy an asset at a low price in one market and then immediately attempt to resell it at a higher price in another market.

Finding niche markets

Plenty of opportunity also exists in specialist markets such as the *spread crack* used by the large US oil and gasoline producers. I explain this particularly attractive 'niche' in Chapter 13.

Accepting the risks of commodity investing

A popular myth says that most commodities, especially energy and food based ones, have shot up in value in the last few decades but economic data suggests otherwise. Using real commodity prices (in other words, adjusted for inflation), oil has indeed increased by just under three times in cost between 1900 and 2011, but the price of most industrial metals is still below 1900 levels (at about 90 per cent) and agricultural products have collapsed in value to barely half 1900 levels (50 per cent).

Another big concern is that commodity markets may have fundamentally changed in the last decade as investment levels increased. Hedge funds and big fund-management institutions have piled into the commodity markets, fundamentally changing them in quite possibly unknown ways.

This evolution opens up some potentially very worrying issues about scale. Take gold and the huge success of just one US-based exchange-traded fund, the State Street Tracks Gold Trust (GLD in the US). Launched just a few years ago, it's already worth a staggering US$72 billion and sits on 1,337 metric tonnes of the stuff, which is more than that held by the Bank of England and most other central banks.

According to a report, this one fund is buying up 13–14 per cent of the annual mine supply every year and has more assets than the next five largest gold mutual funds combined. Such a huge concentration of physical ownership, especially by a legion of private investors through a fund, raises the possibility that a sudden loss of confidence in gold may spark a run, with the exchange-traded fund selling huge quantities of gold overnight, causing prices to plummet even further.

Keeping Current: Investing in Currencies

Many hedge funds like to dabble in currencies – they positively adore the depth and liquidity of these markets – but you don't find many private investors (or pension funds for that matter) popping more than a tiny percentage of their portfolio in foreign currencies or an FX-based fund. Investing in currencies remains a slightly esoteric pursuit, strictly for the more adventurous.

Yet this lack of interest in currencies is a tad perplexing. After all, the currency foreign exchange (FX) markets are truly global in scale, with massive liquidity. Average daily turnover in the global FX market is US$4 trillion, which is 12 times the average daily turnover of the world's share markets and 50 times the turnover of the New York Stock Exchange. The annual turnover of the FX markets is currently running at around ten times world GDP!

Surprisingly, despite the general reluctance of private investors to jump into the currency pool, ordinary investors now account for 8 per cent of investment trading volume according to research firm Aite Group, up from less than 1 per cent a decade ago. A variety of reasons may explain this increase: the cost of trading (many firms don't charge commissions), trading hours (round the clock), the relatively small amount of money you need to get started, and the growing sophistication of the private investor.

Introducing the products and structures

Loads of different structures are available, including s*wap-based contracts* (privately negotiated, over-the-counter contracts in which you trade principal and fixed-rate interest on a loan in one currency for an equal loan in another currency), which grab the lion's share of daily turnover; *spot transactions* (purchasing a currency for immediate, or 'on the spot', delivery), the next biggest category and used for most physical foreign exchange requirements; futures contracts; and *conventional/unconventional* swaps (most swaps are in effect IOUs issued by big banks, but more unconventional swaps are available that have lots of detailed options built into them).

This diversity of trading structures means that the FX markets are deep and broad with tiny bid–offer spreads and so easily accessed by ordinary investors. But that sophisticated global infrastructure doesn't always mean that they're necessarily efficient, which is why hedge-fund managers say that these markets offer up plenty of opportunities.

The US dollar is involved in over 80 per cent of all FX transactions, equivalent to over US$3.3 trillion per day.

Swotting up on FX basics

Currency trading is fairly simple and involves a trade in which you buy one currency and sell another – betting that the first is going to rise in value against its counterpart. Buying 'euro/US dollar', for example, means that you buy a unit of euros and sell the equivalent amount in US dollars, profiting if the euro subsequently rises in value against the greenback.

This binary relationship between investment opportunities means that most trades take place in 'pairs' such as the following (see Table 5-3 for the currency codes):

- ✔ **Majors:** EUR/USD (accounts for about 28 per cent of the global pairs trade), USD/JPY (14 per cent of global trade), GBP/USD (commonly called the 'cable'; 9 per cent of the trade) and USD/CHF (under 10 per cent).
- ✔ **Commodity currencies:** USD/CAD, AUD/USD and NZD/USD.

Table 5-3	Currency Codes	
Code	**Name**	**Notes**
AUD	Australian dollar	Not available
CAD	Canadian dollar (also called the *Loonie*)	Not available
CHF	Swiss franc	Not available
EUR	Euro	Accounts for 20% of daily turnover
GBP	British pound	Accounts for 13% of daily turnover
JPY	Japanese yen	Accounts for 19% of daily turnover
NZD	New Zealand dollar (also called the *kiwi*)	Not available
USD	US dollar	Accounts for 42% of daily volume on global markets

Source: BIS Triennial Survey 2010

Crucially, because returns from currency trading are likely to be small in absolute terms (gains of much more than 10 or 15 per cent from one trade are very unusual), many FX investors use leverage to increase their profits.

Retail currency traders, for example, often borrow enough to turn a mere US$1,000 in principal into a US$50,000 bet. As a comparison, in the stock market the same trader would typically be able to leverage the same stake into just US$2,000 if she's lucky and has access to a margin account.

You can also trade currencies directly or use exchange-traded funds (ETFs, which I discuss in Chapter 16). You can go long (buy) a particular currency with a standard currency ETF or 'short' (sell) a currency, by shorting the particular ETF or buying an 'inverse' ETF that changes value in the opposite direction to the underlying index. You can also leverage positions with ETFs that offer 2 times leverage to the underlying currency's index. Finally, ETFs that simulate the action of currency pairs are available that can replicate the trading action of the underlying FX pairs.

FX trading is a zero sum game (you get no aggregate return from simply holding currencies), in which one country's currency benefits from another nation's economic misfortunes. An appreciation in the value of one currency can be expressed only by reference to another currency, which necessarily experiences a corresponding depreciation.

Making money from FX markets

In simple terms, FX markets offer the perfect environment for the active trader: liquid, deep markets that offer cost-effective trades, simple structures and lots of leverage – you simply have to supply the winning strategy!

Professional hedge-fund investors use these currency markets to take a *macro* decision (a big picture view, as I discuss in Chapter 15) and then implement it quickly and efficiently. What's even better, they can implement that macro investment decision using leverage to gear up their returns (for more on leverage and gearing, see Chapter 10).

Hedge funds and specialist FX traders have emerged as a very popular alternative asset for many institutional investors, with impressive results. One research firm that tracks hedge funds has had a Currency Traders index in operation since 1987 which tracks all the main US-based players. This index has logged only four down years, without a double-digit loss, whereas the S&P 500 has been down six times over the same period, with four of those years boasting losses exceeding 10 per cent.

Data from this index also suggests that those returns have been fairly consistent, if not exactly monumental in scale; in other words, don't invest in a currency-based hedge fund if you expect returns of 30 per cent or more in a good year. Many of the leading funds successfully chisel out positive returns of 2–9 per cent a year with a remarkable degree of stability.

Over the past decade, currencies have been half as volatile as stocks and have tended to move in a direction that's largely distinct from the trading patterns of stocks and bonds. In other words, they can provide you with non-correlated returns.

Deciding on hedge-fund strategies for FX markets

Hedge-fund managers operating in FX markets tend to fall into two big camps: discretionary and systematic.

Discretionary currency strategies

Most hedge-fund managers use discretionary currency strategies. These fundamentals managers believe that they can exploit price inefficiencies using models and processes in which economic and financial data are used as the variables, including balance of payments, capital flows, price levels and monetary conditions.

They use these fundamentals measures to work out the attractiveness (or otherwise) of a major FX market, usually based on a top-down analysis of key macro-economic variables. They may for instance look at the relative attractiveness of a currency measured against the local economy and local prices, or the volatility of a particular currency, and take a view that that situation may continue for some time.

Or they may copy famed investor George Soros and decide to take a contrarian view of a currency; that is, they may think that despite all the market concern about the future of the Eurozone, the euro is cheap versus the dollar or the pound.

One of the most contrarian strategies of recent years is based on the Chinese renminbi currency. The conventional view is that emerging market currencies eventually appreciate in value as their local economy grows in size and affluence. The contrarian view asks what happens if this broad trend is wrong. What if Chinese exporters are disproportionately suffering from a slowdown in demand from their western customers? Perhaps the Chinese currency will be badly hit and fall below consensus levels.

If you're a contrarian, you typically use leverage to boost likely returns.

Systematic currency strategies

This group of investors (also known as *technical managers*) tend to ignore external economic variables and argue that price and price history provide the most effective mechanism for exploiting inefficiencies. They use mathematical, algorithmic and technical models, with little or no influence of individuals over the portfolio positioning.

These fund managers may look at markets with a trend in operation, such as the market displaying 'momentum' as prices keep on rising across the board. Or they may look to find arbitrage opportunities where markets aren't being terrifically efficient (see Chapter 8).

Whatever opportunity they use, these fund managers typically employ quantitative processes that focus on statistically robust or technical patterns in the return series of the asset, concentrate on highly liquid instruments and maintain shorter holding periods than discretionary managers.

Currency overlay strategies

You may run into a distinct group of managers who aren't trying actively to make money from speculating on the FX market but simply looking to hedge their exposure; that is, to dampen down the effect of currency moves on their wider portfolios. This *currency overlay* strategy is conducted by specialist firms who manage the currency exposures of large clients, usually pension funds, endowments and corporate entities. Typically, the institution has a pre-existing exposure to foreign currencies, and is seeking to limit the risk from adverse movements in exchange rates.

Selecting strategies for success

In reality, currency hedge-fund managers are a bit more magpie-like than the preceding section implies, because they willingly borrow ideas from all over the place to make their investors a relatively stable return. Most fund managers in FX admit that in essence four fairly big trades pre-occupy most FX investors.

Carry trade

The carry trade is hugely popular among hedge funds and big institutional players. With this kind of trade in currency markets, you borrow in the currency with the low interest rate and then invest that in the currency with the higher interest rate. If the exchange rate doesn't change, this strategy generates a positive return.

Over the middle part of the last decade (especially up to 2007 and the global financial crisis), this strategy involved borrowing at low interest rates in Japanese yen and then using that loan to buy higher-yield assets elsewhere in places such as the US. Anyone borrowing for next-to-nothing in yen and putting the money into US government bonds at the time received a double pay-off: from an interest rate difference of more than 3 percentage points and from the dollar's rise against the yen. Investors made their profit when they reversed the trade and paid back the yen loan. I look in much more detail at this strategy in Chapter 14.

Convergence trade

The convergence trading strategy consists of two positions: buying one asset forward – that is, for delivery in the future (going *long* the asset) – and selling a similar asset forward (going *short* the asset) for a higher price. You hope that, by the time the asset has to be delivered, the prices have become closer to equal (converged) and you profit by the amount of convergence. Of course, the big risk is that the expected convergence doesn't happen, or that it takes too long – the hit you take can be especially big because convergence trades nearly always involve some form of leverage using a short position.

Forward rate bias

Another popular strategy among FX traders, the forward rate bias is based on the observed tendency of higher-interest rate currencies to outperform lower-interest rate currencies. This forward rate bias is a great example of what's called *currency beta* – currency investors are prepared to hold 'weaker' or 'higher inflation' currencies only if they offer a superior (real) interest rate.

The FX forward rate for such a currency pair (expressed with the higher-interest rate currency as the denominator) will always be at a discount to the spot rate, because the forward rate is determined by the ratio of the two currencies' interest rates. The difference between the spot rate on the forward date and the forward rate is known as *currency surprise*.

Momentum strategy

Many hedge funds focus on FX and *momentum*; that is, the propensity of exchange rates to trend in the short to medium term. In this strategy, you trade on momentum (which direction the currency pair is moving) rather than price.

Discovering the downsides of currency trading

You can see why many smart investors pump part of their portfolio into the FX markets. Investors poured US$4.7 billion into currency-related funds in 2011, even as they pulled money from domestic and foreign stock funds.

Most of that hot FX money goes into hedge funds, but even mainstream asset managers muscled in with a vast range of new funds, ETF issuers being particularly active. These outfits targeted ordinary DIY investors who want to develop their own strategies and trades.

That's good news for the FX business but not necessarily for many of the investors concerned, especially in mainstream FX-based mutual funds. Research firm Morningstar reckons that investors in mainstream currency mutual funds lost 3.3 per cent in 2011, after fees. That return is massively down on funds that tracked the US equity market (the S&P 500 was up 2 per cent, including dividends over that period). And that poor performance is no aberration: currency mutual funds have lost their investors' money four years in a row.

Unsurprisingly given these poor returns from FX mutual funds, many investors run their own DIY approach to FX investing. In the main US market, DIY currency trading volumes increased to more than US$310 billion in 2011, up from just US$6 billion in 2001.

When it works, FX investing can provide fairly stable, low-cost uncorrelated returns, but don't ignore the following big risks:

✔ Most FX traders use leverage to gear up returns; good news when they get it right but terrible when they get it wrong.

✔ FX markets may be deep and liquid, but without leverage you're unlikely to get big double-digit returns on a consistent basis, unless you have a great manager.

✔ Many FX trades such as the carry trade (see the earlier section 'Selecting strategies for success') look impressive and robust until they aren't – at which point investors lose a packet. The big successful trades are well known and very popular but that doesn't stop them being hit badly by a general retreat from anything deemed risky.

✔ FX markets are, by and large, fairly predictable and efficient. That makes it mightily difficult for an FX manager to make money by swimming against the tide. Some do, most don't – and that's especially true for private investors.

Research firm Aite Group reckons that only 30 per cent of all US retail forex trading accounts are profitable in any given quarter. You've been warned.

Chapter 6

Assessing the Hedge-Fund Industry: Don't Believe the Hype

· ·

In This Chapter

▶ Understanding that markets are mostly efficient

▶ Tackling trading costs

▶ Reading the charges against hedge funds

▶ Itemising hedge-funds pros

· ·

*I*n this chapter I peer under the bonnet of the hedge-fund sector and investigate the huge amount of hype and misinformation surrounding the whole area. I explain how the theory of efficient markets counts against hedge funds making money and that their management and trading costs are too high. I lay out a series of claims against hedge funds from sceptics, but balance that with a section on hedge-fund positives.

Despite some great funds and managers producing truly remarkable numbers, in general the claims made by the industry are suspect and open to challenge. Listen to the criticisms and avoid the worst excesses of the hedge-fund sector. But also learn from the smart managers who buck the major trends.

Investing in Hedge Funds: Better than Gambling?

Hedge-fund managers – and to be honest all professional fund managers – face an uphill challenge as regards managing money on an active basis. Understanding why is important, because if you're going to hand over your hard-earned cash to someone you want to know the difficulties that the person is struggling with.

Understanding the efficiency of markets

Over the last few decades academic economists have spent thousands of hours staring at returns from fund managers the world over. They looked at hedge-fund managers, ordinary fund managers and even managers who run accounts full of cash (money-market accounts).

Their findings reveal the main challenge for hedge-fund managers: the markets are mostly efficient and these managers haven't been enormously successful. Put simply, stock markets are incredibly sophisticated weighing machines involving thousands of individual players and a gazillion different trading ideas. Through the sheer quantity of all these individual transactions, markets get the price of a security or stock just about right. With most stock markets working efficiently, consistently beating Mr Market day in, day out is almost impossible.

Understanding the efficient markets hypothesis

According to the efficient markets hypothesis, stocks almost always trade at their fair value because their prices inherently reflect all relevant information. The basic outline of this hypothesis was developed by professional economists, such as Paul Samuelson and Eugene Fama, who tirelessly mined the huge mountains of financial data to discover how investors make a profit from investing in risky stuff like shares. Their conclusion is that investors make money from that income (via dividends and bond coupons) and from taking extra risk, not by second-guessing the markets, largely because those markets are efficient.

You may think that you know better, but the stock market is largely efficient and you probably won't be able to add much value through *stock-picking*, selecting a series of stocks or bonds to go into a portfolio based on all manner of technical factors but also more than a fair share of going with the 'gut'. Although picking individual stocks or bonds can be a rewarding pursuit if you're lucky and manage to choose right often, the odds are that most of the time you're going to get it wrong. The huge mountain of academic research constantly says the same thing, time and time again: stock-picking is a risky strategy that most of the time, for most investors (private or institutional), doesn't pay off.

Looking at the nature of efficient markets

Of the huge amount of academic research on this subject, you really need to understand just a few simple ideas about these supposedly efficient markets. According to economists such as Eugene Fama, financial markets have a relatively simple structure as follows:

✔ The primary role of the capital market is the allocation of the economy's capital stock: that is, your savings.

✔ The market requires accurate 'signals' to allocate correctly those scarce capital resources.

✔ Those signals are determined by the spread of news very quickly around the marketplace.

✔ The outcome of all this activity is called a *capital allocative framework*: a market in which prices always fully reflect the available information (that is, it's an efficient market).

✔ An *efficient* market is therefore one in which large numbers of rational profit-seekers (you and me plus a few thousand professional hedge-fund managers) are actively competing, each trying to predict future market values of individual securities.

✔ In an efficient market at any point in time the price of a security or stock is a good estimate of what it's actually worth.

✔ If a market is efficient, no information or analysis can be expected to out-perform any other.

An alternative to stock-picking: Buying the market

ETFs effectively allow you, the investor, to *buy the market*. In other words, instead of picking an individual stock in the benchmark S&P 500 index (based in turn on the New York Stock Exchange) you buy all the stocks in that index.

The focus is on indices because something like the S&P 500 contains the most valuable companies on the local stock market. Companies such as Apple and the like dominate that index because they're worth a vast amount of money. And they're worth hundreds of billions because they're successful and lots of investors want to buy their shares.

As a company becomes more successful, it becomes more valuable and its *market capitalisation* (number of shares in issue times the price per share) increases. As that market cap increases, it becomes a larger chunk of the total value of the index or market. So the market rewards successful companies that become dominant parts of a market, which is in turn reflected in the composition of the index.

By buying the market you're explicitly accepting that, most of the time, the other players in the market have assessed that value for Apple and all the other companies in an index about right. You may have your own views about Apple's true worth, but in a sense your views don't count. What matters is that the market has decided on Apple's value and you can agree (buy its shares) or disagree and buy some other stock.

Most academics believe that most of the time you're better off agreeing with the consensus and buying the market. Any attempt to force a readjustment in the value of Apple by you (the lone sceptic) will be rewarded by derision and a stony-faced broker who simply wants to know whether you accept the prevailing price or not.

Bucking the implications of the efficient markets hypothesis

The simple insight into how markets are largely efficient most of the time prompts some important insights. If you aren't terrifically good at spotting great investment opportunities, don't worry because neither are most other investors – institutional ones included.

The efficient-markets body of academic research has also spawned a huge body of theory that argues that the price of shares is almost random, and that what matters is the constant flow of news and its impact on shares. At its most ambitious, the theory even suggests that government intervention in the economy is largely outdated and unnecessary and that investors can be trusted to self-regulate.

Notice that I use the word 'theory'. By and large most academic economists accept the idea of efficient markets, as do most professional investors, but many disagree. These critics think that markets aren't efficient and that you can make above-average returns by diligent use of strategies and careful analysis. These critics are convinced that markets don't always get it right and that a fund manager in particular (running a hedge fund or ordinary mutual fund) can help the investor by avoiding (or shorting) the worst stocks and investing in the best stocks. In other words, even though the markets may be efficient overall, inefficiencies do occur and knowledgeable investors can use these inefficiencies to maximise their returns.

Working with the reality of efficient markets

The efficient-or-not-markets debate rumbles on and truth be told both sides have valid points of view. Most of the time, markets probably are fairly efficient weighing machines constantly putting a price on something that's about right. But they don't *always* operate as efficiently as economists like to think they do. Sometimes markets overreact and lunge into a bubble. Some sectors are also ignored by the wider market and all those news flow processes imagined by academics begin to break down. Out of this debate and analysis a consensus has started to emerge.

The home truths in this section represent the middle ground of most debate around markets, with a particular emphasis on the role of a hedge-fund manager. This massive industry has become bloated and expensive, passing on huge charges to the end user. These concerns serve to remind you, the investor, to consider the issues and think carefully about where you place your money.

Recognising that beating the market is difficult

You don't have to believe that all financial markets are completely efficient to believe that active stock-picking, especially by professional fund managers, is an expensive pursuit that largely produces little extra value. This statement isn't to deny that some investors and managers do profit some of the time, just that most of the time, with most active fund managers, you end up paying more for less.

Acknowledging that stock markets are mostly, but not always, efficient

Imperfections exist even within supposedly efficient markets: saying that markets are mostly efficient is a long way from saying that they're always perfect. Even the most ardent fans of efficient markets accept that certain types of share – with certain risk profiles – can outperform the main market much if not most of the time. This acknowledgement doesn't mean that this inefficiency and these market imperfections are easy to capture.

Inefficiencies have a tendency to change over time and mutate. A rigid adherence to a fixed set of criteria in, say, a *black box* – an analytical computer-based system – full of variables can be a risky tactic if the markets adapt and evolve.

Many of the most successful investors – in hedge funds and mutual funds – are contrarians who believe that the greatest opportunities come when markets behave most irrationally. By following their lead and looking for opportunities wherein 'crowd' behaviour has lead to inefficient pricing, you can maximise your returns.

Constructing strategies that deliver above-average returns

If hedge-fund managers are quick, nimble and able to look into the nooks and crannies of the supposedly efficient markets, they may be able to construct strategies that capture above-average returns some of the time, although those returns may be at the expense of higher potential risk.

Making a sensible long-term bet: Copying an efficient market cheaply

The bigger the market, the more liquid it is, and the more liquid the market, the more likely it is to be relatively efficient. In these circumstances the key is to cut costs and track these large, efficient markets as effectively as possible. This means trying to copy the market most of the time, because most of the time the market is right.

Getting to Grips with Hedge-Fund Costs

Hedge-fund managers are playing against a system that's jolly difficult to beat. Working out how and where the markets are inefficient is tough and even when they do perceive an opportunity they need to be quick and trade like crazy. That requirement alone brings with it a nasty sting in the tail.

The innovative trading strategies designed to beat the market almost always involve extra expense, such as trading costs and the clever research effort to spot the special 'system' that provides abundant profits for the brave and adventurous. The inevitable result is that hedge-fund managers charge more than their peers for the privilege of managing your money.

Considering hedge-fund charges

The traditional hedge-fund charging model is sometimes called *2 and 20*: you're charged 2 per cent per year in fees plus a performance fee that takes 20 per cent of the fund's profits when a certain performance target is met. That target may be the return from holding cash (usually expressed via the interbank lending rate of LIBOR yield (the wholesale interest rate that banks charge each other for borrowing cash over the short term) plus, say, 2 or 4 per cent per year.

Add these costs up and an efficient hedge fund can make 3 or even 5 per cent in a good year in charges on your fund. Yet the average total expense ratio (TER) for many hedge funds remains stubbornly above 2 per cent per year, whereas the average exchange-traded fund (ETF) charges less than 0.5 per cent per year. When you look at the charges made by a fund, focus on the total expense ratio because it comprises all the costs of running a fund, including the trading charges for buying and selling shares within a fund. Frankly, any TER of more than 2 per cent per year is unacceptable unless the manager is frankly a super star!

You also need to be especially careful about performance fees, which are in turn based on slightly suspicious-looking hurdles and targets. A LIBOR plus 4 per cent hurdle (which means the fund charges performance fees of 20 per cent of any gains if the fund goes past this hurdle rate) may sound sensible but what if that LIBOR rate is just 1 per cent per year? In that case, a 4 per cent hurdle rate may mean that any gain above 5 per cent per year incurs a 20 per cent performance fee (on any gains above 5 per cent).

So a 7 per cent return triggers a performance fee of 0.40 per cent in addition to a 2 per cent annual charge. Add these two charges together, and your TER can amount to as much as 2.5 per cent (including additional dealing and administration costs) on a return of just 7 per cent per year.

In this example, these charges mean that you're giving away more than one-third of your total returns to your hedge-fund manager. In contrast, an average ETF may produce the same 7 per cent profit but charge you only 0.50 per cent per year in charges.

In recent years the 2 and 20 charging system has broken down somewhat. Many hedge funds now charge a good deal less, with more progressive managers charging less than 1.5 per cent per year, especially if you're able and willing to invest a very large amount of money with them. Always shop around and look to see if there's a way of accessing the fund using a cheaper mechanism.

Accepting that these extra costs matter

The academic number-crunchers reveal why you need to be concerned by the hedge-fund costs and extra expenses of over-active trading.

Behavioural finance professors Terry Odean and Brad M. Barber at the University of California, for instance, researched the portfolios of 66,400 ordinary investors at massive investment bank Merrill Lynch between 1991 and 1997. They concluded that two specific factors reduced returns: lousy stock-picking and high transaction costs. In fact, they discovered that the most active traders averaged 258 per cent portfolio turnover annually and earned 7 per cent *less* per year than a buy-and-hold investor in an ETF, who averaged 2 per cent turnover.

Put together these numbers and an awful truth emerges. Over-active trading involves extra costs that can amount to two-thirds of a per cent per year.

To see the effect this figure has on a typical pension over the very long term, assume that you have a £50,000 savings pot (your portfolio) and that you expect an annual return of 8 per cent. The results in Table 6-1 detail the cost of a seemingly small difference in the annual management charge of a fund.

Table 6-1	Effect of the Annual Management Charge on a Hedge Fund with £50,000			
Fees (%)	5 years	10 years	20 years	30 years
1	70,128	98,358	193,484	380,613
1.5	68,504	93,857	176,182	330,718

These data suggest that the difference of just 0.5 per cent per year in charges over 30 years results in a reduction of more than £50,0000 in final returns (that is, the difference between £380,613 and £330,718 from the table). Just imagine what difference 2 or 3 per cent per year in extra costs has on your portfolio and your retirement income (remember that the smaller your retirement pot, the smaller your likely stream of post-retirement income). Ask yourself whether you really want to destroy as much as a third to a half of your long-term savings by trusting a hedge-fund manager.

Describing the Charges against the Hedge-Fund Industry

To put things bluntly, many academic economists believe that hedge funds are a giant sham, designed to rob investors blind. Here's a selection of the awkward questions they pose about the sector:

- ✔ How can an industry hope collectively to produce absolute returns on a consistent basis?

- ✔ With thousands of different funds running, is it mathematically possible for the average hedge-fund manager to produce positive returns year in, year out?

- ✔ If everyone is trying to achieve this seemingly impossible feat, aren't they all chasing the same strategies and trades to diminishing effect?

- ✔ How can hedge-fund managers possibly hope to dig up new tactics or strategies when rivals follow their every action, thus eliminating that advantage?

Over-charging and being over-paid

The most important accusation levelled at the industry is that hedge-fund managers charge too much in management and trading fees (I crunch the numbers in the earlier section 'Getting to Grips with Hedge-Fund Costs'). Hedge-fund managers have a well-deserved reputation for being appallingly well paid and driving around in fast, expensive sports cars.

Some modest, prudent hedge-fund managers don't lavish vast amounts of money on parties and generally keep a low profile, but these paragons of virtue tend to be over-shadowed by the 'whales' of the hedge-fund world, who earn countless millions managing your money. These fees may be all fine and dandy if the returns justified them, but the sceptics say that reality suggests otherwise, as the next section reveals.

Looking at the financial figures

A great deal of statistical evidence on hedge-fund performance is available and the message is unambiguous: certain hedge-fund managers and strategies do produce impressive numbers *some of the time*, but over the long run those returns tend to look a little feeble.

A crucial aspect when considering these statistics is deciding what constitutes a benchmark against which to measure the returns from a hedge fund. Many hedge-fund managers would love to use a conventional index such as the S&P 500 and say, 'Hey, we produced more reliable, less volatile profits than this equity index!' Which is probably true except that this isn't what hedge funds are set up to do: they're supposed to produce absolute returns in all markets (a positive gain in most years).

Therefore perhaps a better benchmark is the return from an investment class such as bonds or even cash deposits. On this score many, if not most, hedge-fund manager's fail, especially after fees.

Bad news about returns

So what do the data reveal about the relative returns from investing in hedge funds? Table 6-2 shows returns data from the widely respected HFRX index of hedge funds from 2008 to autumn 2012, with recent years broken down into different individual strategies. The bottom line shows returns from the benchmark S&P 500 index as a comparison. If you look at the table carefully, you discover that a strategy of just buying a low cost index tracking fund that followed the S&P 500 index would have delivered better returns over many years than most hedge funds. You can see more data and more recent numbers at www.hedgefundresearch.com/hfrx_reg/index.php.

Table 6-2	HFRX Hedge Fund Indices Data as at 24 October 2012				
Value	*Year to date (YTD) to 24 October 2012 from 1 January 2012 (%)*	*2011(%)*	*2010 (%)*	*2009 (%)*	*2008 (%)*
HFRX Global Hedge Fund Index	2.32	−8.87	5.19	13.4	−23.25
HFRX Equal Weighted Strategies Index	1.42	−6.18	5.29	11.44	NA
HFRX Absolute Return Index	−0.32	−3.72	−0.12	−3.58	NA
HFRX Aggregate Index	Not available (NA)	−4.05	7.52	13.34	NA
HFRX Market Directional Index	2.20	−18.86	9.32	29.34	NA
S&P 500	12.35	2.11	15	26	−37

The HFRX index looks at the publicly reported returns from a huge variety of hedge funds from around the world. The HFRX is the industry equivalent of a benchmark index such as the FTSE 100 or S&P 500. It doesn't include hedge funds that fail miserably and no longer report their data! However much hedge-fund advocates dice the data in Table 6-2, the figures don't look too good for the industry:

✔ You'd have beaten most hedge funds every year except for 2008 simply by investing in a boring S&P 500 tracker.

✔ Hedge funds haven't delivered absolute positive returns in every year over the last five years. In fact, on average they produced positive returns in only three out of five years.

✔ Hedge funds in aggregate *lost* money in 2011 while the S&P 500 index made 2 per cent in profits. They also lost money in the great crash of 2008, when in aggregate terms hedge funds lost 23 per cent (against 37 per cent losses for the S&P 500).

✔ These returns aren't even solid and certainly not predictable. One year they're up, next year they're down. To be fair, these returns aren't as volatile as the markets, but they're very far from being consistent.

More bad news for the industry

Not surprisingly with data about poor returns (like that in the preceding section) lurking around, critics of the hedge-fund model have multiplied, with many hedge-fund researchers and traders turning prosecution witness.

Perhaps one of the most famous in recent years is a certain Simon Lack who used to research hedge funds for a big US investment bank. He looked in detail at returns from a large number of hedge funds from the 1990s through to today. *Financial Times* writer Jonathan Ford described the results as 'miserable', continuing:

> *Mr Lack concluded that investors would have been better off putting their money in US [government] Treasury bills yielding just 2.3 per cent a year. Roughly 98 per cent of all the returns generated by hedge, he estimated, had been eaten in fees.*

The IMA (the industry association in the US) has gone to great efforts to rubbish Mr Lack's data, but its efforts haven't been entirely convincing. The distinct impression remains that hedge funds generally charge too much and deliver too little when compared to benchmark returns.

Assessing other arguments against

In this section, I run through a few of the other charges laid at the hedge-fund door.

Taking too many risks with your money

This damaging criticism against hedge funds says that too many managers take unnecessary risks with your money. On paper, hedge funds are supposed to be doing the exact opposite: competing with each other to notch down volatility and produce a better risk-adjusted rate of return.

To be absolutely fair to hedge funds, most do their very best to enforce strict risk-control procedures. The big hedge-fund houses in particular have beefed up risk departments, with specific risk budgets and a determined effort to control traders. But the horrible truth is that the fee structure is skewed towards taking big bets on big investment ideas. Hedge-fund managers don't get rich by sticking with an index and adding a few percentage points in additional return. No, hedge funds get noticed when they have a blowout year or two and beat the competition hands down.

That striving for success, and extra fees, is fine, but the dangers are immediately obvious. Hedge-fund managers can be encouraged to trade too often, making lots of risky bets and then using leverage to amplify returns. Hedge funds all too frequently implode in these circumstances, with some notorious examples strewn throughout history; certain traders have made cataclysmic investment bets that destroyed their investors' wealth on a massive multi-billion-dollar basis.

Wondering whether the industry has become too big

Perhaps the most damning critique of hedge funds is the most mundane, which is that it's become too big with too many clever people chasing the same set of ideas. As I reiterate throughout this book, some fairly predictable herd-like behaviour goes on in hedge-fund land, with large clusters of specialists in spaces such as long/short equity, merger/arbitrage and macro funds.

Of course this variety is sensible, because hedge funds cover a vast array of different strategies, and practitioners sharing best practice is a good thing. And yet an awful lot of funds are ploughing the same furrows, in exactly the same way.

The cold logic of mathematics reveals that virtually everything in the real world conforms to the power of *mean reversion*: that is, if you do something enough times, your performance probably ends up being fairly average over the long term. Of course, great consistent out-performers exist but they're the exception rather than the rule.

Academics who've spent a great deal of time looking carefully at hedge-fund strategies largely conclude that most of these strategies are over-populated by traders who mostly don't make much of a profit. In fact, they go further and suggest that the anomalies and inefficiencies that hedge funds are supposed to thrive on are being over-exploited and beginning to fade away.

Making a profit is becoming more difficult

Many of the most successful hedge-fund managers have started to close their doors to new money, and in some cases even hand money back to investors. George Soros, for instance (fabled as the man who 'broke' the Bank of England), recently returned all his money. The really smart managers know that finding that extra advantage is incredibly difficult in a world where hundreds of other managers and traders are watching your every move.

Another indicator of this industry-size trap is *style drift*, which simply means that over time fund managers end up investing in a different way than they were supposed to at the beginning (their philosophy changes over time).

This book looks at a wide variety of absolute returns strategies but in reality simple common ideas apply to all funds. On paper, funds should make money in all markets, be largely market neutral and be investing in fairly liquid underlying assets.

Many hedge funds have decided that these ideas are a bit old school and need freshening up. The result is managers setting up large *private equity operations*, which use vast amounts of debt to invest in long-term, illiquid private assets to generate a return substantially above those on offer from public equity markets.

Certainly money can be made from private equity – some of the time – but it's a very different world to that of hedge-fund trader desks, one that these managers don't always fully understand. Private equity:

- ✔ Needs lots of operational expertise and copious lashings of management consultants.

- ✔ Invests in illiquid assets that take anything up to ten years to produce a profit.

- ✔ Uses massive amounts of leverage and generally avoids the public, liquid markets, which means that when markets suddenly seize up and investors want their money back, the fund manager can't return the money because it's tied up in illiquid underlying assets.

Despite private equity being far from a typical hedge-fund strategy, hedge funds have been piling funds into illiquid private equity in recent years, demonstrating that the managers' core area of expertise is now saturated and over-populated.

Defending the Hedge-Fund Industry

The charge sheet against hedge funds is long and detailed, and many investors may conclude that it's sufficiently damning for them to give up investing in these alternative funds altogether. But on balance that would probably be a mistake, as I explain in this section.

Favouring the best managers

The obvious selling point of the industry is that enough funds exist for a few incredibly talented managers to shine through. The industry itself may be facing huge issues, but that doesn't mean that good managers aren't out there and worth backing.

As an example, look at the chart in Figure 6-1 showing the share price of lead-ing British-based hedge fund Brevan Howard Macro set against the returns from investing in the UK FTSE 100 benchmark index.

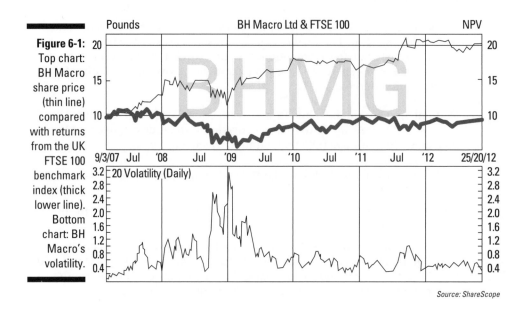

Figure 6-1:
Top chart:
BH Macro
share price
(thin line)
compared
with returns
from the UK
FTSE 100
benchmark
index (thick
lower line).
Bottom
chart: BH
Macro's
volatility.

Source: ShareScope

As you can see, since late 2007 the share price of the BH Macro fund has con-sistently moved ahead of the benchmark. Over the five years that share price doubled whereas the benchmark index is essentially back where it was in 2007. Also take a look at the bottom chart in Figure 6-1 – it shows the volatil-ity of the share price of BH Macro. The daily variance of BH Macro's shares shot up during 2008 and 2009 but since then crashed back down, with volatil-ity levels well below what you'd expect from a mainstream equity.

Funds like this massively popular one have delivered on their promise, giving steady positive gains with relatively low levels of daily volatility.

Arguing for hedge funds

But I can do better than simply defend the hedge-fund sector by picking the best of a bad bunch. A stronger argument in favour of hedge funds is to start with the disciplines and strategies that traders and managers use and then identify where the real opportunities lie amid the general poor performance and high fees.

Markets aren't always efficient

This simple argument is perhaps the most powerful. As investors pile into ETFs that track major indices, they're essentially saying that markets are always efficient and that you can't beat what Mr Market thinks. But this isn't always necessarily true, as I discuss in the earlier section 'Working with the reality of efficient markets'.

The fact is that markets and investors overreact to outside factors and move through cycles of irrational exuberance (where lots of stuff is overpriced) and maddening despair and capitulation (where decent assets are left at ridiculously low prices). More generally on a day-to-day basis, market inefficiencies can emerge, hang around for months on end and then vanish. The fleet-of-foot hedge-fund manager can make steady money by capturing these market opportunities.

Hedge funds can be flexible

The problem for most conventional (non-hedge) fund managers is that they have a mandate, which says that Mr X must run a fund that's bullish (long) US or UK shares, for example. The mandate, which is simply a fact of business established when the fund is set up and the regulators give approval, is to invest in these shares and that's all that the manager can do. This is a sensible form of specialisation, but it has limitations. What happens when US or UK shares are hugely expensive and unappealing? The poor fund manager can't do much more than say, 'stick with it Mr X, it'll all come right in the end, trust me'.

Hedge-fund managers by contrast can take a different view because their mandates are usually very wide. They can short US stocks, or invest in another country where more opportunity exists. In fact, they can pretty much do anything they think of to make a profit.

Similarly, the conventional fund (agreed change) manager is focused exclusively on shares. He can't suddenly turn around and say, 'Hey, I think those corporate bonds look cheap . . . I'll start selling my shares and buy bonds!' (See Chapter 15 for more on bonds.)

But hedge-fund managers can move between individual markets and back and forth between different asset classes, including shares, bonds, alternatives and pretty much anything that makes money.

Hedge-fund managers can think and bet big!

Hedge-fund masters of the universe may sometimes lose their investors' money on certain trades, but they make a far greater amount of money with other supersized bets that pay off.

Sometimes investors want their managers to use leverage and make big bets on big market movements. Great investors such as Warren Buffett and his partner Charlie Munger say until they're blue in the face that they've made most of their profits by taking focused, concentrated bets when they had a strong hunch of an opportunity. Hedge-fund managers can likewise be appropriately unconstrained and use leverage to gear up returns.

Trends exist . . . most of the time

Most academic economists believe three things about modern financial markets:

- They're largely efficient.

- They aren't *always* efficient; sometimes anomalies (such as *value stocks*, stocks that appear cheap based on the ideas of classic value investing, which you can read more about in Chapter 9) can produce opportunities for profit.

- They frequently have strong momentum behind them and lock into a trend that can last for months and months (the so-called *trending market*).

As the herd realises that a trend is robust, investors pile in. That momentum effect takes on a life of its own, and while it powers along you can make money by surfing that trend.

The exact mechanism by which hedge funds make money from market trends varies enormously (some use computing power to make money in a few minutes and others stick with an asset class for weeks), but the same opportunity links them all. Trends can make hedge funds 'loadsamoney' as long as they're willing to be tactical and switch out of the asset class when the trend starts to fade away or jolts to a halt.

Rise of the rocket scientists

Perhaps the most powerful trend hunters are those armed with massive farms full of computers, loaded up with programs designed to spot perceived trends, anomalies and inefficiencies on a minute-by-minute, second-by-second basis.

This form of hedge-fund investing is really a form of data engineering, which unleashes neural networks to scan the markets constantly for opportunity. This is rocket science applied to lots and lots of small trades, with each trade hopefully making a small profit. Leverage may be relatively low and risk levels manageable. In theory, this form of computerised trend hunting is close to modern alchemy . . . until the models don't work, however, and the markets don't behave as expected. This level of computing power can spot trends that the human eye can never see.

Play the cycle of money

The herd-like behaviour of hedge funds can work to investors' advantage, helping them to spot potential opportunities. A typical cycle in hedge-fund land consists of investors getting terribly excited about some new insight or another that suggests the market has something wrong (in terms of a mispricing); that is, an opportunity exists to make a profit.

Many investors react by piling money into these new funds, and all those traders go chasing after the shiny new trend/cycle/anomaly/inefficiency. The early movers make their investors large amounts of money whereas the late movers largely lose, especially after all their fees have been totted up.

Eventually returns from this strategy start to fade away (too much money chasing too little opportunity), investors rebel and ask for their money back, and the herd of hedge funds suddenly turns tail. Funds switch mandates, managers collapse and eventually an opportunity turns into utter capitulation. No sensible manager would be seen dead hanging around in this out-of-favour niche. But at precisely this moment opportunity presents itself again. As capital vanishes from the market, savvy investors frequently start looking anew at the opportunity, especially if it still exists, albeit in a smaller form.

Absolute returns and market neutral

Perhaps the most obvious plus point for hedge funds is that they provide a big opportunity for a manager to run a fund that aims to produce absolute returns through the market cycle. Maybe passing up the opportunity for supersized upside bets is worthwhile if you can guarantee a few percentage points above cash as a consistent return. And maybe the way to do this is to be *market neutral*: that is, have a portfolio that can make money whichever direction the market goes, with balancing long and short bets.

Part III

Thinking and Acting Like a Hedgie: Simple Strategies You Can Employ Yourself

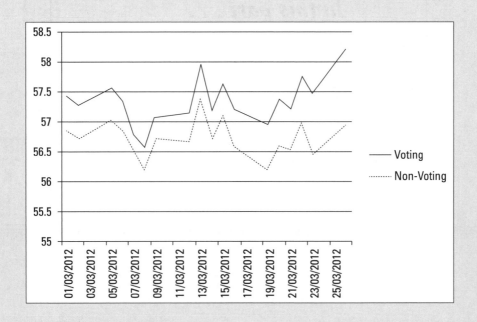

In this part . . .

- ✔ Broaden your investment horizons and learn about the short-selling process, active extension funds and the risks involved.

- ✔ Understand ways of engaging in arbitrage: both popular and controversial methods that you as an investor are likely to encounter and use.

- ✔ Meet famous investors such as Ben Graham and Warren Buffet and see how you can incorporate their successful strategies into your own portfolio.

- ✔ Decide whether the investment leverage approach is for you by exploring the benefits and risks.

- ✔ Get to grips with the basics of shareholder activism and how to use it to your advantage.

Chapter 7

Selling What You Don't Own: Short Selling

In This Chapter

▶ Selling stocks short to make profits

▶ Being aware of shorting risks

▶ Finding companies to short

▶ Activating extension funds

Most people like to think positively and in its conventional form investing is a positive undertaking: investors see a stock, like it and buy it. In the industry parlance, therefore, most investors are fundamentally *long* a stock: they buy it because they see a positive opportunity. They like companies with global markets and high profit rates, where cash is flowing in and lots of dividends are paid out to the shareholders.

Many hedge-fund investors, however, take a more cynical view. They think that opportunity doesn't have to consist in only going long a stock. Using whatever measures take their fancy, they may become convinced that Stock A is under-priced and yet Stock B is over-priced. In other words, they find a potential pair and buy Stock A and sell (short) Stock B.

In this chapter I describe the short-selling process and the risks involved, as well as how to identify a candidate for your dastardly plan. I also introduce you to active extension funds, a less-risky form of shorting. Welcome to the 'dark side' of investing!

Introducing the Art of Short Selling

Short selling a stock sounds rather counterintuitive to many investors. The uninitiated wonder how you can make a profit from something you think is going to fall in value. Well, wonder no more. . . .

Defining short selling

Short selling is incredibly simple to understand: you sell a security (stocks or bonds) now for delivery to a buyer at a future date. You don't own the security – instead, the broker lends it to you for an agreed period of time (plus some obvious charges!). You go *short* when you anticipate a decrease in share price.

The crucial point is that, although you don't own the security at the time of the deal, you receive the sale proceeds and are betting that its value is going to fall over time. At the appropriate point in the future, you buy it (called *covering the short*) at a price lower than the price you originally sold it for, and deliver it to the buyer. As the seller, you retain the price difference as profit on the transaction – assuming that the price does actually fall between the time you sell it and then buy it back.

Of course, short selling isn't without potential challenges:

- ✔ If the price of the stock rises, you have to buy it back at the higher price and you lose money.

- ✔ Brokers don't lend you stock for nothing. They charge for running a margin account (interest), which means that keeping a short sale open for a long time costs you more.

- ✔ If the lender wants the borrowed stock back, you can be forced to *cover*, that is, buy the stock back, even if you must do so for a loss) so that you can return it: known as *being called away*.

- ✔ While you're 'borrowing' the stock (remember, you don't own it), you have to pay the original `ultimate` lender any dividends that he would have earned had he not 'lent' the stock to you.

Carrying out the short-selling process

Many investors think that short selling is the preserve of professional hedge-fund traders. Far from it! You can run a short-selling strategy relatively easily on a standard stock-broking platform, in five simple steps:

1. **Set up an account with your stockbroker and ask for a margin account**. The broker probably wants to make sure that you're an experienced investor and know what you're doing.

2. **Research your potential short.** Use the ideas and tools that I provide throughout this chapter.

3. **Place your order.** If you do so online, you use a box on the trading page called 'short sale' or 'buy to cover'.

4. **The stockbroker borrows the shares.** They may come from her own trading stock, from another client's accounts or another firm, depending on availability. The broker charges you a small fee for this service (it costs them time and money to organise this kind of transaction, if only in administration effort!).

5. **The broker sells the shares on the open market and places the profits of the sale into your margin account.** You have a specified period of time before you have to return the stocks. *Note:* During this waiting period, any dividends that the shares accrue go to the broker or person who actually owns the stock you've sold.

6. **By the end of the period (or whenever the broker calls for the shares to be returned), you buy back the shares and return them to the broker.** If the price of the stock has fallen, you buy the stock back for less than you sold it for and see a profit. If the price has risen – meaning you pay more to buy the shares back –you're out the difference.

Imagine for one moment that back on the morning of 20 April 2010 you decide to short sell BP shares. You hear the terrible news about the oil leak in the Gulf of Mexico and decide that the situation's going to end badly (though you probably don't realise just how badly). Table 7-1 shows how a perfectly timed short sale on BP would have worked out.

Table 7-1	BP's Share Price Falls from £6.50 to £3
Borrow 100 shares of BP at £6.50	£650
Buy back 100 shares of BP at £3	–£300
Your profit	£350

But if you were less clever or clairvoyant and the share price of BP went in the opposite direction (say it rose from £6.50 to £9), your short sale would end disastrously; you'd lose a great deal of money from the share price increasing, as Table 7-2 reveals.

Table 7-2	BP Share Price Rises from £6.50 to £9
Borrow 100 shares of BP at £6.50	£650
Buy back 100 shares of BP at £9.00	–£900
Your profit	–£250

Looking for a company's downside

In order to short sell, you need to find the downside of a company. Although modern globalised financial markets have a myriad risks, at least they're open, largely transparent places where finding information is relatively easy. If you're looking to build a 'case' against a company and thus short its stock, start with the measures I describe in this section.

Downward technical trends in the share price

The chart in Figure 7-1 shows the share price for British oil giant BP over the spring and summer of 2010. The lightning bolt on the chart corresponds to 20 April when the Deepwater Horizon oil rig blew up in the Gulf of Mexico and the share price collapsed from over 600 pence to just above 300 pence. You can see the share price start *trending* aggressively down.

The key measure here is the *moving average*, which is simply the average over a certain period of days (20 in this case) of the share price. This moving average is shown in Figure 7-1 by a thick line that moves down as quickly as the share price. Simple technical analysis suggests that a share price keeps trending downwards if it remains below the 20-day moving average. (For more on using moving averages and technical analysis, check out Chapter 4.)

During those dismal spring days in 2010, short sellers made fortunes from BP shares as the trend moved relentlessly downward.

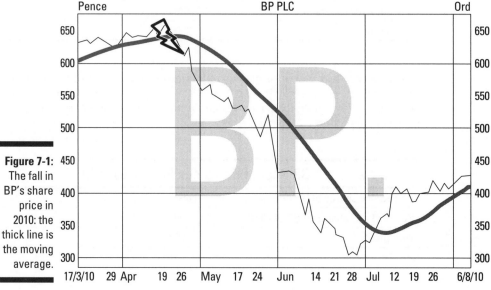

Figure 7-1: The fall in BP's share price in 2010: the thick line is the moving average.

Source: ShareScope

Negative earnings surprises

In Chapter 3, I describe the phenomena of the positive earnings surprise, but you won't be surprised to discover that the opposite can also occur: the *negative* earnings surprise. Astute traders often aim to short sell a stock somewhere between the time it takes the analyst to generate the financial report and its actual release. In other words, they sell a stock short before official reports revealing that profits have fallen cause the stock prices to begin to trend downward.

Many short sellers focus on companies with announcements that profits are unlikely to hit broker estimates. In the City of London an old adage says that profit warnings rarely emerge on their own – instead they're like colloquial red buses and usually come in threes, suddenly, over a short period of time.

Deteriorating fundamentals

Deteriorating fundamentals sounds unpleasant, doesn't it, like a complaint to ask your GP about! But many short sellers are always on the lookout for *deteriorating fundamentals*, which can be anything from declining sales estimates and falling gross margins to crashing cash inflows. (I write more about fundamentals measures in Chapter 9.)

In particular, take a close look at a company's cash book and balance sheet to see whether you can spot *swelling inventories* (lots of stock building up suddenly) and increasing accounts receivables – both indicate that a company is getting into trouble. Increasing receivables is a bad sign because it indicates that a company isn't being paid by its customers on a timely basis. This situation also throws off earnings going forward. If some of these debts ultimately prove to be uncollectible, they have to be written off at some point in the future.

Sector problems

Sometimes the troubles afflicting a company – and pushing down the share price – involve the wider business sector, which may be experiencing an overall slowdown. In the first months of a recession, for instance, especially one powered by declining consumer spending, you're likely to see a sharp slowdown in demand for new cars and expensive summer holidays – these consumer discretionary items are regarded as a luxury by increasingly cash-strapped consumers.

Unsurprisingly the share price of tour operators and car manufacturers (and house builders, for that matter) are the first 'against the wall' in the throes of a recession.

Tax loss selling

In the US, short sellers watch out for *tax loss selling*. This is when, in the fourth quarter of a company's fiscal year, many companies trading at the lower end of their 52-week trading range suddenly experience a sharp drop in their share price. Individuals and mutual funds want to book some of their losses before the year-end to reap the tax benefits, which means that they sell the shares and push down the price. (Holding on to a stock whose value has fallen is called a *book loss*, because, until you sell the stock for a loss, you've only lost on paper. As tax time nears, however, investors sell these devalued stocks because they can use only actual, or *realised*, losses to offset capital gains.)

Short interest measure

Keep a watchful eye on *the short interest*. This is the total number of stocks, securities or commodity shares in an account or in the markets that have been sold short but not repurchased to close the short position. The short interest measure serves as a barometer for a bearish or bullish market. For instance, the higher the short interest, the more people are anticipating a downturn.

I describe how you can monitor this crucial measure in detail in the later section 'Using short interest as a key measure'.

Keep a very beady eye on who's selling the shares and how many shares they're selling. If managers from a company start selling their shares that's usually a very bad sign indeed, perhaps indicating that they have little confidence in the future of their own employer!

Knowing the Risks of Short Selling

Shorting is a very dangerous game and many national regulators in the developed world place severe restrictions on it. As a short-selling investor, you're essentially betting with other people's money and you need to understand that the odds are against you some of the time!

The risks you face are many and varied and include all or any of the following:

- ✔ **You're taking a gamble, because** over time shares tend to *increase* in value.

- ✔ **Your losses can be infinite.** Imagine with the earlier BP example (in 'Carrying out the short-selling process') that the share price shot up to £100 a share; you'd massively increase your losses.

- ✔ **You need to use borrowed money and that costs money in terms of interest.** When short selling, you open a margin account, which allows you to borrow money from the stockbroking firm using your investment as collateral. Losses can easily get out of hand.

- ✔ **You can be hit by what's called a *short squeeze*.** Terrible things happen to short sellers and one of the worst is when the share price inexplicably starts to rise and short-seller losses pile up. This unexpected uptick in the share price foxes the short sellers, who now rush to buy the shares to cover their positions. This rush creates a high demand for the stock, quickly driving up the price even further. Usually, positive news in the market triggers a short squeeze.

✔ **Your timing is wrong.** You may be right that a giant company has over-extended itself and is cruising for a bruising, but if you place your bet at the wrong time you pay the price. For the BP example in the earlier section 'Carrying out the short-selling process', if you bet in April 2009 when the share price was just 450 pence, you'd have spent a long and expensive year watching the share price head up to 650 pence. Ouch!

Locating a Shorting Target

In this section I guide you through finding a suitable company to short, in what can be the often brutal world of short selling.

Spotting the signs

Here are the signals to look for when identifying a company to short sell:

✔ Very popular 'growth' stocks (that is, stock from companies that generate and sustain high profits) are always a good starting place for a company about to be subject to a short-seller raid.

For example, Pursuit Dynamics, a fluid technology company that attracted the interest of one of Britain's most famous bear traders in 2012 (refer to the later section 'Considering the sad case of Pursuit Dynamics' for details), rarely produced evidence of strong revenue growth and its share price seemed to move ahead based on investors' hopes of future contract wins.

✔ Running out of cash and needing a deeply discounted share price placing is also a very bad sign – for the company that is, but it's one that indicates a company may be a good short-selling opportunity.

✔ The interest or lack thereof that short sellers show in a stock can signal that a company is ripe for short selling (more on this aspect later in the chapter in the 'Using short interest as a key measure' section).

✔ Negative announcements followed by talk of a strategic review is usually the nail in the coffin, at which point the short sellers finally claim their scalp.

Introducing the net short

If you fancy yourself as a short seller, one way to find a candidate for your attack is to look for those investors who are net short a particular stock.

The *net short* describes a situation where an investor (usually an advanced trader) has more short positions than long positions in a given asset, market, portfolio or trading strategy. Remember that net short investors benefit when the price of the underlying asset decreases. By attributing a larger proportion of their portfolio to short positions rather than long positions, the portfolio increases as the prices of the assets decrease, because investors are borrowing securities from brokers and selling them on the market in hopes of buying them back later at a lower price.

In simple terms, being net short is the opposite of being net long.

Using short interest as a key measure

Looking for investors with a net short position is easy when you use another key measure called the short interest. *Short interest* is the total number of shares of a particular stock that have been sold short by investors but not yet covered or closed out (that is, bought back and returned to the actual owner), usually expressed as a percentage.

Here's how this percentage is worked out. Short interest is the number of shorted shares divided by the number of shares outstanding. For example, a stock with 10 million shares sold short and 1 million shares outstanding has a short interest of 15 per cent (10 million ÷ 1 million = 15 per cent).

But you don't need to do the sums because most stock exchanges track the short interest in each stock and issue reports at the month's end, thus allowing you to see what the short sellers are up to. Websites such as `http://www.yahoo.com/finance` also publish the short-interest ratio (short interest/average daily volume of the stock) in their Investor Snapshots.

A high (or rising) level of short interest means that many people think that the stock is going to drop (always to be treated as a red flag). Crucially, the short-interest ratio tells you how many days – given the stock's average trading volume – short sellers would need to cover their positions (that is, buy stock) if good news sent the price higher and ruined their negative bets.

The higher the ratio, the more time they'd have to buy – the short squeeze phenomenon – which can actually buoy a stock and send its price rising.

Some people bet on a short squeeze, which is just as risky as shorting the stock in the first place.

Short interest data in the US

In the US a large number of excellent websites track the short interest of major stocks. Top sites include: `www.highshortinterest.com`, `www.nasdaqtrader.com/trader.aspx?id=Shortinterest` and the excellent `www.shortsqueeze.com`. The latter site is especially powerful: tap in a company ticker and you're presented with a huge amount of short-interest data. As an example, see the information in Table 7-3 from `www.shortsqueeze.com` showing data on shares in Microsoft during one week in late 2012.

Table 7-3	Share Data on Microsoft for One Week*
Microsoft Corporation	$29.30
MSFT**	0.76
Short interest (shares short)	92,672,400
Days to cover (short interest ratio)	2.1
Short interest – prior	101,873,600
Short percentage increase/decrease	−9.03

**The ticker symbol for Microsoft Corporation

*Source: `www.shortsqueeze.com`

Short interest data in the UK

Unfortunately short interest data aren't quite so easy to find in Europe and the UK. The US exchanges are very keen to publicise their short interest data but the London Stock Exchange is, strangely, less enthusiastic about that information filtering down to private investors.

Most big institutional investors do still get access to short-interest data but they have to acquire this info from specialist vendors such as Data Explorers. Luckily this British company (owned by MarkIt) makes some data on key shorted stocks available for free via its website. The information in Figure 7-2 is from August 2012 and shows the Data Explorers market snapshot of top shorted stocks as measured by the percentage of outstanding shares on loan – as well as the monthly change in this key measure.

Check out `www.dataexplorers.com/news-and-analysis` for a treasure trove of free information.

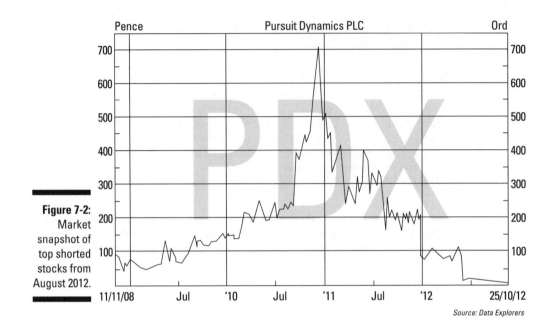

Source: Data Explorers

Figure 7-2:
Market snapshot of top shorted stocks from August 2012.

Data Explorers also provides a series of fascinating market and sector commentaries indicating where short sellers are focusing their attention at the moment. The following paragraph from summer 2012 highlights the massive short interest in the retail sector and (in this month at least) in the US games retailer GameStop:

> *Specialty retail is the best represented sector in the list of the top 20 most shorted shares announcing earnings. Short sellers are keenly aware that the bricks and mortar stores operated by these companies face growing pressure from online competition and a slowdown in consumer spending. The most shorted share announcing next week is video game retailer GameStop with 34% of its shares out on loan. Short interest in the company peaked in April prior to the company announcing disappointing results. It is worth noting that the short covering experienced in the last three months seems to be driven by the fact that long investors who lend their shares have sold their positions, as the available supply of shares has fallen by 20 million shares in the last three months.*

Data Explorers helpfully provides a chart showing the share price versus the changing short interest in the stock (see Figure 7-3).

The Data Explorers surveys also include European stocks. Figure 7-4 shows the top 16 shares in August 2012 with more than one and a half times the level of short interest in the Stoxx 600 index (an index that contains the major European corporations and is equivalent to the US S&P 500).

Name	Industry	Ticker	Earnings Date	% Shares Outstanding On Loan	1 Month % Change
GameStop Corp	Specialty Retail	GME	8/16/2012	33.9	2%
Sales Incorporated	Multiline Retail	SKS	8/14/2012	22.1	1%
KIT digital, Inc.	Internet Software and Services	KITD	8/14/2012	21.1	−7%
Argonaut Gold Inc.	Metals and Mining	AR	8/15/2012	20.5	4%
CACI International Inc.	IT Services	CACI	8/15/2012	20.1	5%
Buckle Inc.	Specialty Retail	BKE	8/16/2012	17.7	2%
InterOil Corporation	Oil, Gas and Consumable Fuels	IOC	8/13/2012	17.6	8%
Hibbett Sports, Inc.	Specialty Retail	HIBB	8/17/2012	15.7	−3%
Bon-Ton Stores Inc.	Multiline Retail	BONT	8/16/2012	15.6	−9%
Parkervision Inc.	Communications Equipment	PRKR	8/15/2012	15.1	6%
The Children's Place Retail Stores	Specialty Retail	PLCS	8/16/2012	14.3	17%
National Presto Industries Inc.	Aerospace and Defense	NPK	8/13/2012	12.9	−3%
Canadian Solar Inc.	Semiconductors and Semicond	CSIQ	8/15/2012	12.7	1%
Eaton Vance Corp.	Capital Markets	EV	8/17/2012	11.9	0%
Photronics Inc.	Semiconductors and Semicond	PLAB	8/14/2012	11.8	−4%
Abercrombie & Fitch Co.	Specialty Retail	ANF	8/15/2012	10.9	131%
Staples, Inc.	Specialty Retail	SPLS	8/15/2012	10.0	39%
salesforce.com, Inc.	Software	CRM	8/17/2012	9.6	−9%
Hot Topic Inc.	Specialty Retail	HOTT	8/15/2012	9.4	−12%
Velti Plc	Internet Software and Services	VELT	8/14/2012	9.2	2%

Source: Data Explorers

Figure 7-3: GameStop share price plotted against the changing short interest.

Figure 7-4: Top 16 European shares in August 2012 with more than 1.5 times the level of short interest in the Stoxx 600 index.

Source: Data Explorers

The Data Explorers surveys are particularly useful for identifying 'unpopular' sectors where the bears are very active. According to the market data firm, renewable energy firms are a particular focus of short-selling attention:

> *Three solar firms feature on the list of most shorted shares, as governments continue to cut the subsidies given to solar producers. German firms Q-Cells and Solarworld have 33% and 10% of their shares out on loan respectively. Short sellers will find it hard to make any meaningful profits from the companies owing to their low market caps of $35 and $182 million respectively.*

Considering the sad case of Pursuit Dynamics

The easiest way to expand on the broad description in the earlier 'Looking for a company's downside' section on how to find a suitable candidate for short selling is to lead you through a real-life example. On initial inspection the chart in Figure 7-5 tells a very conventional story. It shows the share price over four years of a British stock market listed company called Pursuit Dynamics. This was a small company with potentially world-beating technology that at one point (late 2010) suddenly became worth a very large amount of money indeed (hundreds of millions of pounds).

Name	Industry	Ticker	Earnings Date	% Shares Outstanding On Loan	1 Month % Change
Q-Cells SE	Semiconductors and Semicond	QCE	8/14/2012	32.9	0%
Meyer Burger Technology AG	Machinery	MBTN	8/16/2012	22.3	−1%
FLSmidth & Co. A/S	Construction and Engineering	FLS	8/15/2012	12.2	14%
Oriflame Cosmetics SA	Personal Products	ORISDE	8/14/2012	11.8	25%
Solar World AG	Semiconductors and Semicond	SWV	8/13/2012	10.2	−6%
Galencia Ltd.	Pharmaceuticals	GALN	8/14/2012	9.0	−5%
SNS Reaal N.V.	Diversified Financial Services	SR	8/16/2012	7.6	−2%
TUI AG	Hotels, Restaurants and Leisure	TUI1	8/14/2012	7.1	−9%
Michael Page International plc	Professional Services	MPI	8/13/2012	6.3	−3%
Asian Bamboo AG	Food Products	5AB	8/14/2012	5.4	5%
Ratos AB	Captial Markets	RATO B	8/17/2012	5.1	1%
Singulus Technologies AG	Machinery	SNG	8/14/2012	4.8	6%
Holmen AB	Paper and Forest Products	HOLM B	8/14/2012	4.8	10%
Deutsche Euroshop AG	Real Estate Management	DEQ	8/14/2012	4.7	5%
Swiss Life Holding AG	Insurance	SLHN	8/17/2012	4.6	5%
BATM Advanced Communications	Communications Equipment	BVC	8/16/2012	4.2	0%

Figure 7-5: Share price of Pursuit Dynamics, showing the sudden increase and equally sudden fall.

Source: ShareScope

A dissident voice

Cawkwell first voiced his concerns about Pursuit Dynamics as long ago as 2005, and yet the share price continued to move north. The company had a large number of huge professional investors as fans, including the Prudential (with 20 per cent), M&G (18 per cent), BlackRock (12 per cent) and the well-respected private investor, John Morley (11.7 per cent). These firms continued to invest in this small company, believing that it was about to be a great example of world-class technology. They even supported a number of discounted rights issues to help raise extra money for the company.

And then, like so many 'growth' companies with oodles of promise, its share price crashed back to earth and it returned to being a tiny, micro cap company (companies worth between US$50 million and $300 million).

But Pursuit Dynamics was and is a special case. The company boasted a unique advantage, namely, world-class fluid technology, but was the victim of a massive bear raid involving a small legion of short sellers, with a certain Simon 'Evil Knievil' Cawkwell leading the baying pack (the nickname and the spelling are his own).

Background

Cawkwell made no secret of his interest in Pursuit Dynamics's shares because he discussed them in great detail on his various Internet-based forums. His basic contention was (and as far as I know still is) that this much hyped little company was simply not worth the price attached to it by many institutional and private investors. Obviously, as a successful short seller and professional bear raider (someone who believes certain stocks are heading down and shorts them on a very regular basis), he had a large number of detailed reasons for not liking the company, including its unproven contracts with leading international corporations such as Procter & Gamble and its need for large amounts of cash to support the business – see the nearby sidebar 'A dissident voice'.

Suddenly in the summer of 2012 everything fell apart for Pursuit Dynamics. The share price collapsed from over 100 pence (already well off the highs of more than 700 pence a share) to less than 10 pence. The obvious cause of the price crash was that US consumer goods giant Procter & Gamble decided to end an agreement to use Pursuit's technology. This caused a strategic review by the company and a warning that profits would be 'materially below' previous expectations. Just days before this announcement the company had told the London Stock Exchange that it 'knew of no reason for the share price to fall'.

Of course, the short sellers knew plenty of reasons, founded on concerns that had intensified after a rights issue in December 2011. At the time of that placing of new shares, Cawkwell had warned that the stock would be changing hands at below 20 pence in six months' time.

Following the share price collapse in 2012, he noted that:

> *It's quite extraordinary. Today's statement coming immediately after Friday's borders on criminality. The company is obviously run by morons. At no time was there any realistic evidence that Pursuit could ever tie up a deal with Procter & Gamble.*

> www.spreadbetmagazine.com/blog/2012/5/22/
> pursuit-dynamics-spot-the-odd-one-out-in-the-
> announcements-b.html

Short seller activity

The short-selling story is obvious. Cawkwell and his bearish colleagues had been watching Pursuit Dynamics for many years and, expecting a downward spiral for the company's share prices, put a short-selling strategy in place.

Initially, the share price rose consistently to its peak in December 2011, and they failed to make big profits on shares in the company – remember that a rising share price is terrible news for short sellers. Plus, a solid institutional bias appeared to be in favour of the company.

But the subsequent collapse in the share price confirmed their worst fears (and best hopes). They bought the shares back for significantly less than they sold them for and made vast profits.

The short sellers involved with Pursuit Dynamics made a very large amount of money betting that the company would ultimately stumble. Quite possibly, some lucky souls 'bought' shares at, say, 700 pence and sold out at 20 pence, in which case they made truly gargantuan profits.

Not every short-selling raid is as successful as the Pursuit Dynamics example. In fact, many short sellers can end up losing an absolute fortune if they find themselves caught in a short squeeze (which I describe earlier in 'Knowing the Risks of Short Selling'), when a company surprises to the upside; for example, wins that contract it's been talking about for years.

Entering the World of Active Extension Funds

Not many professional hedge-fund investors spend all their time shorting markets like Simon Cawkwell (refer to the earlier section 'Considering the sad case of Pursuit Dynamics'). That's a very precarious game and, although you can make huge profits short selling, the chances are that sooner or later you get caught in an aggressive short squeeze and are forced to take huge losses.

Instead, many hedge funds take an alternative tack, using shorting as part of a more modest ambition: to give you the return from holding a major asset class but with special enhancements. Welcome to the world of *active extension funds*, which aim to modestly outperform a given benchmark. These strategies are essentially a 'smarter' way of going long an equity class but with extra oomph! They use short selling and leverage, but to all intents and purposes they're like more conventional long-only peers.

The key to understanding how active extension funds work is to look at their beta exposure, which is usually close to 1. The beta of a stock is a technical measure of how its share price moves relative to the wider market. A beta of 1 indicates that the share's price will move with the market whereas a beta of less than 1 means that it will be less volatile than the market. A beta of greater than 1 indicates that the share's price will be more volatile than the market.

Meeting active extension portfolios in practice

To maintain a beta of 1 while adding a short leg to the portfolio, the manager has to leverage up the long leg by an equal figure. Therefore, if a manager decides to set up a portfolio with 30 per cent of the portfolio value in the short positions, the long positions must be leveraged up by 30 per cent as well, to 130 per cent of the portfolio value.

A typical active extension fund may earmark 100 per cent of its assets for investment in long-only prospects, as usual. It then takes a short position on the identified unattractive shares, typically up to a value equivalent to 30 per cent of the total assets.

The proceeds from the short-sell contract are added to the fund, which now has 130 per cent to invest in its long-only bets. In this way, for each £100 invested, subscribers are getting £130 exposure to the markets. Hence this kind of fund structure is also sometimes called a *130/30 portfolio*. The net exposure of the portfolio (that is, its beta) is calculated by subtracting the short leg from the long leg: £130 – £30 = £100, which is a beta of 1. The leverage can be from long 100 per cent (and short 0 per cent) up to long 200 per cent and short 100 per cent.

To comply with investment fund legislation in the US and Europe, the maximum leverage allowed is 100 per cent of net asset value. This limits the leverage in practice to an interval from 100/0 to 150/50.

A commonly sold type of active extension fund is the '130/30' fund. As with its active extension siblings (those with more or less leverage, like 120/20 and 140/40 funds, for example), 130/30 funds involve the fund manager short selling stocks to the value of 30 per cent of net asset value (NAV), with the proceeds used to acquire additional long positions, bringing the total exposure to 130 per cent long and 30 per cent short. (The NAV refers to a fund's per share price.)

Enjoying the benefits for the private investor

Active extension funds have become popular with many investors. They made their debut in the UK in July 2007, having been pioneered in Japan, Australia and the US. Their popularity in the US, in particular, rose quickly, and by the latter part of 2007 some US$50 billion of funds were under management there. These funds proved popular because they not only provide market exposure (beta) but also enable the fund to generate additional *alpha* (extra return).

Much of that alpha comes from the leverage provided by shorting, which increases the level of participation in market changes and boosts the potential outperformance of the market. In effect, managers previously constrained by a long-only strategy can now profit from securities that lose value, as well as from those that rise.

These relatively new structures give you as a private investor access to the kind of investment strategy that was formerly available only to institutions (because of the high cost of entry set by minimum investment levels). Even better, active extension funds bridge a gap by taking the kind of long/short strategy employed by hedge funds and placing it within a transparent, regulated framework. On paper these funds allow greater diversification – and mitigation of risk – within a portfolio!

Table 7-4 compares the features of active extension funds with other funds so that you can see the pros and cons side-by-side (I discuss pairs trading in Chapter 3).

Table 7-4	Comparisons of Different Fund Structures		
	Long Only	*Active Extension*	*Long/Short Market Neutral (Pairs Trading)*
Returns	**Relative**	**Relative**	**Absolute**
Uses short selling	No	Yes	Yes
Beta	1	1	0 (market neutral)
Leverage	No	0–100% of value of fund	Unlimited but usually 300–400%

Understanding the dangers of active extension funds

If hedge-fund managers are going to be successful in the active extension fund space, they need to know everything about the shares they're dealing with, especially because they're shorting the stocks. Here are some of the risks involved:

✔ Long/short funds such as active extension funds aim to have a market exposure of a beta equal to 1, and therefore don't provide protection in a market downturn. Consequently, to participate you need to have a positive view on the general market over time.

✔ Many professional investors are suspicious about the downside risks when fund managers get their short selling wrong. With long-only funds, the potential loss is limited to the amount of the original investment: in effect, when it's gone, it's gone. By contrast, the potential loss on these short positions is uncapped.

✔ The extra leverage that shorting brings to the mix can work in both directions: if it boosts returns by increasing a fund's participation in the upside, it has a similar gearing effect when the market's heading south.

✔ Shorting as a central plank in this strategy is only effectively deployable in developed, populous markets, which rules out active extension funds investing in emerging markets.

Remember that long-only managers don't necessarily have adequate shorting skills, which is why hedge-fund managers with experience in short selling find themselves frequent targets for recruitment.

Discovering another Short-Selling Option: Exchange-Traded Funds

You can use short selling for virtually any kind of liquid, underlying asset. Most short selling is concentrated on ordinary shares issued by individual companies, but a growing number of firms also short sell *exchange-traded funds*, funds that track an index or a commodity yet are traded the same way stocks are traded. Chapter 16 explains these ETFs in greater detail, but for now I consider just one key attraction of ETFs: they allow you to take a view on a whole market or asset class via an index; for example, when you're interested in taking a view on, say, Chinese shares.

ETFs are very liquid and hugely popular in the hedge-fund community because they allow this form of 'shortcut investing'; if you hate Chinese shares, you short Chinese ETFs. This big-picture style of investing can turn into a macro-investing strategy, which I discuss in Chapter 15.

Working out which ETFs and asset classes potentially have the highest short interest is interesting. The data may then allow an investor with big blocks of asset classes (equities, bonds, alternatives, commodities) to alter her exposure to 'risky' assets; that is, asset classes that are being heavily shorted. In the US, short interest data is readily available on all ETFs but Europe has a distinct lack of information outside the big institutions. Luckily, you can find this data by using the ETF issuer's own website.

 Visit the UK website of major ETF player iShares (www.ishares.com) to find information quickly about its huge range of individual funds. On each of the fund data pages you can see a Securities Lending tab. Clicking this tab enables you to use a series of data tools to view who's 'borrowing' the underlying shares in this particular ETF.

Some funds don't show much borrowing of stock from the portfolio, especially if institutions are confident that that asset class is about to increase in value. But fund managers will be lending out a great amount of underlying shares and bonds if the asset class is likely to fall in value. The iShares data tables tell you the level of borrowing for all funds in the range, and as a short seller you may find yourself drawn inexorably to those with the most borrowed assets.

Chapter 8

Understanding Arbitrage: Big Name, Simple Idea

*I*magine that you spot someone walking along the street dropping crisp new £20 notes onto the ground. Obviously, as an honest citizen you'd chase after the person and point out his error! But how long do you think that obvious opportunity (go on, pick them up and treat yourself to a free lunch!) takes to get noticed by passers-by? Five seconds . . . ten?

Now, see that person as being the financial markets. But surely that's ridiculous, you say – according to academic economists the markets aren't in the habit of nonchalantly dropping piles of cash into the path of professional investors. These experts think that the chance of making big profits from market inefficiency is fleeting to the point of being almost nonexistent. Many hedge-fund investors, however, beg to differ. They think that markets constantly throw up opportunities in the shape of inefficiencies and they capitalise on those opportunities through arbitraging stock and bond markets.

Arbitrage is the practice of taking advantage of a price difference between two or more markets by simultaneously purchasing and selling an asset to make a profit from a difference in the price. In one kind of arbitrage, an investor may spend some cash initially without risking losses later (as in the currency trade). In the second type, no cash flows now but it offers a positive chance of making money.In this chapter, I introduce you to the world of arbitraging and how it works. I describe two different ways to engage in arbitrage: the popular version using convertibles and the recent, controversial innovation of using powerful computers (known as high-frequency trading). I focus on these two types because they're the methods you, as a private investor, are most likely to encounter and use.

Introducing Arbitrage: Pricing Models and Arbitrage Options

In one sense arbitrage forms the basis of everything that hedge funds do. The key idea is that they look for market inefficiencies, anomalies and mispricings and then aim to make a profit from these small price differences by using leverage, short selling and options-based products (see Chapters 3, 10 and 16).

On paper this all sounds fairly straightforward but most arbitrage opportunities aren't easy to find or exploit, which creates some pretty big obstacles to you getting involved. These barriers come in many different shapes and guises, for example the need for:

- **Patient research:** Arbitrage is not a game for the casual or novice investor. To be successful at exploiting market inefficiencies, you need to know a lot about the sector you're trading in and specific companies within those sectors.

- **Absolute knowledge about a specialist field:** Although theoretically arbitrage is risk free, risk is involved in many of the specific types of arbitrage strategies. One example is convertibles (a way that companies raise money by issuing income-based securities, as I describe in more detail in the later section 'Investigating Convertible Arbitrage'). To execute these competently, you need to understand how that strategy works and the risks inherent in it.

- **Super-powerful computers:** To spot fleeting opportunities that last for only seconds or minutes – the basis of HFT (check out 'Getting Up to Speed with High-Frequency Trading' later in this chapter).

- **Lots of money and expertise in making the various arbitrage opportunities work:** Bridgewater Associates, for example, one of the world's largest hedge funds, has advanced computer systems costing tens of millions of pounds to set up and run, which scour world markets looking for mispriced assets. This massively expensive deployment of human skill and computing prowess means that hedge-fund investors are often in effect 'walking the streets' every day looking for fools dropping their £20 notes!

Despite the costs and barriers, arbitrage opportunities still sometimes become overcrowded and hazardous to the wealth of investors: if everyone is looking for the same opportunity, hedge funds can lose money when arbitraging. Unsurprisingly, therefore, many hedge funds involved in arbitrage opportunities have an aversion to so-called transparency (or openness) in financial markets because they make their money from the cloudy, opaque nature of the markets!

Some arbitrage amounts to short selling the most liquid financial assets and going long the more illiquid assets. That can work a treat in some bull markets but can get dangerous when bearish times emerge. Arbitrage hedge-fund managers claim to be operating a market-neutral opportunity (that is, taking matching long and short positions, enabling money to be made whether prices are rising or falling), but in reality they still get hurt if for instance equity markets head steadily downwards in value.

Getting all mathematical

Arbitrage is a simple idea but hedge-fund investors who use these so-called arb techniques base their trading on remarkably complex mathematical models.

Tipping your CAPM: The traditional pricing model

To lead into a discussion on the mathematical model that powers arbitrage trading, I want to introduce you to a core concept in financial markets: the *capital asset pricing model* (CAPM).

The CAPM is an economic model that describes the relationship between risk and return and helps you work out the true value of any investment-based asset. It allows an investor to calculate the rate of return on an asset, such as a share, if it's to be added to an already well-diversified portfolio, given a certain level of risk.

The CAPM is based around the deceptively simple idea that higher returns are possible only if you take on higher risks.

The following equation sits at the heart of this model:

$$E(R_i) = R_f + \beta_i(E(R_m) - R_f)$$

where:

- $E(R_i)$ is the expected return on the share or security
- R_f is the risk-free rate of return from an asset such as bonds or cash
- β_i is the beta (a market fundamental as a real price movement)
- $E(R_m)$ is the expected return of the market
- $E(R_m) - R_f$ is sometimes known as the market premium or risk premium (the difference between the expected market rate of return and the risk-free rate of return)

The CAPM assumes that investors:

- ✔ Are rationally risk-averse

- ✔ Intend to maximise their *utility*, or benefit (satisfaction gained from owning an asset)

- ✔ Are price takers (that is, their transactions don't influence prices and therefore don't have any effect on the market itself)

- ✔ Can lend and borrow as much as they like using the risk-free rate of interest

- ✔ Trade with shares and securities that can be sub-divided into small pieces

- ✔ Won't incur any transaction or taxation costs, such as brokers' commissions and spreads

The CAPM allows investors to work out whether any share or asset class sits sensibly in their portfolios, given their appropriate level of risk.

A great many analysts don't subscribe to this model, thinking that the assumption that investors are rationally risk-averse is ridiculous and ignores a large amount of evidence that suggests that investors are anything but rational – that is, emotion plays a large part in investment and trading decisions; because this rationality is a core principle of the CAPM formula, that formula doesn't quite capture the true value of an asset. For this reason, investors who use arbitrage rely on different formulas to determine an asset's value.

Discovering APT: The arbitrage pricing model

Sophisticated investors involved in arbitrage strategies express criticisms of the CAPM model of the preceding section. They think that it's too 'broad brush' and doesn't help them work out what's incorrectly priced at the security or stock level. Such investors prefer to use a model that tells them how a share (or bond) price differs from the theoretical price predicted by economic models.

This *arbitrage pricing theory* (APT) doesn't rely on measuring the performance of the market – after all, many hedge funds who use it like to make money in all kinds of market conditions. Instead, APT directly relates the price of the security to the fundamental factors driving it.

This all sounds fine and dandy in theory, but in reality those fundamental values need to be empirically determined; that is, it must hold true in actual practice as well. They may include macro (that is, large scale) factors, such as economic growth and interest rates, or look at sector or company specific statistics, such as trying to get under the skin of consumer-spending patterns in retail markets.

The potentially large number of risk factors means that lots and lots of betas need to be calculated. Plus, no guarantee exists that all the relevant factors have been identified.

Arbitrage pricing theory: How apt!

The APT model was created in 1976 by Stephen Ross. In the technical language of economists, the theory predicts a relationship between the returns of a portfolio of assets (such as shares) and the returns of a single asset through a combination of many independent macro-economic variables, such as interest rates, unemployment rates and inflation rates. The resulting 'answer' derived from the model tells the investor where a mispriced asset is expected to be.

Whereas the CAPM formula from the preceding section requires the market's expected return, the APT model uses a risky asset's expected return and the risk premium of a number of macro-economic factors.

The APT model can be summed in an equation as follows:

$$r = r_f + \theta_1 f_1 + \theta_2 f_2 + \theta_3 f_3 + \ldots$$

where

- ✔ r is the expected return from a share or security
- ✔ r_f is the risk-free rate
- ✔ Each f is a separate factor
- ✔ Each θ is a measure of the relationship between the security price and that factor

By using the APT model, you can identify mispriced securities (those whose actual price differs from the APT price) to make money.

Meeting some different types of arbitrage

Arbitrage throws up an array of investment opportunities, with lots of different individual strategies, including:

- ✔ **Capital structure arbitrage:** Perhaps the biggest opportunity within the arb space, it involves looking at the different types of securities (equities, bonds and a hybrid class called convertibles) issued by corporations. Probably the most popular part of this strategy focuses on these hybrid convertibles (flip to the later section 'Investigating Convertible Arbitrage').

- ✔ **Fixed-income arbitrage:** Tries to exploit inefficiencies in the pricing of bonds and other income-producing securities. Arbitrageurs use bonds, interest-rate swaps, US and non-US government bonds, US Treasuries and mortgage-backed securities in their trades.

- ✔ **Liquidation arbitrage:** Where the arbitrageur bets that the break-up value of a business (all the assets minus its liabilities) is bigger than the current market value of the company. The arbitrageur is hoping that someone will come along and buy the company at a price that reflects its true value.

- ✔ **Model arbitrage:** Where a fund takes advantage of mispricings, usually of fairly exotic derivatives and structured products.

- ✔ **Reverse distressed debt:** Where you buy credit default options on 'highly rated' securities that are likely to become credit impaired. A credit default option is one in which the payoff is linked to the credit worthiness of the underlying entity. By buying this type of option on a highly rated security that's heading for a downgrade, you maximise the money you can make. (*Note:* A *highly rated security* is, by classification, financially strong and able to pay principal and interest on time.)

- ✔ **Reverse merger:** Involves an announced deal not going through – spreads are so tight on most deals these days that the profits on one deal breaking down can more than pay for other losses.

- ✔ **Statistical arbitrage:** A highly technical, short-term strategy that involves large numbers of securities (hundreds to thousands, depending on the amount of capital at stake), very short holding periods (days or even seconds), and huge computational, trading and information technology infrastructure. This strategy grew out of pairs trading (see Chapter 3) but is now driven by immense computing power. For more, read the 'Getting Up to Speed with High-Frequency Trading' section later in this chapter.

Viewing a typical example of an arbitrage opportunity

In the core North American financial markets, arbitrage opportunities emerge on a regular basis. A great way to help understand arbitrage is to take a look at how one such real-life opportunity arose.

Telus Corporation (ticker TU), one of Canada's major telecommunications companies, had long boasted a dual-share structure, involving shares with or without voting rights. In February 2012, the company announced that it wanted to consolidate this structure into one. Its aim was to make life simpler for its investors by converting the non-voting shares into voting common shares, along the way increasing liquidity and fairness – both types of shares had long enjoyed the same dividend payments! The spread between the voting and non-voting shares represented an obvious arbitrage trade opportunity.

Had it gone through (Telus eventually withdrew its proposal), this strategy would have involved buying the non-voting shares and shorting the voting shares (to eliminate the company-specific risk), capturing the 'spread' between the two classes of shares that had stood at about $1.26 a share, or 2.2 per cent. The chart in Figure 8-1 shows this consistent spread in prices between the two classes of shares over March 2012.

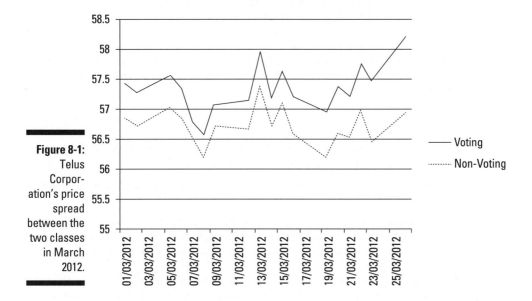

Figure 8-1: Telus Corporation's price spread between the two classes in March 2012.

Obviously the strategy involved risks, including worries about Canadian foreign ownership restrictions – would the government intervene and try to stop the consolidation of shares? (The Canadian government was and still is hugely concerned by foreign ownership of key companies – in the case of Telus Corporation, that foreign ownership couldn't exceed 33.5 per cent of shares outstanding).

Another obvious risk was that the vote may not have gone to plan and the consolidation be voted down. In fact, a leading US hedge fund called Mason Capital did turn up on the share register, eventually owning 19 per cent of the shares. It argued that the consolidation wasn't in shareholders' interests, although a majority of external shareholders had approved the deal.

Arbs can be caught short if their chosen event doesn't happen. The Telus consolidation looked like an obvious way to make a small but useful profit, but Mason Capital evidently thought otherwise and tried to torpedo the deal. This example highlights a key risk with any form of arbitrage, which is that when an opportunity sours losses can escalate quickly, wiping out the small initial profitable opportunity.

Assessing the risks

Arbitrage is a way to make money off of price fluctuations. Because the fluctuations tend to be small, this strategy relies on making so many trades that the cumulative gain will be substantial. And therein lies the risk. To maximise exposure and increase potential gain, many arbitrageurs use leverage.

With leverage, you use borrowed capital, or credit, to increase your earning potential. But just as leverage multiplies gains, it also multiplies losses. (In Chapter 10, I explain leverage – its advantages, disadvantages and risk – in detail.)

Other risks exist as well:

- **Execution risk:** When, in not closing multiple transactions at the same time, a small price shift reduces your profits.
- **Mismatch risk:** When you incorrectly assume that assets are correlated when they're not.
- **Liquidity risk:** When you face a margin call but your money is held up because you can't move the assets. Even though the position may eventually make you money, you can end up bankrupt before it does so.

Arbitrage has become increasingly popular in recent years as investors seek alternative investment options, which has reduced the effectiveness of the strategy.

Investigating Convertible Arbitrage

One of the most common and popular forms of arbitrage involves convertibles. The beginnings of convertible arbitrage trade go back as far as the second half of the twentieth century, when the first convertible securities were issued. The key part of this strategy is to look at the pricing of something called a convertible security (nothing to do with safety worries about hitting the highway in an open-top car!).

A *convertible security* is one that can be converted into another security at a pre-determined time and a pre-determined price. In most cases, the term applies to a bond that can be converted into a stock. *Convertible bonds* are neither bonds nor stocks, but hybrid securities with features of both. They may have a lower yield than other bonds, but this is usually balanced by the fact that they can be converted into stock at what's usually a discount to the stock's market value.

Companies usually finance their activities through a complex combination of equity (shares), preferred shares, convertible bonds (which have the option to be converted into shares) and bonds. The key insight is that in theory when a company has many different securities that are all linked to the performance of one asset (the company), these securities *should* trade in a similar fashion. But arbitrage traders realise that they don't necessarily do so!

You can view a convertible bond as a corporate bond with a stock call option attached to it. Corporate treasurers of large companies usually look on convertibles as a relatively inexpensive financing tool, because the bond's coupon is often much lower than straight debt. The price of a convertible bond is determined by the interplay of three factors:

- ✔ **Interest rates:** When rates move higher, the bond part of a convertible bond tends to move lower, but the call option part of a convertible bond is worth more.

- ✔ **Stock price:** When the price of the company's stock moves higher, the price of the bond tends to rise as well.

- ✔ **Credit spread:** If the company's creditworthiness deteriorates, the bond price tends to move lower.

Profiting from convertibles

Convertible securities *usually* trade in line with the underlying stock value, because they represent options to purchase that stock. If the convertible somehow gets out of line with this trend, however, an arbitrage opportunity opens up – frequently a company's convertible bonds are priced inefficiently relative to the company's stock. Convertible arbitrage attempts to profit from this pricing error.

A typical trade involves being long Company A's convertible security (for example, a bond or preferred share) and short Company A's stock. Instead of purchasing and shorting stocks, however, convertible arbitrage takes a long position in, or purchases, convertible securities. It simultaneously takes a short position in, or sells, the same company's common stock.

A hedge fund can run a convertibles-based strategy by buying a company's convertible bonds at the same time as it shorts the company's stock. If the company's stock price falls, the hedge fund benefits from its short position. In addition, the company's convertible bonds are likely to decline less than its stock; they're protected because they're regarded as less risky fixed-income instruments. On the other hand, if the company's stock price rises, the hedge fund can convert its convertible bonds into stock and sell that stock at market value, thereby benefiting from its long position and, ideally, compensating for any losses on its short position.

Although convertible arbitrage typically involves US corporate convertible bonds, significant convertible-bond markets also operate in Europe and

Japan, as well as niche opportunities in other regional markets, such as Asia (ex-Japan) and Canada. In fact, hedge funds are thought to hold more than 60 per cent of the outstanding convertible bonds in the US, which means that a potential lack of liquidity exists in falling markets. As a result, the price of all convertibles may fall together regardless of the underlying convertible-bond valuations. If you plan to make convertible arbitrage part of your strategy, be aware of this possibility and make sure you carefully control your risk levels and don't expose much capital to the trade idea.

Historically, the leverage used for a convertible arbitrage strategy varied considerably by manager, from 4 to 9 times capital. However, the average leverage for this strategy has recently been estimated to have fallen to as low as 2 times. This reduction translates to smaller potential profits but also lower levels of risk

If all goes well, a typical hedge-fund convertibles strategy may produce the following cash flows:

- ✔ Cash inflows from coupon payments of the convertible – remember that they pay income via regular coupons.
- ✔ Cash inflows from the short interest credit on the short stock account.
- ✔ Cash outflows due to dividend payments on shorted stock; that is, the fund has to pay the dividends owed on the ordinary shares it borrowed.

Assessing the strategy's recent performance

In recent decades convertible arbitrage has become hugely popular among many hedge-fund managers. Although it has been one of the most successful hedge-fund strategies in the past, consistently providing double digit returns, its performance has deteriorated in recent years.

The number of convertible arbitrage hedge funds is believed to have grown from about 28 in 1998 to about 121 in 2007, with assets under management shooting up from US$0.8 billion in January 1998 to about US$12.9 billion in June 2004, before dropping back to US$9.4 billion in December 2007. The average annual return over the period 1998–2007 was 9.05 per cent – by comparison, during the same period the average total annual return of the S&P 500 was 6.84 per cent. After 2007, many convertible funds' results plummeted, although some funds have produced robust positive returns since 2010.

Many commentators suggest that the deterioration in performance from the middle of the last decade can be explained by stable equity markets (before 2008), rising interest rates (again, before 2008) and withdrawals from funds, as well as increased competition in the hedge-fund industry and lower volatilities in the main capital markets.

In recent years convertible funds have turned in a volatile performance, with big losses in 2008 followed by massive gains in 2009 – returns from 2011 and 2012 have been a tad lacklustre (see Table 8-1).

Table 8-1	Recent Returns from Convertible Arbitrage (%)				
	2012	*2011*	*2010*	*2009*	*2008*
Annual Return of Dow Jones Credit Suisse Core Convertible Arbitrage Hedge Fund Index	5.90	−7.66	11.16	46.23	−30.34
S&P 500	16.44	2.11	15.06	26.46	−37.00
Merrill Lynch All US Convertibles Index	11.83	−5.18	16.77	49.13	−35.73
Dow Jones World Index	10.74	−9.91	11.89	31.97	−42.85

Source: www.hedgeindex.com – accurate as at 1 November 2012

Convertible arbitrage trades represent more than half of the secondary market trading in convertible securities. This statistic indicates that hedge funds are a very important liquidity provider in the convertible market.

Finding the opportunities

Unlike many strategies used by hedge funds, arbitraging isn't phenomenally complicated, which perhaps helps explain why it's become so popular in recent years. Most convertibles arbitrage managers follow a three-step process:

1. **Identify undervalued convertible securities.** Convertible arbitrageurs seek undervalued convertibles with good liquidity. They also like to focus on specific convertible bond attributes such as convertible bonds with a high reward-to-risk ratio. All managers must be able to borrow stock to short as a hedge, and also need protection against sudden dividend increases.

2. **Establish the hedge ratios.** After managers select a suitable convertible, they need to determine the appropriate hedge ratio (that is, the amount of shares to sell short). With the right hedge ratio, the position can be profitable if the stock rises or falls.

3. **Manage the risks.** The last stage involves the manager working out the main risks involved in a bond trade. These can include:

   - **Credit:** Most convertibles are below investment grade or not rated, and so significant default risk exists.

   - **Interest rate:** Longer maturity convertibles are sensitive to interest rates.

   - **Manager:** Managers may incorrectly value a convertible and/or short an incorrect amount of stock.

   - **Leverage:** Borrowed funds magnify returns from the generally stable relationship between the long bond and the short stock. However, borrowed funds also magnify the risk of losses.

   - **Liquidity and execution:** The manager's ability to enter/exit a position with minimal market impact directly affects profitability.

   - **Stock loan:** An effective hedge depends on how reliably and cost-effectively the manager can borrow and sell short shares.

Diversification is the simplest way to address these numerous risks. Many managers also use credit derivatives such as credit default swaps (CDSs) as a form of insurance policy against a company defaulting on its debts and going bust. I discuss CDSs further in Chapter 15.

Being aware of the risks of convertible arbitrage

Convertible arbitrage isn't without risks. In fact, arbitraging convertibles is trickier than it sounds. You generally have to hold convertible bonds for a specified amount of time (before they can be converted into stock), and so you need to evaluate the market carefully and determine in advance whether market conditions will coincide with the time frame in which conversion is permitted.

Convertible arbitrageurs can also fall victim to unpredictable events. In 2005, for instance, many arbitrageurs held long positions in General Motors (GM) convertible bonds and short positions in GM stock. They suffered losses when one big investor tried to buy GM stock at the same time as its debt was being downgraded by credit-rating agencies. Because the arbitrageurs were long on the debt but short on GM stocks, they suffered losses on both positions as the bond value fell and the stock value rose.

Getting Up to Speed with High-Frequency Trading

In contrast to convertible arbitrage (see the preceding section), which has largely escaped media attention because it involves specialised securities that most individual investors ignore, high-frequency trading (HFT) has become the subject of massive public controversy. This computerised form of arbitrage is very similar to its convertibles-based siblings but its impact has been felt far and wide.

In this section I look at HFT, which is so contentious that fear about it contributing to sudden market crashes has caused many regulators to call for a curb on the activity of algorithmic-based arbitrageurs.

Appraising the brave new world of computerised trading

For much of Wall Street's history trading in shares was fairly easy to understand: buyers and sellers gathered around desks on an exchange floor and shouted orders at each other. Then, in 1998, the Securities and Exchange Commission (SEC) authorised electronic exchanges to compete with marketplaces such as the New York Stock Exchange. The idea was to open up the market so that anyone with a new idea and a powerful computer could access these hugely important markets.

This sensible reform didn't turn out quite as planned, though. In simple terms, the US stock markets rapidly discovered that not all computers are created equal! Some investors deployed tens of millions of dollars buying super-powerful machines that can churn through a mountain of market data in a matter of seconds. All they needed was a set of ideas to power the computer program used by HFTs; arbitrage theory provided that and a massive new hedge-fund sector emerged. Today, these computing-based trading systems use software to analyse huge amounts of incoming market data and then run trades based on the data.

In addition, high-frequency traders also benefit from competition among the various exchanges, which pay small fees that are often collected by the biggest and most active traders – typically a quarter of a cent a share to whoever arrives first. Those small payments, spread over millions of shares, help high-speed investors profit simply by trading enormous numbers of shares, even if they buy or sell at a modest loss.

These high-frequency traders usually don't have any positions open at the end of a given trading day! They carry out incredibly short-term trading.

Some of these computer-based trading programs rely heavily on the processing capability of computers to find and analyse relevant market data – usually based around the fundamentals of a particular share. Other HFT algorithms simply respond to the hectic world of the electronic trading floor; that is, they respond to price-based technical data and not company fundamentals. They can spot trends before other investors can blink, changing orders and strategies within milliseconds. Regardless of how the programs identify their opportunities, a typical HFT system can run as many as 165,000 trades in a matter of a few seconds.

You're probably wondering whether all this speedy trading makes anyone any money. Well, the answer is yes, for a small few. In 2012 profits from HFT in American stocks was due to hit US$1.25 billion, down 35 per cent from 2011 and 74 per cent lower than the peak of about US$4.9 billion in 2009, according to estimates from the brokerage firm Rosenblatt Securities. That decline may sound worrying, but US$1.25 billion is still a large amount of money from just one specialised strategy.

Many believe that HFTs increase market liquidity because of the way this type of trading works – the traders exploit small price inefficiencies across thousands or tens of thousands of trades a day and close out their positions at the end of the day. Others argue that it also increases market volatility and name it as a contributing factor to market crashes. You can read more about these opinions in the 'Stating the argument for HFT' section later in this chapter.

Discovering different HFT strategies

Hedge funds use a number of core arbitrage-based, algorithmic-based strategies:

- ✔ **Market making:** Places buy or sell orders on various securities in order to earn its bid–ask spread, thus creating a new market by acting as a counterparty to incoming market orders.

- ✔ **Ticker tape trading:** Uses superfast computers to analyse ticker quotes and volumes to glean information not yet reported.

- ✔ **Event arbitrage:** Uses recurring events and past price history to forecast short-term market moves and profit accordingly.

- ✔ **Statistical arbitrage:** Attempts to take advantage of predictable deviations in stable statistical relationships between securities. (These mathematical models used to determine predictable deviations from these 'stable statistical relationships' are highly proprietary and may be questionable.)

Stating the argument for HFT

A British government study concluded in 2012 that the rise of HFT may be a good thing for ordinary investors, arguing that HFT strategies make it easier and cheaper for ordinary investors to buy or sell stock whenever they want. In a sense the researchers backed up the conclusions of many academics that arbitraging away market inefficiencies is positive because it helps keep a market liquid and efficient. Experience shows that a market with a great deal of opacity is usually bad news for the private investor and HFT helps shine a light on those inefficient practices. As HFTs exploit price discrepancies, the prices tend to converge, eliminating inefficiency.

The report did worry that the increasing prevalence of computerised trading may lead to isolated incidents of instability in the financial markets, such as flash crashes. But the researchers firmly rejected the idea that HFT causes greater volatility in markets and manipulates stock prices.

Setting out the objections

Not all regulators and researchers are relaxed about HFT. Andrew Haldane, executive director for financial stability at the Bank of England, is certainly worried by the growth of this form of trading, saying

> *what we have out there now is this complex array of multiple mutating interacting machines, algorithms. It's constantly developing and travelling at ever higher velocities. And it's just difficult to know what will pop out next. And that's not an accident waiting to happen, that's an accident that has been happening with increasing frequency over the last few years. We shouldn't wait for the equivalent of the Space Shuttle disaster before remedying the situation. We already have enough light on the dashboard flashing red to want to do something differently.*

> www.bbc.co.uk/news/magazine-19214294

But high-frequency traders may be struggling with more mundane problems, because general drops in overall trading volume have made it harder for them to make profits. And in this new technology arms race, many traditional institutional investors have upped the ante and invested billions of pounds in new technology that allows them to recapture any advantage – measured in shaving milliseconds off trade times.

The biggest worry for investors is that the HFT software may malfunction and end up causing chaos. The computers are subject to human errors in software design or mistakes in execution on the parts of the traders, which can create serious complications for major stock indices. The *New York Times* reckons that:

> *high-frequency trades make up about 60 percent of the near 7 billion shares exchanged on US stock indexes (about 4.2 billion shares) every trading day.*

So glitches in these systems can move markets dramatically.

Predicting that new regulations are on their way

Perhaps the biggest threat to HFT comes from the regulators. Canada, Australia and Germany have adopted, or at the very least proposed, a wide range of limits on high-speed trading. Regulators in the US (HFT's homeland) have so far been reluctant to curb the trade, although the Securities and Exchange Commission has installed a new program (in October 2012) called Midas that allows the agency to look in detail at real-time market transactions. This new software was designed by an HFT firm and is far from being an 'all seeing eye'. For instance, it doesn't have information on the trades executed in so-called dark pools (trading venues that don't have to follow the same reporting rules as the public exchanges).

If it does work, Midas may help stop future flash crashes.

Chapter 9

Weighing Up Growth Versus Value Investing

I describe enough advanced thinking in this book for you to see why maths-trained, rocket-scientist types make a lot of money with hedge funds. Yet many successful investors aren't especially clever or cutting edge in their methods. They're fairly boring and mainstream and use ideas that have been kicking around for at least 70 years.

The primary (though not exclusive) focus of these old-school investors is on an individual company. They know whether a firm and its shares represent good value or whether the shares are about to grow quickly as profits power ahead. They love talking about fundamental measures and numbers, focusing on balance sheets, profit and loss statements, cash flows, and the assets and liabilities of their chosen company; they deliberately ignore talk about options or volatility.

Within this old-school approach is a wide variety of beliefs, which can be summed up as the growth-versus-value debate:

✔ **Growth:** Investors who focus only on companies that are growing quickly and can deliver massive returns.

✔ **Value:** Cautious types who prefer to buy cheap, quality stuff (they're probably the biggest group in the hedge-fund community).

✔ **Best of both worlds:** Investors who borrow a bit from both sides of the debate; they like to buy cheap shares but only in a good, growing company.

In this chapter I describe these views and show how you can use the ideas within your own portfolio. The stars of this debate are famous investors who've developed their own tweaks and variations on the two basic strategies and turned them into hugely successful funds. Therefore, I introduce you to Ben Graham and Warren Buffett as well as less familiar characters such as Richard Driehaus. You can learn from every one of these investing greats.

Understanding the Key Measures

In order to describe the old-school investment approach, this chapter has to touch on the important company financial attributes that the investors use. These measures take a specific security and then attempt to look at the fundamentals that lie behind the share price or at the share price itself. Here's a brief introduction to the key measuring tools that help you build your portfolio with more confidence:

- ✔ **Profits (or earnings):** Probably the most widely used set of numbers by all forms of equity investors. A business's profits are the result of subtracting the net costs from the total cash sales, and from this figure deducting dividends paid out, capital expenditure and taxes.

  Many company managements manipulate their earnings, regularly exempting supposedly one-off costs from the final profit figure.

- ✔ **Price to earnings (PE) ratio:** A way of relating the flow of earnings to the *market capitalisation* (the total dollar value of the company's outstanding shares) of the firm. If a company is valued at $100 million and produces net profits before tax of $10 million, its share price to earnings ratio is ten. The PE ratio is also sometimes used in an inverse sense via the *earnings yield*. In this example, the earnings yield of the $10 million profit-making company is 10 per cent; that is, 10 per cent of the market value is accounted for by its earnings.

- ✔ **Cash flow:** Many investors focus closely on the cash flow coming into the business because earnings are by their nature a tad suspicious. (Corporate managers and their accountants can deploy hundreds of different ruses to 'reshape' profits.) The purest concept is *free cash flow*, which contains all the net cash profits coming into the business after dividends, capital expenditure and any other exceptional expenses – the company is making large investments (hopefully in things that will yield a high return!), for example – are excluded.

- ✔ **Dividend yield:** Much beloved by cynical investors. Theoretically you can only pay out hard cash dividends if you have enough hard cash profits, and so dividends are the last bit of the cash pipeline that can be handed back to investors as their annual reward. The yield is the dividend payout as a ratio against the market value of the company.

✔ **Book value:** The residual value after everything has been accounted for that belongs to the investors. This measurement forces investors to look at the total assets of the business less all liabilities, which they hope is positive! Curiously, the book value of the business is virtually never the same as the market value of the shares combined.

✔ **Debt:** Closely watched by many investors and simply measured as all the short- and long-term debt facilities versus either the book value of the business or the market value of the business.

✔ **Share price:** Indicated by the market makers. As I describe in Chapter 3, the share price has its own momentum, or lack of it! Many investors like to see a share price that's moving ahead steadily over time relative to the market. In contrast most investors view with suspicion a share price that goes nowhere for long periods or starts steadily falling, although contrarians are attracted to these poor momentum stocks.

Cultivating an Interest in Growth Investing

For many investors, stocks and shares are all about the search for growth stocks, where they can reap huge rewards from a share price that goes up many times in value. In this section I look at this perhaps most excitable group of investors and their hunt for fast-growing companies and spectacular profits.

To help you get under the skin of growth investing, I take a look at the ideas of two of the greats: Richard Driehaus and William O'Neil.

Defining growth-investing basics

Growth-investing guru and professional hedge-fund manager Richard Driehaus has no time for talk about magic valuation methods or the fundamental value of stock. For him, each company's share price is unique and that means investors have to look at the company and what it does, instead of comparing it to anything else.

For Driehaus the key is to buy *high* (when a share price is trending upwards) and then sell *even higher*. This philosophy means that Driehaus tries to buy into a share where the price has already started trending upwards, making new recent highs and showing strong relative strength. He thinks that these features mean that the stock is in demand from other investors like himself.

This strategy is obviously risky: you can end up buying near the top of a share's price cycle. But Driehaus says:

I would much rather be invested in a stock that is increasing in price and take the risk that it may begin to decline, than invest in a stock that is already in a decline and try to guess when it will turn around.

Driehaus's investment company has taken this aggressive growth style and developed a sophisticated investment strategy built around the following simple principles:

- ✔ Aggressive-growth companies, by definition, are the fastest-growing companies in the economy, in terms of revenues and earnings.

- ✔ Earnings growth is the principal factor in determining the prices of common stock over time.

- ✔ The fastest-growing companies also tend to be the most adaptable and dynamic firms within the economy.

Focusing on profits

For Driehaus and his colleagues, the growth-orientated objectives are brought to life by using a number of key measures including an *insistence on earnings growth*. Investors need to start with an understanding of profits generated by a company and how the growth in those profits is the principal factor in determining the share price over the long run.

Only through constant and sustained earnings growth can cash flows be increased, dividends raised and the value of the business 'worth' be expanded. Therefore, investors need to look out for accelerating sales and earnings growth as well as the odd *earnings surprise* (when the company surprises analysts by producing profits above their estimates).

As a Driehaus follower, you need to become hugely interested in a share's technical price data, including price support levels, volume characteristics and relative strength rankings, as well as look at sector and industry relative strength. By combining an analysis of the company and its growing profits plus its technical share data, you can 'make early identification of companies on the threshold of rapid stock price appreciation'.

Following the profits

Many of Driehaus's ideas are echoed by another legendary growth investor, William O'Neil, who says that finding growth stocks is all about examining 'winners of the past to learn all the characteristics of the most successful stocks'. The fruits of this research are contained in the CAN SLIM approach, which I discuss further in the later section 'Getting practical with a growth screen' and which you can examine in greater detail at `www.canslim.net`.

O'Neil passionately believes that stocks sell for what they're worth and stocks with low PE ratios (see the earlier section 'Understanding the Key Measures') are probably correctly priced by the market. What matters to O'Neil is that the firm whose shares you're buying is growing fast and that the markets recognise this fact.

For O'Neil (and Driehaus) the key test of quality is profits. You need to look for a minimum increase of 18–20 per cent in quarterly earnings compared with the same quarter last year. Specifically, you want to find shares where a kind of earnings growth engine is kicking in, and where new products or services are about to be launched.

O'Neil sums up his philosophy as follows:

> *we're buying companies with strong fundamentals, large sales and earnings increases resulting from unique new products and services and trying to time [those] purchases at a correct point as the company emerges from consolidation periods and before the stock runs up dramatically in price.*

Getting practical with a growth screen

O'Neil has gone out of his way to publicise his ideas (he also happens to own a major investment newspaper called *Investor's Business Daily*), so popularising his CAN SLIM ideas. In particular he's helped along advanced investors by spelling out which factors to look for as you 'filter' the market using what's called a *stockscreen*, a tool investors and traders use to find stocks based on criteria they specify; it enables them to analyse hundreds of stocks in a relatively short period of time.

Stockscreens tend to be used with online web tools from places such as www.ycharts.com or www.ft.com, although some of the best technology is available using offline software-based programs such as ShareScope (www.sharescope.co.uk). These programs allow you to use key measures to determine how you filter down through the universe of thousands of individual stocks. These screens are a great way of identifying a small basket of key stocks and then buying them for your portfolio.

The clue to what a typical CAN SLIM stockscreen looks like is in the name. CAN SLIM is an acronym, with each letter standing for a key financial measure:

- ✔ **C is Current Earnings.** The key is to look for companies experiencing major percentage increases in current quarterly earnings per share (EPS) when compared to the quarter from the year before: quarterly earnings growth of at least 18–20 per cent. Sales should also increase by at least 30 per cent in the last reporting period compared to previous period.

✔ **A is Annual Earnings.** Meaningful growth is required over the last five years, with a 4–5-year annual growth rate of between 20 and 50 per cent per year.

✔ **N is New Products.** O'Neil reckons that new products or services cause the big earnings acceleration. He cites innovations such as Rexall's new Tupperware division, in 1958, which helped the stock rise from $16 to $50.

✔ **S is Supply and Demand of the shares.** If not many shares are in circulation, a small amount of buying can push prices up quickly, and so in the US investors should look for companies with 5–25 million shares outstanding. For UK investors, the equivalent number is around 1 million shares.

✔ **L is Leader or Laggard.** O'Neil passionately believes that so-called expensive shares are worth it because they carry on rising in value, whereas shares that seem cheap usually get even cheaper. Relative strength in the share price matters.

✔ **I is Institutional Ownership.** O'Neil likes some, but not too much, *institutional ownership* (when a large amount of shares in a company is held by entities such as financial organisations, endowments and pension funds). Look for 5–25 per cent.

✔ **M is Market Direction.** Very few stocks go up when the market is going down. O'Neil advises investors to buy individual stocks only when the market as a whole (that is, the S&P 500 index) is going up.

Tracking down great growth companies introduces lots of risks:

✔ You can end up overpaying for these wonder stocks. That expensive price turns into a bubble and eventually investors become disenchanted.

✔ The company may make mistakes. It may not carry on increasing its profits, consequently issuing profits warnings with the inevitable impact on the share price.

✔ Companies can simply change and become boring. The wonder growth stocks may mature, start paying dividends, give up on risky expansion and become ex-growth. One example that springs to mind is Microsoft, a very popular stock that matured into a huge giant whose share price has gone virtually nowhere for many years.

Searching for the elusive tenbagger

The hunt for amazing-performing growth stocks sometimes translates into one much used, and abused, word – the wonderfully elusive tenbagger of stock-market lore! A *tenbagger* is a stock where the share price has gone up at least tenfold during the period it's in your portfolio.

The originator of the term, Peter Lynch, lists his key criteria for finding these slippery tenbaggers, including:

- ✔ Look at small companies because 'big companies don't have big stock moves . . . you get your biggest moves in smaller companies'.

- ✔ Look for fast growers where earnings are growing by more than 20–30 per cent per year.

- ✔ Look for insider buying and share buybacks (that is, look for people inside the company buying shares or repurchasing shares they sold earlier, both of which indicate that those in the know are investing in themselves).

- ✔ Diversify and hold plenty of stocks and different kinds of risk in your portfolio.

But Lynch also has two other criteria waiting in the wings, which aren't so widely referred to by breathless growth fiends because these criteria seem diametrically opposed to what growth investors typically look for:

- ✔ Buy stocks from dead industries with dull products and dull names. The reason? Companies that don't inspire excitement, either in their products or in their industry, generally have lower share prices and can therefore be good bargains.

- ✔ Buy stocks from sectors where analysts don't bother looking. A spin-off or a fast-growing company in a no-growth industry, for example, rarely attracts attention from other growth investors.

So Peter Lynch isn't a growth investor in any real sense of the word. True, he likes to find great investments (who doesn't!), but in temperament he's much closer to the value investors that I describe in the next section.

Entering the World of Value Investors

Many investors instinctively find themselves balking at excited talk of growth stocks and tenbaggers, such as in the preceding section. Deep down they sense that they're being sucked – or even suckered – into an economic bubble of the type I discuss in Chapter 4. More to the point, they think that a better way of building an investment strategy exists, one not anchored on projections of where volatile earnings may be headed in the future, as I discuss in this section.

Most of the time value strategies probably deliver you better returns growth strategies, if only because they tend to focus on picking companies that pay out a nice, boring dividend every year! You probably aren't going to make large absolute losses from value investing, but you may lose out, in relative terms, in a bull market phase. You still make money, of course, but growth strategies may have delivered huge returns.

Origins of value investing

The value school of professional investing started in one of the greatest boom and busts of history: the Wall Street Crash of 1929. At that time Ben Graham was working on Wall Street as a stockbroker. He noticed the mania for growth and was horrified. For him, the crowd was a dangerous beast and certainly not one to be trusted because it piles into whatever is hot.

Graham believed that the market gets things wrong because of its obsession with growth at all costs.

Using value as the key criterion

Value investors believe that the stampede towards growth companies is almost inevitably a recipe for disaster, and instead they advise investors to look at the underlying value of the company. Value investors start from a very different, contrarian place when compared to growth investors. They look for a company whose shares are great *value*; that is, cheap relative to their prospects. They instinctively hate paying-the-odds for anything and think that most people are probably wrong most of the time.

Looking at value investor loves

The first great value investor Ben Graham (read the earlier sidebar 'Origins of value investing' for more) believed that you make money by focusing. The path to true riches lies in a relentless focus on good value and a margin of safety. When you choose to invest hard-earned money in a share (a real-world business, not just a piece of paper) ensure that the company and its shares are cheap.

Getting great businesses at bargain prices

Cheap indicates a great many things to value investors. On a surface level it can mean that the vital statistics (the fundamentals) of the company's share price are cheap in relation to the wider market, or that the PE ratio (which I explain in the earlier section 'Understanding the Key Measures') is low, or that the ratio of sales to share price is unreasonably high.

But the word suggests more than simple ratios: it also means that a safety margin is built into the shares. Look at the company's balance sheet and consider which assets back the shares – is the share cheap in relation to these assets?

Other value investors like to look at future prospects as well and consider whether future profits growth and cash generation are going to add to the intrinsic value of the business. They ask whether the stock is cheap relative to its future growth prospects.

Loving that dividend

Value investors are rigorous folk and they make the effort to acquaint themselves with all sorts of measures of shareholder wealth. In particular they love dividends – a juicy dividend can make a big difference to total shareholder returns over the long term.

As an investor, not only do you benefit from any increase in the capital value of the shares (following a re-evaluation by the market of the intrinsic value of the business), but you also get all those lovely dividend cheques. Add it all up and you can make above-average returns.

Buying a solid business with intrinsic value

The bottom line for value investors is that the market all too frequently undervalues decent companies with good prospects. Ben Graham disciple Mario Gabelli sums up the core of this philosophy in Peter Tanous's book *Investment Gurus*:

> We're buying a business and a business has certain attributes . . . as surrogate owners there are certain characteristics with regard to the franchise, the cash generating capabilities of the franchise and the quality of the management . . . . You also have a notion of price. Where are you buying that stock within the context of what I call 'private market value' – what others might call intrinsic value? And within that framework, Mr Market gives you opportunities to buy above that price and below that price, that intrinsic value.

Focusing on this *intrinsic value* means looking at what you believe the assets and liabilities of the business are worth. Think like an informed industrialist and ask what such a person would pay to buy this business. Consider the total business value: cash, *receivables* (that is, all day to day debts owed to the company), inventory and goodwill, earnings power, plus some modicum of future value potential. If the total is something you can view as cheap, you stand a better chance of making a profit.

Finding fallen angels

Ben Graham famously advises investors to 'fish where the fish are'. In other words, if you spot lots of seemingly cheap companies in a particular sector, start investing because some of those stocks are probably cheap.

Graham's core insight is that, despite wild speculative variations, shares do have a fundamental economic value that's relatively stable and can be easily measured by the term intrinsic value. Over the long run, performance of companies and share prices generally reverts to a mean: the lowly priced cheap stock no one seems to like eventually rises in price as the market comes to love its intrinsic value in relation to the share price.

Only buy shares when their market price is significantly below that of the calculated intrinsic value.

Value investing in practice

James Montier, investment strategist, asset allocation guru and Ben Graham acolyte, is keeping the master investor's ideas current. He sums up his take on Graham's views as follows:

> At the heart of Graham's approach was the concept of an appropriate margin of safety. That is to say, investors should always seek to purchase securities with a large discount between intrinsic value and market price . . . . Indeed, Graham's own best loved criterion was a price less than two-thirds of net current assets.

James Montier was a research strategist for a large French bank and is now a fund manager at investment house GMO. He believes that behaviour matters and so investors should always endeavour to better understand their own weaknesses, biases and traits.

In order to qualify as a value opportunity, Montier advises looking for the following measures (for more details on some of these items, take a look at the earlier section 'Understanding the Key Measures'):

- ✔ A PE ratio of less than 40 per cent of the peak PE ratio based on five-year moving average earnings (look beyond just the last year's earnings figures).
- ✔ A dividend yield at least equal to two-thirds of the AAA bond yield.
- ✔ A price of less than two-thirds of tangible book value (look at tangible assets rather than intangible ones).
- ✔ A price of less than two-thirds of net current assets.
- ✔ Total debt less than tangible book value.
- ✔ A current ratio greater than 2 (the current ratio, an indicator of a company's liquidity, measures how able a company is to repay its short-term obligations, like money borrowed and owed payments).
- ✔ Total debt less than (or equal to) twice net current assets.
- ✔ Compound earnings growth of at least 7 per cent over the last ten years.
- ✔ Two or fewer annual earnings declines of 5 per cent or more in the last ten years.

Reading the value bible according to Tweedy, Browne

New York investment house Tweedy, Browne has turned many of Ben Graham's ideas into modern-day investment strategies. Here are the partners' practical value-investing tips:

- ✔ **Search for a low share price in relation to asset value.** Stocks that sell for below their book value are great and stocks that trade below their net current asset value (cash and easily realisable assets) are even better.

- ✔ **Seek a low share price in relation to the PE ratio.** The PE ratio turned around and expressed as an earnings yield – that is, a PE ratio of 10 becomes an earnings yield of 10 per cent – should be at least twice that of the yield obtained by investing in triple AAA-rated corporate bonds (the highest – best – rating indicating financial health).

- ✔ **Value confidence:** Love evidence of the directors buying their company stock.

- ✔ **Be a true contrarian:** Go out of your way to look for stocks where the share price has dropped back recently.

- ✔ **Focus on small-cap investing:** Investing in small caps produces better long-term results.

Using the balance sheet for real value

Joseph Piotroski (an associate accounting professor at Stanford University Graduate School of Business) has quietly emerged as a new champion of Ben Graham's theories (for more on Graham, check out the earlier sidebar 'Origins of value investing') with an updated idea of deep value investing. He's keenly aware that dirt cheap firms selling well below their asset base are increasingly hard to find. His great innovation is to re-focus attention not on the earnings and dividends statements but on the balance sheet.

Modernising the value investing idea

Piotroski undertook a huge research study that found that the performance of conventional value stocks is wildly skewed, with a few big winners and lots of losers. Emboldened, he devised a points system to spot these unloved gems (see the later sidebar 'Using points for good behaviour' for details). But Piotroski noticed something else, too: economists generally define boring value stocks as those in the bottom 20 per cent when companies are ranked according to price/book ratios.

TECHNICAL STUFF

Using points for good behaviour

Piotroski's concepts form a relatively easy-to-understand points system, with a point awarded for each of the following:

- One point for a positive return on assets (defined as net profits before exceptional items divided by the total assets of the firm).

- One point for a positive cash flow.

- One point for an improvement in return on assets over the last year.

- One point for a company where cash flow from operations exceeds net income (because depreciation and non-cash expenses normally reduce the net profits but have no impact on cash flow).

- One point if the measure of financial leverage, ratio of total debt to total assets, declined in the past year.

- One point if the current ratio increased over the year.

- One point to companies that haven't issued any new shares in the current financial year – firms that issue too much debt may be struggling to manage liquidity and running short of funds.

- One point for an increase in gross margin.

- One point if *asset turnover* (total sales divided by total assets at the start of the financial year) has increased during the year.

The sum of the scores indicates a company's financial strength, with a higher result corresponding to better financial health.

Piotroski is convinced that the market singularly fails to price solid financial backing adequately into the current share price and as a result consistently undervalues some company shares. He believes that markets are too swayed by the wild gyrations and ephemera of speculative investing. Investors, institutional and private alike, are victims of their own short-sightedness – they react to every bit of rumour and gossip and neglect the hard evidence of past returns and strong finances.

Looking at the reports and accounts

Piotroski believes that investors should stick to the hard facts represented by the reports and accounts. They should scrutinise profit and loss, cash flow and balance sheet carefully, making full use of the full range of financial measures including specialised ones such as the *current ratio*: working assets or current assets divided by current liabilities.

When he applied the analysis to the US stock market, the results were compelling. The better a firm fits his criteria – I lay out his points system in the nearby sidebar 'Using points for good behaviour' – the better its shares perform. In fact, an investment strategy that bought the expected winners and shorted the expected losers would have generated a 23 per cent annual return from 1976 through to 1996. Applying just a long strategy – only buying stocks not selling or shorting them – also produced above-average returns: a portfolio of high-scoring book-to-market (BM) firms made at least 7.5 per cent beyond the market over the same time frame.

The Tao of Investing

James Montier (see the earlier section 'Value investing in practice') is a value investor through and through. He believes that private investors can absolutely apply value investing to their investing strategies. For Montier, the only relevant aspect of investment is maximum returns, and so 'the question becomes, how should we invest to deliver this objective?'. Therefore, he developed his own ten-point plan for future investing success, pithily called his Tao of Investing:

✔ **Tenet I – Value, value, value:** Value investing is the only real safety-first approach. By putting the margin of safety at the heart of the process, the value approach minimises the risk of overpaying for the hope of growth.

✔ **Tenet II – Be contrarian:** As [investor and mutual fund pioneer] Sir John Templeton observed, 'it's impossible to produce superior performance unless you do something different from the majority'.

✔ **Tenet III – Be patient:** Patience is integral to a value approach on many levels, from waiting for the fat pitch, to dealing with the value manager's curse of being too early.

✔ **Tenet IV – Be unconstrained:** Although pigeon-holing and labelling are fashionable, they don't aid investment. Investors should be free to exploit value opportunities wherever they may occur.

✔ **Tenet V – Don't forecast:** Investors have to find a better way of investing than relying upon their seriously flawed ability to soothsay.

✔ **Tenet VI – Cycles matter:** As [American investor] Howard Marks puts it, 'we can't predict but we can prepare'. An awareness of the economic, credit and sentiment cycles can help with investment.

✔ **Tenet VII – History matters:** The four most dangerous words in investing are 'this time is different'. Knowledge of history and context can help avoid repeating the blunders of the past.

✔ **Tenet VIII – Be sceptical:** Questioning what you're told and developing critical thinking skills are vital to long-term success and survival.

✔ **Tenet IX – Be top-down and bottom-up:** Both a top-down viewpoint (wherein investors look at the big economic and financial world picture and then select stocks based on that information) and a bottom-up viewpoint (in which investors focus on the company specifics rather than industry specifics) matter; neither has a monopoly on insight.

✔ **Tenet X – Treat your clients as you'd treat yourself:** Surely the ultimate test of any investment is, would you be willing to invest with your own money?

Considering the risks of value investing

Two words beautifully sum up the worries of many mainstream investors as they approach value investing: *value* and *trap*. In layperson's language, you can discover an undervalued gem, with a wonderful balance sheet, and buy the share. You know the share is probably unloved but you don't care; you think it's cheap. Unfortunately, many value stocks remain good value and cheap longer than investors can stay solvent, leaving you without the gains you were expecting.

You may well think that a stock is wonderful value, but if no one else shares that insight you end up losing money because the company's shares become a *value trap*: that is, they stay cheap for a very long period of time.

 Many value investors are by nature long-term investors and are willing to sit tight for many years. But many of the smartest investors also ruthlessly adopt what's called a *stop loss* procedure, in which they sell a cheap share if it keeps getting cheaper.

Minding the GARP: The Best of Both Investment Worlds

In the debate pitting racy growth fiends against boring value types, many professional investors believe that both approaches have virtues and that investors can have the best of both worlds: that is, a bit of growth and decent value! This middle-of-the-road school has even been given a name – GARP: Growth at a Reasonable Price (see Figure 9-1).

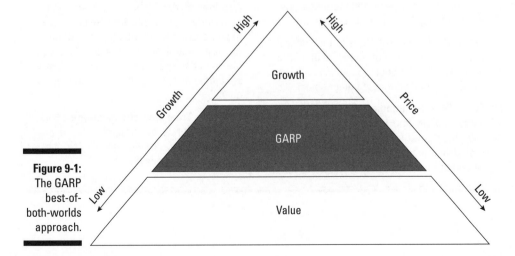

Figure 9-1:
The GARP
best-of-
both-worlds
approach.

A typical GARP strategy asks the investor to focus on companies where earnings are growing steadily but the shares are reasonably priced. If you can find such companies you can SWAN (sleep well at night), another term associated with GARP investors!

As a sensible investor, recognise that markets change rapidly and sentiment moves with the economic cycle. The only way to protect yourself against this real risk is to diversify and mix and match styles. So perhaps for every two value screens you operate, have one growth screen (I explain stockscreens in the earlier section 'Getting practical with a growth screen'). Or for every two value stocks, have one growth stock. If the markets are entering an optimistic bull phase, you can consider switching this ratio – two growth stocks for every one value share. But always mix and match styles and screens.

Getting to know GARP

At the core of GARP is a simple desire: to benefit from a double whammy of growing earnings and a growing PE ratio that reflects this growth of earnings (check out the earlier section 'Understanding the Key Measures' for a discussion of the PE ratio).

As a chosen company's earnings per share grow, the PE ratio of the company falls if the share price remains constant. But faster-growing companies usually receive a premium rating from investors – remember that they like the look of these enticing firms. So an astute GARP investor can not only benefit from a rising share price prompted by the increasing earnings (the PE ratio stays constant), but also benefit from a re-rating upwards as investors reclassify the previously boring stock as growth and *increase* the PE ratio. That is, the analysts start to suggest that Quality Company X can now safely trade at, say, 20 times (growing) earnings rather than the previous 15 times earnings.

Truth be told, quibbling with this best-of-all-worlds strategy is difficult: it's simply advising you to find the best companies at cheap share prices. The problem is that such mythical beasts are rather hard to track down, especially in the large-capitalisation universe.

Remaining sceptical

GARP investors like to see positive earnings numbers over the past few years, coupled with positive earnings projections for upcoming years. Yet they retain the value-investment scepticism of companies that are growing too fast, with earnings accelerating at an unsustainable rate! GARPers think that these shooting-star companies are too risky and unpredictable.

Classic GARP-influenced investors look out for companies where the earnings growth is ticking along at a steady 10–25 per cent per year rate.

Desiring sustainable growth

GARPers like to reassure themselves by making certain that a firm's sustainable growth is also reflected in the cash flow statement, which means looking for positive cash flow at the operating level to accompany earnings increases. But that's not all – cash flow needs to be greater than earnings, indicating that the firm is throwing off cash at a generous rate.

If a firm is growing at this perceived sustainable rate, GARPers may well accept a higher PE ratio than traditional value investors; perhaps buying into firms with a PE ratio of 15–25, a level that's far too pricey for value investors (who'd prefer a low PE ratio, say under 10).

Finding out-of-favour sectors

GARP investors tend to home in on so-called out-of-favour shares; that is, ones where market conditions aren't favourable or the financial community doesn't properly perceive the true worth of such companies.

You then hold the stock until a fundamental change in the company's nature takes place or it grows to a point where it's no longer growing at a faster rate than the economy as a whole.

Focusing on smaller companies

Most GARPers focus on medium- and small-capitalisation stocks. Although the market does a pretty good job of pricing in expectations of future growth for large companies, a great deal more inefficiency applies with smaller companies. Only a small number of brokers may cover the stock, which means that the big institutional players don't always have accurate information on which to base their share-buying decisions. This kind of market inefficiency – in the form of imperfect knowledge – can produce stunning price anomalies.

This focus on smaller stocks brings a greater potential risk. Many smaller stocks have limited analyst coverage, sometimes just one 'house broker' who's effectively employed by the company to make forecasts. Therefore your estimate of future sustainable growth is based on a slightly dubious source, as opposed to the dozens of relatively objective estimates you find for larger companies.

Getting some Zweig appeal

Martin Zweig is widely regarded in the US as one of the greatest stock-pickers of all time and his easy-to-replicate approach, detailed in his book *Winning on Wall Street*, has delivered consistently above-average returns. Zweig is a classic GARP investor in that he doesn't like overpaying for shares he regards as exciting. Zweig's primary purpose is to identify high-growth firms at a reasonable price, or as Zweig himself puts it 'reasonable gains in sales and earnings'.

To invest like Zweig, you want growth but not at any cost. Chase fast-growing companies with consistently rising earnings but that are also sustainable and backed up by a share price showing some recent strength. Remember that value investing has a role to play in that you don't want to overpay for poor fundamentals. Growth shouldn't be compromised by paying too much for the stock – you want PE ratios (see 'Understanding the Key Measures' earlier in this chapter) that aren't too far above the average for the market.

Like many growth investors, Zweig's looking for evidence of earnings acceleration. Over whatever period you choose to concentrate on – quarter by quarter basis, or six monthly – he's after companies that are increasing earnings above trend. He wants earnings stability (not overly influenced by seasonal factors), earnings persistency (persistent rising earnings) and earnings momentum (growth over the short and long term). For more details, see the sidebar 'Zweig's quantitative requirements'.

Zweig's quantitative requirements

Zweig wants earnings that are growing faster than they were (i) a year ago during the same period, (ii) in the preceding three quarters and (iii) over the preceding three years. For Zweig, same period growth last year is crucially important because it strips out seasonal factors and gets to the heart of how a business is responding to change. He wants a fast-growing firm that's been growing earnings pretty much consistently for the past five years.

But Zweig is also profoundly interested in sales growth and share price momentum. He specifically demands that sales should be growing as fast as or faster than earnings, because cost-cutting and other non-revenue-producing measures alone can't support earnings growth forever. Most Zweig fans reckon that sales growth should be at least 15 per cent.

Zweig also doesn't want to fight the market. Although he cares about paying over the odds

for a stock – he ideally doesn't want to pay more than three times the market average PE ratio – he's concerned to buy only shares where sentiment is positive. Hence his requirement that, whatever your measure of momentum, it should be at least positive in the last six months.

This quantitative level of screening is only the first and most basic stage for Zweig. He uses the metaphor of the 'shotgun and rifle' approach: the quantitative aspects are the broad screening measure whereas the rifle approach is to then zero in on the shortlisted companies, and use more detailed qualitative analysis that focuses on the quality of the balance sheet as well as the share price and how it's moved up and down in the market, relative to the broader market.

Performing tonight: Joel Greenblatt and the Magic Numbers

Earnings growth is at the core of many GARP approaches – a company with long-term, steadily rising, sustainable earnings growth, with a reasonably rated share price, is the absolute ideal. Some of these approaches involve quite complicated strategies, with many different measures including earnings used as a way of spotting the right company.

But many successful investors think that an alternative way exists, which looks at how efficiently a company uses its capital – are the company's managers generating enough in the way of profits and earnings to justify the investment in equity (and debt) in the company? This relatively simple approach has been championed by a certain Joel Greenblatt (see the sidebar 'Are you smarter than a 10 year old?' for the background).

Greenblatt's approach is easy to understand and relies on two simple rules. Seek out companies with:

- High return on invested capital, based on the generation of decent profits.
- Low share price, low PE ratio and a high earnings yield (the PE ratio expressed as a percentage).

In essence, Greenblatt's formula is 'buy a good business at a bargain price'.

Are you smarter than a 10 year old?

With his *The Little Book That Beats the Market*, Greenblatt set out to develop an approach that was apparently simple enough for his children to understand and use, yet that also reflects the core values used by Greenblatt to manage his portfolio.

To understand Greenblatt's success and the appeal of his Magic Numbers, note the marketing blurb used to sell his books: 'two years in MBA school won't teach you how to double the market's return. Two hours with *The Little Book That Beats the Market* will. Let Joel Greenblatt, Founder and Managing Partner at Gotham Capital (with average annualised returns of 40 per cent for over 20 years) show you how "beating the market" can be made simple and easy.'

The 'Little' book has been a huge success both in the US and the UK, where bank RBS has even introduced an index based on this approach. Even ultra-cautious financial analysts and researchers have taken notice, curious to see whether Greenblatt's novel approach really can deliver huge returns moving forward.

Identifying good businesses

The first key foundation to Greenblatt's approach is to identify the strength of a business by examining the return on capital (ROC). This requirement measures the operating profit of the total investment (equity and debt) used by the company to generate a profit. If a company is able to earn a high return – say 25 per cent or more – the business is desirable.

Turning to the share price, Greenblatt takes the popular PE ratio and inverts it – he calculates the earnings yield by dividing earnings before interest and taxes (EBIT) by enterprise value. The *enterprise value* is simply all the equity invested in the business plus all the debt.

Greenblatt uses a very particular measure, namely, return on capital invested (ROCE). Whereas most investors use alternative measures to assess the profitability of a business – such as return on equity (ROE, net profit divided by equity) or return on assets (ROA, net profit divided by total assets) – he determines return on capital by dividing EBIT by the tangible capital employed (net working capital plus net fixed assets) and includes all the debts inside the business.

Finding Magic Number companies

Using these basic principles, Greenblatt runs a very simple screen as follows:

1. **He eliminates foreign companies, banks, finance firms and utilities.**

2. **He looks only at the 3,500 largest companies, because he suggests that trading less liquid, micro-capitalisation stocks is costly.** This cut-off is roughly equal to a market capitalisation minimum of US$50 million.

3. **He runs a screen based on return on capital and ranks them from 1 to 3,500, based on that measure.**

4. **He ranks that 3,500 again using the earnings yield, where the share with the highest earnings yield is ranked number 1 and 3,500 is assigned to the stock with the lowest yield.**

5. **He adds up these two rankings, giving you a Magic Number with the lowest combined rank bought.** Thus a share with a rank of, say, 100 for return on capital and an earnings yield rank of 431 would have a combined rank of 531.

Deciding whether it works

Greenblatt says that he's tested his system in enormous detail. He claims that buying the 30 best-ranked companies, holding that portfolio for a year and then repeating the screening process the next year would have returned 30.8 per cent annually over the last 17 years. By contrast, the S&P 500's annual return over the same time frame was only 12.4 per cent.

The great risk with any simple system like this one is what some critics call the garbage in, garbage out syndrome. Just because two numbers seem to produce a series of correlated returns doesn't mean that a real-world mechanism is at work, a method within the numbers that hints at a real cause for the out-performance. Statisticians frequently warn of these data-mining risks.

But to be fair to Greenblatt the value ideas behind this approach are easy to conceptualise – you're buying a company that's efficient, works its assets hard, produces good profits and has cheap shares.

Hearing the gospel according to Buffett

One famous investor's approach has come to typify an archetypal form of GARP investment style. His name is Warren Buffett and he's probably the most famous investor in the world. His success in finding great, quality companies at a reasonable price is legendary. Using his own secretive strategy, Buffett has delivered huge profits for investors in his Berkshire Hathaway group.

Precisely because he doesn't spell out his exact criteria or likely investment targets (that is, after all, how he makes his money), his acolytes are the ones to spell out Buffett's stock-selection strategy.

The classic Buffett philosophy is take your time to find the right stock, use painstaking research and screening, and then stick with the share until its intrinsic value is realised. As Buffett would say, 'buy great companies not great stocks' – which means approaching buying a single share as if you're buying the entire business.

The Buffett strategy

At the heart of Buffett's analysis is his dislike of what he calls commodity-based firms – ones where price is king and the cheapest company and products always wins out. These firms are characterised by low profit margins, low returns on equity, little brand name loyalty, excess capacity within the industry and erratic profits.

Consumer monopolies, on the other hand, are very much Buffett's forte. He likes firms with significant pricing power, partly through strong brand recognition or significant intangible but unrecognised value. These 'monopoly' firms can easily build shareholder value by making the intrinsic value in the company become more open.

Buffett is a discriminating investor who researches companies in great depth (he believes that investors end up owning a bit of the business). He doesn't run a few quantitative screens – low PE, high dividend yield – and then buy all the stocks identified (for more on stockscreens, check out 'Getting practical with a growth screen' earlier in this chapter). In as much as anyone can know a typical Buffett screen, based in part on studies of his methodology, it involves many different layers and different themes.

Profits first and foremost

Investors need to examine the underlying profitability of the business. For Buffett, that doesn't mean taking for granted the profit and loss account and the quarterly earnings per share (EPS) figures. Those quarter-on-quarter figures, miraculously showing a steady increase, really tell you very little about the business and its underlying profitability. Ultimately you want to discover the underlying intrinsic value of the business. The only way to do so is to dig deep and uncover the business's underlying profitability. Earnings of course matter when you start to investigate a business. You're looking for companies that, at a minimum, produce profits over the medium historic term.

Like many investors who start off as value investors, Buffett appears to care about the *current PE ratio*, which is the share price measured against the current level of profits per share. Judging by his sage-like pronouncements before the dot.com meltdown, he doesn't like firms with a high PE ratio, and so any strategy probably should have a maximum PE value – anything much above twice the market average (or mean) is likely to be a bit too rich for Warren.

Follow the cash

Despite an interest in the current PE ratio, earnings matter very little to Buffett followers. The important aspect is whether the business produces the hard cash you'd expect it to.

Therefore you need to look at the cash flow statement and ask, 'Can the company fund its growth sustainably and pay dividends as well as fund its capital expenditures (called capex for short)?'

Focus on the balance sheet

Like cash flow, return on equity (ROE, net profit divided by equity) is a positive way of examining underlying profitability. Buffett watchers suggest that he probably prefers an ROE of at least 12 per cent, though some suggest it may be as high as 15 per cent per year. Plus he likes that ROE rate to be consistent in historical terms, with a trend upwards if anything. One implication of high returns on equity is a net margin that's likely to be well above average.

Remembering Buffett's 'training' in value investing, you also need to look at the balance sheet to check the asset backing of the firm. Buffett is quite liberal in using measures such as price-to-book value (PBV) – he has to invest his giant mountain of money in stock markets, where a share with a PBV below 0.5 is almost unheard of.

Buffett is suspicious of excessive debt – when looking for a quality business, examine the net gearing (which compares the company's capital to its debt) and interest cover (which indicates how easily a company can pay the interest on its debt) as your best measures of 'affordability' of debt. A net gearing rate above 100 per cent is likely to trigger alarm bells and interest cover of at least 1 is pretty much essential.

Chapter 10

Gearing up to Use Leverage

*I*nvestment leverage means borrowing to invest: using someone else's money to achieve your investment goals. If you think that sounds a little odd, you're not alone, and in this chapter I provide a discussion on differing views about the approach – from those totally opposed to leveraging to economists who encourage young people to borrow money to invest in the stock market (what has the world come to!). Overall, however, I suggest a middle way: that borrowing other people's money to improve your own returns can be a good idea in the right circumstances and if you're a relatively sophisticated investor.

After all, many institutions use leverage to improve their returns. In fact, leverage is so common that you'll struggle to find a bank or fund management company in the developed world that doesn't use it in some form. In that sense, leverage sits at the heart of the global financial capitalist system. Not that these firms borrow heavily all the time, and I'm certainly not suggesting that you go out and binge on debt in an attempt to amplify your returns ten-fold. But some borrowing, leveraging and *gearing up* (that is, magnifying) your returns can make sense if you understand the risks.

As a small investor, you can make use of leverage easily through a margin-based stock broking account. To help you decide whether the investment leverage approach is for you, I guide you through the benefits and risks and remind you of the always-important role of cash in your investment portfolio.

Understanding Investment Leverage

Many people already engage in some form of leveraging, borrowing money carefully and diligently – having a mortgage is an example. But you don't just buy any old house with hundreds of thousands of other people's pounds.

You're careful with leverage and homes, just as you need to be with an equity or a bond that looks to be equally compelling value.

Leveraging: The theory

In abstract terms, leverage can be defined as the creation of exposure greater in magnitude than the initial cash amount posted to an investment, where leverage is created through borrowing, investing the proceeds from short sales or using of derivatives.

This rather dry definition does remind you that leverage can broadly be understood as any means of increasing expected return or value without increasing your out-of-pocket investment, that is, your money upfront.

With leveraged investing, you take out a loan and make a single large investment purchase on day one. Then you set aside a portion of your income each month to make interest payments on the loan. If all goes to plan, your investment increases in value over time and eventually you can sell the asset, repay the loan and make a handsome profit. At least that's the plan!

Imagine that you decide to buy a £200,000 house with a £20,000 down payment and a £180,000 mortgage. The £20,000 is your equity investment in the home, and the rest of the purchase price is covered by the lender's loan of £180,000. If the home's value increases to £220,000, you're able to pay back the £180,000 loan and keep the remaining £40,000. You make a 100 per cent return on your £20,000 investment.

Throw interest into the mix and your return is less, but the idea is the same: borrowing lets you increase your return beyond that which would have been possible with your initial investment alone. Without borrowing the £180,000, for example, your initial £20,000 could never have brought you a return of £40,000. In a world without leverage (that is, without loans from friendly, compliant banks!), you'd need to find the full £200,000 in cash. The return on your investment? Just 10 per cent!

Leveraging: The practice

Opponents of investment leveraging maintain that putting other people's money into housing as an investment (via mortgages) is very, very different from putting borrowed money into stocks. After all, houses only ever increase in value, don't they? House prices aren't that volatile, are they? Well, no! Recent experience shows that house prices can and do fall sharply in value, as do shares. Arguably house price volatility is lower than equity volatility but not by much.

Critics also point out that shares aren't predictable; they don't always go up in value. Granted nothing is predictable about risky assets such as shares, but shares (equities) have in the past risen in value quite considerably over the long term. Considering what works over the long term in terms of returns is important when thinking about investment leveraging, and so I examine this issue in more detail in the later section 'Perusing what works over the long term'.

If that history of positive returns for shares holds true in the future (a big if, of course), why not use leverage to improve your returns, especially if you're willing to be patient and look to compound your returns.

Compound returns refers to the fact that investment growth accelerates over time as the growth from one year is added to your initial investment to create a larger investment that can grow the next year, and so on. With leveraged investing, you contribute a much larger amount on day one and then hope that the whole amount grows substantially over the long term. The effect of compound returns is much greater with leverage, but so is the risk.

The key to successful compounding is having the largest possible amount growing at the beginning and then leaving it alone for as long as possible.

Tax can also help with leveraging. In some countries, such as the US, you can write off the interest you pay on a loan, that is, it's tax deductible. In the UK, however, the rules are more complicated. Home buyers may qualify for mortgage interest relief but it applies to only a percentage of the interest paid, is capped at a certain maximum amount and the benefits end after the seventh year.

Considering the types and forms of leveraging

Not all forms of leverage involve spending someone else's money; it can work in different ways. Three main forms of leverage operating exist:

- ✓ **Financial leverage:** The most obvious type, this is created through borrowing leverage in your portfolio (through margin calls, see the later section 'Buying on margin') or at the company level (through using corporate debt).

- ✓ **Construction leverage:** This is created by combining securities in a portfolio in a certain manner; that is, you may use short positions within a portfolio or hedge certain assets.

- ✓ **Instrument leverage:** Virtually all options and most futures-based contracts have some form of gearing built into them; that is, you may invest in a gold option that magnifies any increase in futures prices three-fold.

One example of leverage that doesn't involve borrowing works at the company level, through buying shares in a firm that uses leverage in its own business.

Imagine a company that's involved in mining gold from large mechanised operations in Southern Africa. Although you can invest in a fund that tracks the price of gold, or even buy a few gold coins individually (a *direct* exposure to gold), investing in a gold mining company through shares via the stock market is an *indirect* form of exposure to gold; that is, if gold increases in value, you hope that the value of shares in the gold mine increases too. Plus potential exists for even greater returns if gold prices rise substantially. A bump in gold prices is likely to give an exponentially huge boost to a gold producer's top line revenue.

This example demonstrates two forms of leverage:

- ✔ **The shares are linked to the gold price and their value may shoot up if gold increases.** The costs of digging gold out of the ground are fixed (the producer doesn't have to put a whole lot of additional labour or capital into digging out increasingly valuable gold). Therefore, any extra profits from rising prices feed through into a geared increase in the profit margin.

- ✔ **Gearing (debt) on the company balance sheet works in the investor's favour;** especially if profits increase and the book value of all assets in the company starts rising.

Buying on margin

As a private investor you can't run a private equity fund, but you can use a margin account to take advantage of leverage. Most stock brokers willingly set you up a margin account that lets you borrow money at a pre-agreed interest rate; generally you can borrow up to 50 per cent of the cost to purchase stocks.

Assume that you have £100,000 to invest and you use it to buy 500 shares of a £200 stock. If the stock's price goes up to £250 in 12 months, you end up with a £25,000 gain and a 25 per cent return. That's known as your *unlevered* return.

With leverage, however, you still have £100,000 to invest but your broker allows you to borrow up to 50 per cent of any stock purchase at an interest rate of 10 per cent. Now you can buy 1,000 shares at £200 per share, for a total investment of £200,000 (£100,000 of your cash plus that £100,000 margin loan). The stock goes up in value to £250 over 12 months as before and you sell up. You get back £250,000, pay back your loan of £100,000 plus 10 per cent interest (£10,000) and you have £140,000 in your hand – a pretty nifty 40 per cent return.

Appreciating the Risks

Clearly the main leverage risk is what happens if you borrow too much money and the cost of leverage starts to work against your investment.

The vast majority of investors think that a leveraged asset (that is, one bought through leverage) is always riskier than an unleveraged asset (that is, you haven't borrowed to buy), even if the leveraged asset has low risk and the unleveraged asset is highly risky. Yet in reality the key issue may not be the use of leverage, but the *risk* of the underlying asset.

Leverage can be risky but it's just one risk among many. You need to understand all the risks of investing an asset (bond, equity, commodity or currency) and work out whether the potential reward for taking that risk is worth it. But no one gets a free lunch (except maybe celebrity chefs) and you rarely make a positive return without taking some form of risk. Check out Chapter 2 for much more about this vitally important subject.

Determining leverage risk

To help understand leverage risk, consider this simple example:

- ✓ **Scenario 1:** Investor A puts her money into FX (that is, currency) based assets, which typically move up and down by no more than 5 to 15 per cent over a few months, or even a year. This investor decides to gear up her returns by using 2 times leverage; that is, for every £1 she puts in from her own money, she borrows another £2 from someone else.

- ✓ **Scenario 2:** Investor B buys into very volatile commodities that can increase and decrease in price by more than 50 per cent in a matter of a few months, but doesn't use leverage; that is, he invests £1 of cash in the investment hoping for a big increase in value for his financial asset.

Six months later the currency investment in Scenario 1 (say a pair between the US dollar and UK sterling) has fallen by 15 per cent, giving investor A a 30 per cent loss (2 times leverage). The commodity investment of Scenario 2 has also fallen in value, but the underlying asset is much more volatile and has decreased by 30 per cent in value. Investor B has made a 30 per cent loss, which is the same loss as Investor A, who owns a much less volatile asset.

This example illustrates a classic hedge fund quandary. What's more risky:

- ✓ A fund invested in a volatile asset but with borrowing leverage of 2 times capital (Scenario 1)?

✔ A fund with 100 per cent market exposure and a beta of 3 times but no borrowing leverage (Scenario 2)?

In essence this quandary involves looking at risk using two different measures:

✔ The market risk (beta) of the asset being purchased; that is, how much the price of the asset moves in relationship to the wider market.

✔ The leverage that's applied to the investment.

The answer? Neither.

Each tactic – buying riskier assets and increasing the leverage ratio applied to a given set of assets serves to increase the *risk* of the overall investment. This means that if a portfolio has very low market risk (invested in lower volatility, lower beta assets), higher leverage may be a better idea than investing in an unleveraged fashion in assets that have a higher beta and are much more volatile.

As top fund manager Ray Dalio puts it: 'If investors can get used to looking at leverage in a less prejudicial, black-and-white way – as in "no leverage is good and any leverage is bad" – I believe that they will understand that a moderately leveraged, highly diversified portfolio is considerably *less* risky than an unleveraged non-diversified one.'

The relationship between risk and leverage is complex. In particular, when comparing different investments, a higher degree of leverage *doesn't* necessarily imply a higher degree of risk.

Asking the question: Isn't gearing up risky?

Using leverage – in effect, using other people's money – is almost self-evidently risky and apparently today's world is a slightly grim place in which everyone's deleveraging like crazy. Or at least that's what some stock-market analysts think. For debt cynics like Gary Shilling (author of *The Age of Deleveraging* (Wiley, 2012), and he's far from being a lone voice), debt is bad and cash is good. Read the nearby sidebar 'A warning from history' for the historical justification for this view.

The brutal truth is that, although leverage can certainly help to gear up your returns, any losses are also correspondingly greater. If you invest £25,000 of your own money and your portfolio drops in value to £15,000, after 15 years, you've lost £10,000. But if you borrowed £25,000 to purchase that same portfolio, you're out of pocket by much more. If, for example, you paid for your investment by taking out a home equity loan with a 15-year term at 6.5 per cent, you've also paid £14,200 in interest. In this case, your total loss is £24,200 (£10,000 + £14,200) – almost 150 per cent more!

A warning from history

Leverage has certainly gone horribly wrong in the past, especially when applied to investing in shares using margin accounts. The orgy of margin buying during the 1920s' boom helped precipitate the Stock Market Crash of 1929 and the resulting depression as thousands of investors couldn't make their margin calls. Back then, margin requirements were quite lenient and investors were able to purchase huge blocks of stock with very small upfront investments.

When the stock market began its deadly spiral in 1929, scores of investors received margin calls. They were forced to deliver additional money to their brokers or their shares would be sold. Because most individuals were leveraged to the hilt, they didn't have the money to cover their leveraged positions, which forced brokers to sell their shares. The selling precipitated further market declines and more margin calls . . . and so on. And everyone knows what happened next.

Using leverage shortens your time horizon and doesn't give you the long-term time to bounce back. Also, come what may, you still have to pay the interest on the loan, even if your investments are falling in value.

Few events are worse than receiving a margin call from your stockbroker. A *margin call* is when your broker demands that you deposit enough of your own cash into the account to bring the balance up to the minimum maintenance margin requirement.

Investors must put up a minimum initial margin of 50 per cent, but they also need to always run a maintenance margin of at least 25 per cent. This margin protects the broker if the value of the investment declines. If your value of equity in shares or bonds drops below that 25 per cent barrier, your stock broker needs to make the margin call.

Thinking Seriously about Leverage

If the preceding section on its risks and dangers has put you off leveraging, for balance I suggest you read this section on the argument of the strategy's advocates.

In 2010, *Time* published a fascinating article called 'Why Young People Should Buy Stocks on Margin' (you can check it out at www.time.com/time/business/article/0,8599,1982327,00.html).

Writer Barbara Kivia talked to two respected economists, Ian Ayres and Barry Nalebuff, who created quite a stir by suggesting that *debt could be good* and that young people should consider using leverage to increase their investment returns.

Their central insight is that investors need to be committed to investing over the long term with a proper diversified mix of assets. Although young people don't tend to have enough money to build a healthily diversified portfolio, leverage can help them get the money they need.

That the cost of borrowing is so low helps, of course: since the global financial crisis of 2008, interest rates have collapsed globally and even rates on margin accounts are now at all time lows, although those costs increase as leverage moves beyond 3 times. According to Ayres, the benefits of diversification are 'lost' when the cost of borrowing increases through increased gearing.

Perusing what works over the long term

Obviously Ayres and Nalebuff's argument in the preceding section (that if you're going to take a risk using leverage, spend your borrowed money investing in shares) depends on the fact that shares have been a great investment for those investors willing to stick with them over the *very long term*. The historical evidence does indeed back up this argument. In virtually every study of extremely long-term data on returns from the global stock markets, shares have walloped both bonds and cash (see the nearby sidebar, 'Examining the research').

Examining the research

The most definitive source proving that shares have largely moved upwards since the middle of the nineteenth century (with a long-term trend return of just above 6 per cent per annum) is by a group of British academics based at the London Business School: Professors Elroy Dimson and Paul Marsh and Dr Mike Staunton. They've delved back into market data and looked at comparative returns – and, in a series of papers and books, reached fairly unequivocal conclusions. For instance: 'over the last 109 years, the real value of shares, with income reinvested, grew by a factor of 224 as compared to 4.5 for bonds and 3.1 for bills'. Other long-term studies for the US market vary slightly, but the message is unambiguous: shares worked in the past as a risky investment. If the average cost of margin loans has been just over 5 per cent for the last 100 years, but the returns from shares have been between 6 and 7 per cent, using leverage would have kicked in an additional 1 to 2 per cent in extra returns over the last century. That would have equated to a massive gain for a committed long-term investor using leverage over many decades.

Just because shares have been worth betting on based on historical data, however, doesn't mean that you aren't taking a risk that they may fall in value. Shares can and indeed have fallen by much more than 20 per cent in any one year. And they can also be a hideous investment not only for just a year, but also a whole decade. Over the 20 years between 1989 and 2009 shares have been a lousy investment compared to bonds.

Investing in shares isn't *guaranteed* to be a successful approach over the long term!

Yet on balance the historical evidence suggests that, in recent times, investing in shares has been worth the risk compared to supposedly safer assets like bonds and cash – in fact, in the UK, the return from shares has been worth about 4 per cent extra on average since 1900.

The bottom line is that, if you had to bet on an asset increasing in value by an average of between 5 and 10 per cent per annum, in a compound manner over the very long term, you'd probably start with shares. That means that if you do use leverage to increase your gains from an investment, think about starting with shares.

Making leverage work for you

Using leverage is probably suitable only for professional investors (such as hedge funds) or affluent, sophisticated investors. Here's what you need:

- A high tolerance for risk.

- A long investment horizon.

- An excellent credit rating and low interest on the loan (these two factors tend to be in tandem with each other).

- A healthy personal cash flow and the ability to absorb any potential losses. Even if you meet all these demanding criteria, I suggest that you adhere to the following simple rules when using leverage within an investment strategy:

- **Invest for the long term:** The amount of risk involved in leveraging decreases as your investment horizon increases.

- **Commit to the strategy:** Even for long-term investors, short-term market volatility carries the risk of emotional decision making – that is, selling at the first sign of trouble – which can derail an investment strategy before it has time to work. Make sure that you're committed to a particular leveraged-based strategy for the long term.

✔ **Borrow less than you can afford:** The last thing you want to worry about is being forced to cash out early because of an unforeseen change in your ability to make interest payments.

✔ **Consider a 'no margin-call' loan:** Many investment loans now offer a 'no margin-call' feature (sometimes at a slightly higher interest rate). Unless you can easily come up with cash to cover a margin call, choose a loan with a no margin-call feature. For all about margin calls, flip to the earlier section 'Asking the question: Isn't gearing up risky?'.

✔ **Diversify your investments:** Don't increase your risk by investing in a single investment or by investing in high-risk investments.

✔ **Make the repayments on the principal:** Reduce the risk by repaying the loan gradually over time.

Remembering to hold some cash

You have one almost failsafe way of controlling the risks involved with leverage: always try to make sure that you have a lot of cash sitting around in your portfolio! In fact, many investors use a dual strategy involving lashings of leverage alongside a healthy cash reserve. In Chapter 16 I look at how you can use options to gear up returns: in the following example the leverage is built within the product structure.

The idea is simple. Limit your downside risk by keeping cash, but use a small amount of leverage for a part of your portfolio. Perhaps 5 to 10 per cent of your portfolio assets is about right, committed to one main investment idea based on a market view expressed using options.

If the options-based bet using leverage goes wrong, you end up losing at most 5 or 10 per cent of your portfolio's value, but the rest of your assets are safe in cash. If your bet's right, and the market moves your way, your small bet on a market move can yield massive, leveraged profits!

By all means use leverage, but also remain cautious by keeping a large reserve of cash. Mix and match absolute returns strategies (plenty of cash as an absolute safety net) with leveraged strategies with the potential for geared returns. For more on the idea of *value investing* (selecting stocks that trade for less than their assumed intrinsic value), check out Chapter 9.

Chapter 11

Stepping into Structured Investments

....

....

*M*aking a profit when shares rise in value is, of course, par for the course; but imagine also being able to receive a positive return even when a market falls in price without getting involved in the complexity and risks of a hedge fund. If this possibility sounds too good to be true, read on.

In this chapter I introduce you to the humble *structured product*, otherwise known as a *structured investment* (the two terms are used interchangeably). Structured products contain within them a promise that's common to any hedge fund (which I discuss in Chapter 3), namely, the potential for an absolute return in all markets and market conditions.

I show you how structured products deliver on this promise of returns in most, if not all, markets, in a number of different shapes and guises, ranging from the humble synthetic zero and the auto-call to the racy accelerator. I also lead you through call and put options and zero coupon bonds, and the different ways in which the varying returns are powered, including:

✔ A hefty bet on volatility (which I describe in Chapter 4).

✔ Plenty of potential risks – banks going bust, for instance.

✔ Interesting ways of leveraging returns (flip to Chapter 10 for more on leveraging).

Introducing Structured Products

At its core a *structured product* involves a simple trade-off based on risk and return, which then translates into a series of options that are used to power the eventual payout. A good, well-thought-through structured product can deliver on nearly all the promises of a hedge fund or *absolute return fund* (a fund that aims to produce a positive return in every kind of market) but with a little less complexity.

Unfortunately not everyone is enamoured of the humble structured product. Many experts are keen to rubbish this class of investment as the work of the Devil or, at the very least, clever rocket scientists out to design complex toxic structured products that inevitably benefit them rather than their end investors. US and UK regulators have also taken an interest in poorly constructed structured products from time to time, with the simplest incarnations sold on the high street through to the big retail banking networks receiving much close scrutiny.

Because structured products aren't uncontroversial or universally popular, many supposedly sophisticated private investors eagerly hand their money over to expensive hedge fund managers who then end up investing in – guess what – structured investments! Don't be fooled; many hedge fund managers and professional investors make extensive use of structured products within their portfolios, and so ultimately no reason exists why you shouldn't also take advantage of the kinds of investment structures the professionals use.

The structured product you buy very much depends on what you want out of an investment, with your own requirements perhaps ranging from an annual income through to some upside (capital gains!) over a period of as much as six years.

Any upside inevitably comes with the potential for risk, and so like any strategy in this book, you can end up losing your shirt! The key is to understand the risk and then decide what works for you. Refer to Chapter 2 for help in understanding risk and determining how much investment risk you can tolerate.

Investigating investments with a defined return

Structured products and investments can also be sensibly termed 'defined return' strategies, in that they attempt to provide the investor with a . . . wait for it . . . defined return that in some cases mimics an absolute return. In this section I provide some gloss on this idea of a defined return and take a look at two such structured products in more detail: zeros and autocalls.

All structured investments involve taking a view on equities, usually expressed through a benchmark (or reference) index such as the S&P 500 or the FTSE 100. Take a look at the following two possibilities:

- ✔ **You're bullish:** You think that American equities are due to shoot up by a huge amount over the next four to five years. In this case you're probably looking to leverage your upside to the maximum through something called agrowth or accelerator structure (I discuss accelerators in the later section 'Using bear and bull accelerators to gear up your returns').

- ✔ **You're bearish:** You reckon that the FTSE 100 is due a thorough thrashing, with falls of 10 or even 20 per cent on the cards. In this case you may start looking down the list of products for a bear accelerator; that is, to increase your profits as markets fall back.

Most investors probably sit somewhere in the middle of the above spectrum of opinions and so are wary about betting on any large outcome. Perhaps they think that markets may spend the next few years going nowhere; that is, the S&P 500 benchmark index of big American blue chips (which I define in Chapter 3) is going to be at the same level in five years' time. Investors may also be willing to bet that markets are going to be *range bound* (that is, they'll *tick up* (rise slowly in price) in some years and then down in others but always remain in a range of, say, 20 per cent either way of the current level of the index). This view may also find its way into your demand for income; notably, that you're not hugely bothered by the direction of this range-bound market, but you'd quite like a decent, above-average income above all else.

These views can be articulated into an investment using different structures. The key with each variant is to understand that a trade-off is likely to come with your defined return. For instance if you want an income above all else, that may mean that you don't share in any capital upside if the index does suddenly shoot away from you. Alternatively, if you only want to gear up (leverage) that return in rising markets, you may have to forgo the dividends paid out by the companies that are contained within the benchmark (or reference) index. In Chapter 10 I discuss leverage and gearing in more detail.

This leveraged form of defined return may also come with another risk: if the markets fall unexpectedly you can end up losing all your money. Remember that just because you 'define your return' doesn't mean that the investment comes with no risks!

Zeroing in on the popular yet humble zero

In this section I take a look the simple zero – which contains many of the standard features of structured investments – and explain why it makes sense for so many investors.

The zero's origins lie back in the late 1990s, when fund managers in the UK investment trust sector realised that many investors were happy to receive a fixed annual return that could be rolled up and paid out at a date in the future. This longing for a defined annual return, not paid out as income but at maturity, was eventually – by the power of financial alchemy – transformed into a *zero share*. The zero share was one among a bundle of share classes that these early financial engineers invented, with some shares paying out an income every year while others participated in the upside via leverage (called *capital shares*).

By the early part of the new millennium, however, dark clouds began to gather. This complex bit of the UK investment industry – nicknamed the *split capital movement* – ran into trouble as the global stock markets foundered on the rocks of dot.com mania. The underlying assumption of this fund structure (that equity markets would always go up in value) collapsed under an equity market bubble, and suddenly a whole host of funds were unable to make those defined returns promised by the humble zero.

Flash forward a few years after this terrible event and imagine yourself in a small conference room at a large investment bank. The 'blue-sky' person in the corner has been charged with coming up with new fund structures that the bank salesperson can sell on.

'Remember those zeros issued by the investment trust guys?' he asks. Everyone nods in recognition. 'Investors liked that idea of a steady 6 per cent a year return over, say, five or six years, rolled up at the end – didn't they?' Again much nodding but also furrowing of brows as they try to work out where this conversation is going.

'Why don't we come up with a new form of zero that isn't in a fund or investment trust, but is a simple payout based on a defined return?'

And so was born the simple *synthetic zero* – the poster child of the structured products boom. Here are the basics:

- You the investor give your money to the investment bank or fund manager, which issues you a £100 share or certificate.

- The financial institution promises to pay you an annual compound return of 5 per cent a year for the next five years, rolled up as a final payout of £127 per unit.

A number of conditions apply to this payout, however:

- The issuer uses a benchmark index, for instance the FTSE 100 index, to determine the payout. You receive £127 (5 per cent per annum, compound, rolled up over five years) as long as the FTSE 100 hasn't fallen by more than 50 per cent. The key values for this index are the level when the zero was issued and the level when it closes (the investment matures). Your hope is that the final level is well above the barrier.

  This condition is known in the trade as a *barrier*, and if it's breached (the FTSE falls by more than 50 per cent from the level at the time of issue of the zero) you not only don't get that annual return of 5 per cent but also lose more than 50 per cent of the £100 invested. The barrier is, quite obviously, a risk and not the only one.

✔ The IOU that pays for the final maturity payout is probably an IOU issued by a large investment bank. Before Lehman Brothers went bust very few people seemed to worry about banking counterparty risk, but now everyone knows different. Banks can go bust and when they do they don't always live up to their IOUs.

✔ If for whatever reason you, the investor, can't afford to wait until the five years is up and need to sell out in the middle of, say, year three, you face a penalty for cashing out early (no surprise there). But what you probably didn't guess was that the market value in year three is going to be determined by a range of factors that includes the prevailing level of volatility in equity markets plus the markets' estimate of the riskiness of the bank that issued the zero. In sum, the amount of money you get back in year three depends on lots of factors.

I also need to mention two *opportunity costs*; that is, returns that you've sacrificed in order to get that defined return:

✔ If you'd invested in the FTSE 100 through, say, a tracker fund (such as an ETF (exchange-traded fund), which I explain in Chapter 16), you may make a considerably larger amount than just 5 per cent per annum. The markets may shoot up by 50 or even 60 per cent, but you'd still only get 27 per cent with your zero.

✔ If you'd invested in a FTSE 100 tracker comprising lots of large blue chip companies, you'd have also received a series of dividend cheques that may have been worth 2 or 3 per cent per annum. With the structured product you get none of those semi-annual payments.

In choosing a structured product and the so-called defined return, you're forgoing potentially greater returns that you may see from other products.

You do, however, get the following:

✔ The knowledge that you can make a nice, yearly return even if the stock markets fall by 5 or even 20 per cent per annum over those five years.

✔ £127 per unit in five years' time, as long as the barrier isn't breached and the bank is still in business.

✔ A yearly return paid not as income (which may incur income tax) but as a single capital gain in five years' time (subject then to capital gains tax).

This incredibly simple structure has proved enormously popular and over the last ten years all manner of variants on the same theme have been brought to market, but the humble synthetic zero remains rightly popular.

Another reasonably common structure that's similar to the zero is the standard *income plan*. This product looks and feels exactly like a zero in that it pays an annual return over a fixed period (usually five to six years), with the only difference being that the annual return is paid as an income year on year. In all other respects, it's exactly like the simple zero, with a barrier (usually at 50 per cent) based on an underlying index (usually the FTSE 100 or S&P 500).

Seeking a predictable regular return: The autocall

Over the years financial product designers and marketing types have constantly tinkered with the basic zero structure that I describe in the preceding section, with perhaps the most important innovation being the *autocall* (or kick out plan).

The basic idea behind an autocall is nearly as simple as the zero – an annual return in exchange for taking some risk:

1. **You hand over, say, £100 per share or unit, potentially for a period of up to five years.** The level of the underlying or reference index – in this case, the S&P 500 – is noted at issue.

2. **The issuer looks back at that underlying index at the end of year one to see whether it increased (any increase, no matter how small, is relevant) or remained stable.** As long as the underlying index hasn't dropped in value, the structure *calls*: that is, it pays out an agreed upfront return of 5 per cent for the year. Your £100 is now £105 and the autocall matures – that is, closes or winds up.

What happens, you may ask, if the underlying index doesn't advance but falls back? Well, the barrier on a typical autocall is usually set at 50 per cent (at which point your capital is at risk), but if the index has fallen by, say, 10 per cent you don't need to panic. Your autocall simply rolls on to the next year, to the second anniversary of the fund, when again you see whether the underlying index has advanced from the initial level. If it has, you receive a return for both years, in other words, 10 per cent or £110.

Every year over the next five or six years you're presented with a chance to receive an annual income, as long as the underlying index stays stable or advances.

If the index doesn't advance at all over the full five years (based on the initial level of the S&P 500) you simply receive back your initial investment of £100 *as long as* the barrier hasn't been breached (that is, the S&P 500 hasn't fallen by more than 50 per cent).

Returns from autocalls are, like zeros, regarded as capital gains, which can be advantageous for certain investors. Autocalls also carry with them the same set of risks as a zero: counterparty risk of the bank issuer going bust; the barrier being breached in a nasty market downturn; and the opportunity cost of markets rising and of dividends not being paid. Yet the intrepid investor also receives some equally obvious upsides including a potentially steady 5 per cent return plus a capital gain.

Autocalls have also been tweaked over the years, with a defensive version perhaps the most noteworthy. The *defensive autocall* is structured exactly like a conventional autocall with annual call dates and a barrier, but with one key difference – you can receive an annual call return even if the market you're tracking has fallen in that year.

Imagine for one moment that the FTSE 100 is at 6,000 when a defensive auto-call is issued with a 10 per cent annual return. The defensive version may still make that 10 per cent payment in one year's time even if the underlying index falls by no more than 10 per cent. Therefore, as long as the FTSE 100 index is at 5,400 or more, you get a 10 per cent annual return; that is, you may make a 10 per cent positive return even if the stock market falls by 10 per cent over the same period.

The call level used to trigger annual payments may in fact keep on falling every year over the next five years, perhaps settling at just 50 per cent of the initial level of 6,000 for the FTSE 100; that is, it pays out a positive return of 10 per cent per annum even if the FTSE 100 index is at 3,001.

Using bear and bull accelerators to gear up your returns

Not all structured investments are built around the concept of the defined annual return that I describe in the earlier section 'Investigating investments with a defined return'. Some structured products are based on the concept of leverage or geared returns; that is, you receive a multiple of the returns from an underlying index. These *accelerators* can work on the upside (advancing markets) and on the downside.

To help understand the process, imagine the S&P 500 is at 1,200 when an accelerator is issued. The structure offers to pay five times the return of the index (the S&P 500) over the next five years, up to a maximum return of 100 per cent in total. If you put in £100 per share, you could get back a maximum of £200 as long as the S&P 500 increases by 20 per cent over the five years, with a gearing of 500 per cent.

Of course, some form of barrier is probably in operation, which means that your initial investment of £100 is at risk if the S&P 500 falls by more than 50 per cent; that is, if it falls by 51 per cent, you don't get leveraged upside returns and also lose £51 per share or unit.

These accelerators contain two new features that are worth considering:

✔ **A geared upside return:** That is, you get back 5 times the change in the underlying index. This gearing varies enormously between products, with a precious few growth structured products boasting no cap (see the next bullet point) at all but much lower gearing.

✔ **A cap:** This maximum payout stops the geared participation moving beyond a defined return; that is, £200 or a 100 per cent gain. The cap also varies enormously between issuers, with some structured products boasting caps set at very low levels (as little as a 20 per cent gain).

This accelerator structure has evolved into many variants with perhaps the most common being a simple growth plan. This structure has no cap, but a much lower gearing rate. An S&P 500 index growth plan may, for instance, involve a geared participation rate of 120 per cent of the annual price return of the index. This arrangement means that if over the five years of a plan the S&P 500 goes up by 50 per cent, you receive back a total return of 60 per cent (50 per cent × 1.2).

Examining the Components of Structured Products

Opponents love to talk up the risks of structured products and then in a solemn voice intone that they're fiendishly complex and the work of clever rocket scientists out to diddle the poor unsuspecting investor. Some structured investments are, indisputably, poorly built, horribly complex and of debateable value (especially those sold on main street by big banks and mutuals). But, as I describe in this section, in reality most products sold direct to investors through advisers or listed on a stock exchange are fairly transparent in their construction.

Peer under the bonnet of nearly all structured investments and you find a common set of components; you don't need to worry too much that they exist just understand what's involved. Add up these differing components to a structured product and you can quickly see that an issuer can derive a number of different sources of income or capital gain (premiums from issuing the barrier put, forgone dividends contained within the call that tracks an index, plus the difference between the zero coupon bond value at maturity less the sum paid upfront), which all go towards funding the cost of the upside call plus any bank charges and fees.

Discovering the call option

The most important working bit of a structured investment component is a *call option*. This derivative-based option (I discuss derivatives in much greater detail in Chapter 16) pays the upside return via the annual defined return (say, 5 per cent per annum) or the geared participation rate (say, 5 times the index return); see the earlier sections 'Investigating investments with a defined return' and 'Using bear and bull accelerators to gear up your returns', respectively, for more.

Underwriting an option that promises to pay out, say, 5 per cent per annum for the next five years doesn't come free! The call option costs the structured-product issuer real, hard money and other parts of the structure have to pay for it.

Luckily this isn't completely a black and white case of a call issuer funding the 5 per cent per annum for the next five years. The call option may perhaps track the FTSE 100 index, which can be good news for the call option issuer. Some profit is to be had by selling away the likely flow of dividends that an investor would have received if the option had tracked the underlying index. Over a five-year period, for instance, the combined companies within the FTSE 100 index may pay out as much as 20 per cent in compound dividend return. The issuer of the call option pockets that return as part payment for guaranteeing to make an upside return, in turn selling on that dividend participation in the dividend futures markets.

In addition, remember that the call option may never be triggered; that is, markets fall disastrously and the barrier is breached. If that's the case, the call option is never used, no return is ever paid out and the issuer of the (upside) call option simply pockets the premium income and moves on to the next deal. In these circumstances guaranteeing to pay out 5 per cent per annum on the upside may seem like a reasonable bet.

Enjoying the downside: The put option

Another option lurking around is called a *put option*, which is linked to the barrier that's usually set at around 50 per cent or 40 per cent of the initial index level of the FTSE 100 or S&P 500 when the structure is issued.

In reality, this barrier is a *downside* or *put option*, which means that someone (probably a pension fund) has been willing to write an option that pays out a generous premium in return for making a big profit as markets dive by more than 50 per cent over the duration of the structure. If the barrier isn't breached the option expires worthless and the structured-product issuer pockets the premium to help pay its costs and fund the cost of the call option. The premium from writing these downside options isn't huge but pension funds are keen buyers because these options give them some opportunity to make money in a collapsing stock market.

Getting insurance: The zero coupon bond

Sitting at the heart of the zero coupon bond structure is a bond the bank issues behind the structured product. In effect, this bond guarantees that your initial investment (say, £100) is paid back in full as long as the barrier isn't breached. Think of it as the insurance policy on paying you back your initial investment.

But insurance doesn't come free and the bank has to fund it by going to the markets using something called a *zero coupon bond*. This bond is like any other bond issued by a bank with one big exception – it doesn't pay a coupon every year but rolls up the annual cost at maturity.

Assume the bank wants to make a payout of £100 in five years' time to fund your structured product. Given its current credit rating it discovers that it can issue a zero coupon bond that promises to pay out £100 in five years' time but which costs just £80 today; that is, the £20 difference is the cost of funding that loan through annual interest rolled up over five years.

A risky bank (that is, one that is regarded as more likely to have problems repaying its debts by the markets) may discover that its high yields work in its favour – it may only have to pay £70 today to make £100 in five years' time. The key, though, is that the zero coupon bond issued by the bank (it hopes) pays out the initial investment of the investor. The difference between the eventual cost of the zero coupon bond (£100) and the initial cost (between £70 and £80) represents the cost of borrowing, which is in turn ploughed back into the structured investment to pay for the upside call option.

Understanding the Structured Products You Invest In

The talk in the preceding section of peering under the bonnet should alert you to the risks involved – some of the structured products sold on the market can be very complicated and potentially toxic even for a sophisticated investor. Before you even start thinking about using structured investments, you need to understand exactly what you're getting yourself into. Here, arranged in no particular order of importance, are the factors you, as a potential investor, should look at:

✔ **Caps:** Many structured product providers put caps on the maximum return you can make for your investment. If that cap is set too low, you can find yourself very quickly hitting the maximum return over the duration of the investment – especially if the upside participation rate is also very high.

✔ **Counterparty risk:** If the markets believe a financial institution is much riskier (that is, that it may in the future default on its debts), they tend to demand a higher rate of interest for lending to it. But that potential for return comes at a cost – the bank is perceived as being riskier and you can lose your money if it goes bust – and banks do go bust, as recent events testify.

✔ **How the barrier can be breached:** In some structured products, if the barrier is breached on any day within the full term, at any time, you can be in trouble – and your capital protection destroyed. This event may matter if trading during the day on a major index results in an anomalous sudden collapse in prices, which then proceeds to vanish by the end of the day.

✔ **Absence of dividends:** Remember that structured products don't pay out any dividends that you may have made by investing in the underlying equities. For a large blue chip index such as the FTSE 100, this is important; ensure that your return or upside properly compensates you for this loss.

✔ **Tax position:** Autocalls are very popular because they can provide an annual payout that's taken as a capital gain, not taxed as income. I discuss autocalls in the earlier section 'Seeking a predictable regular return: The autocall'.

Here are some other factors to consider:

✔ **Capital protection parameters:** If you're offered capital protection, understand what this really means. Is it contingent on a barrier, and what happens if that barrier is breached? Don't underestimate the possibility that markets can fall by more than 30 or even 40 per cent, and when that happens, many structured product barriers are broken.

✔ **Safety versus the potential for return:** Don't be surprised when you discover that the more 'safe' a product looks, the lower the potential for return. Many building society products, for instance, offer capital security but the returns can be absolutely derisory. Equally, some structured deposits look very safe but the upside is very limited.

✔ **Costs:** Structured products are like any investment – they incur costs throughout the structuring process. The financial institutions issuing the options make a charge, as does your financial advisor.

✔ **Early relinquishment rules:** Nearly all structured products sold through independent financial advisers (IFAs) involve a fixed term – usually around five to six years. You can sell your investments in the plan within that period of time but doing so usually incurs quite substantial charges and dealing is usually restricted to one day every month. For that reason, don't leave a plan early unless absolutely necessary.

Timing your purchase for structured investments

The options and bonds built into a structured investment can come across as a tad complicated on first inspection, but one central insight is hugely valuable if you want to think like a hedge fund: any investment issued in times of high market volatility tends to pay out a bigger potential return for investors.

In essence, structured investments provide the smart investor with a simple way of making money from volatile markets.

Here's how you, as an ordinary investor, can make money in these difficult circumstances. Imagine a structured product issuer coming to market during a period of intense market volatility. This volatility is going to affect various components of the investment hugely, such as:

- **The value of the options used within the structure:** The premiums from issuing puts (check out Chapter 3 for more on puts) on the barrier increase as volatility spikes upwards. As volatility increases, you may reasonably expect large insurance companies and pension funds to seek even greater protection from big losses by buying your barrier-based puts. Increased options-based premium income should hopefully feed through into an increased upside; that is, increased annual returns on an autocall.

- **Counterparty risk:** Increases in volatility may also feed through into increased uncertainty about the viability of a bank and its accompanying bonds. This means that the bank has to pay bigger interest coupons in order to borrow on the zero coupon markets, which translates through into even more generous funding for the structure. In other words, higher bond yields reduce the upfront cost of issuing a zero coupon bond, giving the issuer even more money to pump into the upside via the call option.

But volatility also reminds us that the markets change over time; over days, months and years markets move up and down. The key theme here is time, or what bond investors call *duration risk*. In simple terms, the longer the duration of an underlying option, the greater the cost – this notion of time value is hugely important in understanding structured products.

Autocalls are potentially very popular with some issuers because more than a decent chance exists that the structured products are going to call after the one-year anniversary; that is, equity markets will be the same or have advanced over that year, triggering a call and thus the payout of the product. As a result, the issuer of an upside call (the option that funds the annual defined return) calculates that it stands a good chance of only having to issue an option for one year, which in turn implies lower costs for issuing the call. A promise to pay out over five years, by contrast, involves longer duration risk and thus a smaller coupon – which helps explain why the annual returns on most five-year synthetic zeros are substantially lower than a five-year autocall.

Combine this understanding of how time and volatility interact, and then apply it to an autocall and you can begin to understand what may constitute the 'perfect storm' for a structured product – volatile markets, where investors are worrying about the solvency of a bank, which is in turn issuing a one-to five-year autocall structure.

To see how these factors work to your benefit, consider all those components I discuss earlier in this section, including the call and put options and how they can change in different market conditions. Imagine that the stock markets start to bottom out after a bad fall – in this circumstance many call option issuers will reckon that markets are going to recover fast and be happy to charge a much smaller fee for writing the upside option. Equally, worries about the credit rating of the bank result in a higher annual bank bond cost, which pushes down the upfront cost of issuing a zero coupon bond, increasing in turn the amount of money left over to pay for a call. Last but by no means least, increased volatility pushes up the price of the put options sold to big pension funds and insurance companies looking to make money from falling markets.

The risks from such a perfect storm are all too clear! The most obvious is that the bank issuing the bonds that protect the initial investment does go bust. This counterparty risk potentially increases almost exponentially as volatility increases. Equally, pension funds are willing to pay more money for downside puts for a very good reason; notably, that the risk of a nasty market collapse of 50 per cent or more is likely to increase. If that's the case, your barrier is broken, and you may end up losing your initial investment and any hope of a positive return.

Mixing and matching for maximum impact

Volatility is a horribly double-edged sword, but smart investors can hedge their bets by using structured investments and products wisely. They buy products with a generous structure (falling call levels contained within a defensive autocall can be very helpful) and sensible annual returns (don't always chase the highest possible upside return) that are issued by counterparties where the actual chance of a default is very low.

Crucially, make sure that you understand how different products work in different markets:

- ✔ **Traditional autocalls:** These tend to work well in what investors call *range-bound markets* (see the earlier 'Investigating investments with a defined return' section), in which an index such as the FTSE 100 trades over a number of years at levels that vary between 5,000 and 6,000 (flip to the earlier 'Seeking a predictable regular return: The autocall' section for more details). Zeros can also work well in these markets (see 'Zeroing in on the popular yet humble zero' earlier in this chapter).

✔ **Defensive autocalls:** These may work well for weak markets where investors expect moderate falls in the underlying index of between 5 and 20 per cent. Again, check out 'Seeking a predictable regular return: The autocall'.

✔ **Accelerators:** These work very well in volatile markets witnessing the first stages of a pronounced bull recovery. As markets power ahead you may reasonably expect caps to be hit very quickly – if you've bought a product listed on the stock market, you should be able to sell out almost immediately the cap is hit. The key is then to reinvest back into a momentum driven market through a straight plain vanilla tracker or via a growth structure with no cap on the upside. The earlier section 'Using bear and bull accelerators to gear up your returns' contains more information on accelerators.

Buying and selling structured investments

Many of the advanced strategies and ideas that I describe in this book can be a tad tricky for investors to access without professional help. For instance, I have no doubt that running computer-driven algorithmic-based trading strategies (of the sort I describe in Chapter 13) from my garden office is technically possible, but I'm not sure that it's a great idea or a terrifically easy process to manage on a day-to-day basis!

The good news is that the structured investments I highlight in this chapter are a relative slam dunk in investing terms and you can easily buy and sell nearly all these products via a canny stockbroker. Many IFAs can also buy simplified versions of zeros and autocalls via their own fund-dealing platforms, although the costs can start increasing when you add in their own fees.

Chapter 12

Benefitting from Shareholder Activism

Since the global financial crisis of 2008, discontent with the corporate elite in the UK and the US has grown at an astonishing pace. All manner of activists now scrutinise the major decisions of leading publicly listed companies (PLCs), with hedge funds increasingly joining this motley crowd of vigilant observers.

Although you may struggle to believe that sports-car-driving hedge-fund managers have much in common with anti-capitalist or social and ethical campaigners, in fact they do: both groups believe (though from different standpoints) that company bosses aren't doing the right thing by their stakeholders. For hedge-fund activists, the 'right thing' is whether managers are running the company so that investors and shareholders benefit as well as the amply rewarded senior management team.

When a leading hedge-fund activist shows up on a firm's share register, he may well be planning to bring about real change in the company and its direction in order to boost the share price – good news for the hedge-fund investor, the wider shareholder base in the targeted company and even often for the targeted company. But the real icing on the cake is that as an outside investor you can follow in the trail of these hedge-fund activists.

In this chapter, I introduce you to the basics of this type of activism and two masters of the art. I describe how you can follow these activists to share in the benefits of improved share values. I also discuss a specific subsection of activity connected to investment trusts and turn all Mystic Meg with some predictions for the future of shareholder activism. Note that in this chapter I focus on the UK and the US markets, where activists are most common.

Discovering the Activist Basics

Shareholder activism is when minority shareholders (often hedge funds) exercise and enforce their rights with the aim of increasing shareholder value over the long term.

Hedge-fund activists aren't the first hard-nosed investors to kick up a stink about the way under-valued, mismanaged companies are run but they have become enormously effective. Market statistics paint a powerful picture of their activism, with a huge wave of hedge funds now engaged in a day-to-day struggle with the corporate elite. Between 1994 and 2006, the number of public firms that hedge funds targeted for poor performance grew more than 10-fold (from less than 12 to over 120).

Hedge funds don't engage in activism because they're good guys – far from it! Hedge-fund activists want to buy the shares of a company because they think those shares are cheap. If all goes well, and the judicious application of lobbying, legal threats, PR campaigns and the occasional whiff of mental intimidation(!) pays off, the firm's shares increase in value substantially.

Hedge-fund shareholder activists typically rely on the so-called value approach when identifying their targets, forming in effect a subset of hedge funds that invests in equities in a manner akin to classic, value-orientated investors; that is, they look to increase the intrinsic value of the company's shares. This value-investing approach (which I discuss in greater detail in Chapter 9) usually means that investors buy a company with a decent balance sheet, sound cash flow and a cheap share price.

Evolving activism over time

In the 1970s and 1980s, a whole generation of corporate raiders thrilled the US media, publicly duelling with a star-studded list of the top corporate names in the US business scene. These raiders would buy large numbers of undervalued shares in companies, thus securing significant voting rights that enabled them to force a company to change leadership, management or structure in order to increase the share values. But this confrontational activism alienated many investors and thereafter a subtler form of activism began to emerge. In particular, many big institutional funds noticed that, when a corporate raider turned up on the scene, frequently the raider pocketed most of the gains from shaking up a company and not the fund!

This anxiety spawned a more consensual activism that consisted of encouraging the management of a company to change direction, cut costs, scale back expansion plans and return money to the long-suffering shareholder base through share buy-back offers or increased dividend payments. Leading US pension funds (such as the Californian state scheme Calpers) also muscled in on this game, sometimes working on their own to change companies, sometimes partnering up with other funds including private equity houses.

Although similar in some ways, private equity firms typically invest in companies over longer time periods – three to seven years, for example – with the intent of increasing the value of the company's assets and, therefore, the profit made by the firm's investment. Hedge funds, on the other hand, generally invest in securities solely to make money from the change in the asset's price, without any major intent to change the structure or profitability of the company itself, and therefore hold the assets for much shorter periods of time, sometimes for seconds or fractions of seconds.

This pension-fund activism popped up in the more conservative City of London as well. The pension fund for what used to be called British Telecom (BT) was and is self-managed by a company called Hermes, and over the last 30 years its UK-focused fund has been especially active, cajoling and jostling company CEOs to do the right thing and change the direction of their company. That approach certainly paid off for BT pensioners and the UK fund has produced an annual return of 8.2 per cent for the last 20 years – a good 4 per cent per year more than you'd expect from investing in the FTSE All Shares index.

As a guide to what activists look for in a target company, the BT Hermes UK fund has three selection criteria for picking the companies in which it invests. It asks:

- ✔ Is the firm underperforming?
- ✔ Does the fund believe it can engage with the company's management successfully?
- ✔ Does the fund expect to obtain at least 20 per cent more value over the current share price?

Organising activist campaigns

Theoretically, any shareholder can decide to become an activist. You can, for instance, stand up at the company's shareholder meetings and shout loudly about the misguided direction of its leadership. But the truth is that you probably won't bring about any real change, though you may feel a little better after the rant!

The fact is that most activists are pension funds, corporate raiders, private equity groups and, of course, hedge funds.

Hedge funds become very active only because they think they can make money by moving the share price. To bring about real change, they need to understand the mechanisms by which they can effect change – and these mechanisms vary considerably between different countries.

Tactics and tools

Activists employ two general approaches (for more, see the later section 'Quiet chats or aggressive campaigns?'):

✔ Aggressive campaigns that bully the firm's management into change.

✔ A softer, communicative method.

In practice, activists use a mix of these approaches. Notorious activist Warren Lichtenstein (founder of activist fund Steel Partners II) suggests that a mixed stick-and-carrot approach is most successful. He notes that, 'the best situation is where we find a cheap stock with great management and a great business, and we can sit back and make money'.

Activists use a number of methods to effect change in a company. For aggressive approaches, their campaign weapons include any or all of the following:

✔ Buying a reasonable chunk of shares and then using proxy forms to push for change.

✔ Requesting dissolution of the company; that is, terminating the company's legal existence.

✔ Asking for more detailed information from the senior management, such as how the senior executives are paid, or details about how a business will increase its profits.

✔ Turning up at scheduled investor meetings and also attempting to call extra ordinary meetings.

✔ Requesting that new items be put on the agenda of existing items.

✔ Lobbying PR campaigns for change.

✔ Running general nuisance campaigns.

✔ Holding informal behind-the-scenes conversations.

Many activists focus their attention on key governance-related issues, such as the removal of the CEO and/or the restructuring of the CEO's remuneration package.

Practicalities and legalities

The first key step for most US-based activists is the filing of an initial Securities and Exchange Commission (SEC) Schedule 13D form, where the activist clearly states its purpose in buying the shares. The form is triggered after an investor directly or indirectly acquires the beneficial ownership of 5 per cent or higher of any equity security in a publicly traded firm with the stated intent of influencing the firm's policies.

After the shareholder is on the books, a 'conversation' can commence – although the activist probably discovers quite quickly whether the target management and directors are willing to listen to any ideas for change. The reality is that most company boards can easily resist outside investor pressure if they so desire!

According to US federal and state laws, for instance, the only way a shareholder can force a firm's existing managers to pursue alternative strategies or changes in corporate governance is through a contested proxy fight, which is very costly. Needless to say that as a result of this institutional bias, which automatically shifts the balance in favour of the status quo, most activists choose their battles very carefully.

The UK regulatory environment is much more favourable to incumbent management, meaning that shareholders can much more easily force their will upon a company's management. In the UK, any shareholder or group of shareholders with at least 10 per cent of the voting rights in a firm can call a special shareholders' meeting to introduce a binding shareholder proposal.

As you may expect, many company managers use every trick in the book to battle shareholder activists. One of their favourite tactics is the *poison pill*, which is designed to make the shares less attractive to those wanting to take the company over. Poison pills usually come in one of two forms:

- ✔ A *flip-in*, which allows existing shareholders (except the acquirer) to buy more shares at a discount.
- ✔ A *flip-over*, in which the company's investors are allowed to buy the acquirer's shares at a discounted price after a suggested merger.

Buying discounted shares dilutes the value of the acquirer's shares and makes taking over the company more expensive.

Quiet chats or aggressive campaigns?

Activism isn't easy. The management of many leading publicly listed companies are more than capable of resisting change, especially from investors with only a few per cent of the company's shares. The regulatory framework doesn't help, but another simpler reality also makes life hard for activists: these aggressive campaigns take time and money and often don't work! Some activist investors thus much prefer a softer approach, which is to try to get the management of the target company to co-operate through gentle persuasion and the veiled hint of a threat!

Hedge-fund activists that choose to adopt this quiet approach typically begin by sounding out the company chairperson with a telephone call, letter or email pressing the incumbent board to make changes designed to increase shareholder value. Hedge funds often lobby for finance-orientated changes, such as having a target company squeeze value from the balance sheet by spinning off underperforming non-core assets and by using share buy-backs or a sizeable one-off dividend to distribute 'excess' cash to shareholders.

More radically, a hedge-fund activist may advocate an outright sale of the target, as a going concern or through divestiture of key operations. Hedge funds also sometimes lobby in favour of increased operational efficiency.

Recent surveys suggest that this quiet approach is increasingly popular among activists – one US survey from 2012 suggests that 76 per cent of investors prefer 'dialogue and negotiations with management' compared to 16 per cent who opt for shareholder proxy battles and just 4 per cent who went for litigation. Academic data also show that only 26 per cent of hedge-fund activism is hostile. Far more often, hedge funds work with the management and other shareholders.

Using the hedge-fund advantages

In their battles to improve shareholder returns, hedge funds face stiff competition from pension funds, corporate raiders and private equity groups keen to take their target company private – that is, get rid of its stock market listing. (Many corporate takeovers involve converting the company from a public to a private entity so that shareholders cannot trade their stocks in the open market; the raiders then restructure the company and reissue its stock after the company is profitable again.) But hedge funds have one big advantage over their more conventional activist rivals – they don't need to buy as many shares in a target company to effect change, largely because they're subject to a smaller number of statutory regulations.

Unlike mutual funds (collective investment vehicles that are sold to the general public that limit the ownership of voting shares), hedge funds can hold more than 10 per cent of any firm's stock and invest more than 5 per cent of their assets in any stock. In addition, they aren't required to have sufficient capital to cover redemptions and can restrict investors from exiting their funds – nor do they need to disclose their holdings, investment strategies, shortselling positions or leverage ratios.

Given these regulatory advantages hedge funds have over traditional institutional investors, all kinds of activists now call themselves hedge funds. You, too, can take advantage of these favourable rules. Just be aware that the very things that make hedge funds more flexible may also make them less transparent and, therefore, more risky.

After setting up their lightly regulated shop, the hedge-fund activist needs to start buying shares. Even at this step, hedge funds have an advantage. Academics reveal the surprising conclusion that some of the most successful activist hedge funds own as little as 2 per cent of the shares of a publicly quoted company, although the most common stake is about 10 per cent. Therefore, to be successful an activist doesn't have to deploy a huge chunk of capital to effect change in a company.

With these advantages to help them, hedge-fund activists are pretty successful in their stated aim of changing the direction of a company – and boosting the share price. In about 40 per cent of campaigns, hedge funds succeed in their stated aim of making a corporate change and in another 26 per cent they achieve partial success, gaining significant concessions from their targets.

Examining who benefits from activism

Hedge funds aren't altruistic: they shake things up at the corporate level in order to make money! But sometimes their activism benefits other groups as well.

Research concludes overwhelmingly that hedge-fund activism is positive for all the major parties – except perhaps the small group of departing CEOs who find themselves on the wrong end of the campaign. I quote some of the relevant research results in this section.

The company

One definitive study of shareholder activism finds that:

> *hedge fund activists improve both short-term stock performance and long-term operating performance of their targets. The most dramatic changes in performance accrue to targets where activists seek corporate governance changes and reductions in excess cash.*

Nicole M. Boyson and Robert M. Mooradian

The wider company investor base

Researchers looking at 888 activist campaigns (launched by 131 different funds) between 2001 and 2005 reveal that:

> *the announcement of a programme of activism by a hedge fund . . . results in large positive abnormal [share price] returns, of between 5 to 7 per cent, during the announcement window and that these returns are not reversed one year after. . . . The events which generate these positive returns tend to involve changes in business strategy (such as refocusing and spinning off non-core assets) or the sale of target company.*

Alon Brav, Wei Jiang, Frank Partnoy and Randall Thomas

The hedge fund and its investors

Unsurprisingly, this group benefits! One study looking at 151 hedge-fund activist campaigns between 2003 and 2005 reports that:

> *Hedge fund targets earn 10.2 per cent average abnormal stock returns during the period surrounding the initial Schedule 13D.*

April Klein and Emanuel Zur

Another study came to the same conclusion, suggesting that the risk-adjusted annual performance of hedge funds seeking changes in corporate governance is about 7–11 per cent higher than ordinary (non-hedge) investors.

Another way of looking at the same data is to track the performance of activist hedge funds within broader hedge-fund indices (which track returns from different strategies). The HFRX index series separates out shareholder activists (under the category 'event driven strategies') and finds that in 2012 they returned 6.6 per cent, but lost 16 per cent in 2011 (2010 returns were +15 per cent and 2009 returns +44 per cent).

Selecting Target Companies

The sad truth is that not every company listed on the UK or the US markets is run well. Even more importantly, many companies are technically well run (in that the managers are perfectly competent) and yet the share price is marooned at a low level because a key part of the corporate strategy isn't working. As a result, thousands of potential activism targets are available.

Not all targeted companies are badly managed. Sometimes activists pick on companies where the strategy for growth isn't working, no matter how diligent the management may be. In particular, many activists examine carefully how a company is looking to grow and generate more revenues.

Watching out for activist quarry

Despite an extensive list of potential candidates, the vast majority of companies are never targeted by an activist. Working out who the activists may hit next isn't easy, but as a private, though ambitious, investor you can profit from shareholder activism in two general ways:

- ✔ Locate potential target companies *before* hedge funds show up on the share register.
- ✔ Wait for evidence that a hedge-fund activist is on the share register and follow its lead (the most common approach).

Getting a head start on the activists

If you're determined to buy into a potential target company before any evidence of hedge funds on the share register. look for some or all of the following common characteristics:

✔ Hedge funds like to target profitable firms with decent profits or earnings.

✔ Many hedge funds are especially keen on companies with a strong cash flow and growing cash reserves on the balance sheet. Many activists think that this hard money should be returned to the shareholders rather than wasted on other deals or projects.

✔ Some activists look at the main investment strategies, such as capital expenditure (capex) spending (used to acquire or update the company's physical property or equipment), or identify companies engaged in extensive merger and acquisition activity.

✔ Hedge-fund activists tend to target relatively small companies. Median assets for firms targeted are about US$200 million in the US.

Hedge funds don't like investing in companies in distress; that is, where the target is close to bankruptcy. The risk of failure and total capital destruction is just too great.

You're going out on a limb when using this approach. Although getting ahead of activists can yield more profit, the risks are clearly higher. After all, no one may follow your lead.

Keeping a beady eye on hedge-fund activists

If you're willing to wait for evidence of hedge-fund activity before investing, you need to keep on top of the activist hedge funds. The good news is that monitoring these market movers online isn't difficult.

In the US market, start by looking at the shareholder register of large companies and scrutinise the latest Schedule 13D filings lodged with the SEC regulators at www.sec.gov/answers/form13f.htm. In the UK, all companies are required to keep current registers that list company members (shareholders) and, among other things, how many shares they hold. To gain access to a register, you submit an application to the company, stating why you want the information and disclosing who, if anyone, you plan to share the information with. The company has five days to comply with the request (or deny it after having sought a court order). You can find application forms at a government organisation called Companies House, which is accessible online at http://www.companieshouse.gov.uk.

When digging around in shareholder data, remember that as well as investing in companies through its ordinary shares, many activist hedge funds also use fairly complex derivatives and spread-betting positions (that aren't always declared on the regulatory forms).

If becoming an activist ambulance chaser appeals to you, a growing number of resources online let you track activist battles, almost in real time. You can find the two best research sites at `www.hedgetracker.com/directory/Shareholder-Activist` and `http://activistinvesting.blogspot.co.uk`.

Knowing when to get out

As I mention earlier, investing in a company that has attracted the attention of activist shareholders can yield very positive returns. The changes spurred by the activists' involvement breathe fresh life – and increased share price – to already strong, but possibly stagnant, companies. Having said that, not all companies will go on to see greater growth nor are all activists ones to follow. Following are signs you can use to decide which activist funds and companies to steer clear of:

- Attacking too many companies over a relatively short period of time (say, a year) might indicate a lack of focus

- Attempting to make the company take on too much debt can ultimately end in disaster for all shareholders

- A lack of sector specialism; that is, the hedge fund tries to target companies in all sorts of sectors without really understanding any particular sector in great detail

- Lining their own pockets rather than the fund's.

Monitoring Master Activists in Action

The best way to discover the practical techniques of hedge-fund activists is to take a look at a couple of expert practitioners, which is precisely what I do in this section.

Waging war by letter: Dan Loeb

Few hedge-fund activists are as outspoken or articulate as the inimitable Daniel Loeb. Many private investors carefully track his dangerous adventures through corporate America and buy into his latest epic struggle with company managers. They're all on the lookout for a profound change in company strategy – and a resulting increase in the share price.

Loeb is a great character and superb investor. His hedge fund is called Third Point LLC and he's built up a fantastic track record and a loyal following.

Shareholder activism is just one of the many strategies that his US$8 billion hedge fund uses. Truth be told, deep down Loeb is a value investor with enormous respect for the investing disciplines developed by Ben Graham (whom I discuss in detail in Chapter 9).

Most successful hedge-fund activists are value investors who decide that only some form of direct action can force a company management to boost the value of the share price. They also tend to use activism as just one part of a wider multi-strategy approach.

Shareholder activism has made Loeb legendary, largely because of his sense of humour (at the expense of boards), his lampooning of corporate egos and his wonderfully caustic letters to target boards and their CEOs (you can read many of them at `www.businessinsider.com/dan-loeb-letters-2011-12?op=1`).

Most of Loeb's funds aren't open to new money, but UK investors can invest in a London stock market-listed fund called Third Point Offshore, which co-invests as a feeder fund alongside Third Point's main outfit. The website is at `www.thirdpointpublic.com` and the ticker is TPOG.

Targeting Yahoo

Loeb's appearance strikes fear into the hearts of corporate America, but until fairly recently he focused on companies that few people had heard of. Not for him, the David and Goliath task of humbling a global corporate that strayed from the path. But in 2011, Loeb upped the ante and declared war on a company known to hundreds of millions of consumers around the world – Yahoo.

Yahoo was an Internet pioneer and its online investing service (see `uk.finance.yahoo.com`) is still a massive success. Yahoo epitomised the first wave of Internet revolutionaries, but rather like Microsoft (another IT pioneer in its day), this tech giant lost its way. Founder Jerry Yang went through a number of new CEOs as the company struggled to find a new sense of direction against deadly competitors such as Google and Facebook. Offers to buy the group came and went (including one from Microsoft) and the board persisted with its strategy of battling on as many fronts as possible.

One autumn day in September 2011, Loeb turned up on the share register declaring a 5.1 per cent interest – making him the third-largest shareholder. By itself that stake wasn't large enough to force change, but Loeb is never frightened of launching a proxy shareholder battle (which I describe earlier in the 'Organising activist campaigns' section) using his two most powerful weapons: his letters to the board and his ability to generate wider media interest (based in part on those wonderful letters).

Writing to the Yahoo board

In this section I quote and comment on extracts from a letter Loeb sent to Yahoo's board. You can see his first full letter at `http://management.fortune.cnn.com/2012/04/02/yahoo-activist-investors/#more-10025` or `www.businessinsider.com/dan-loebs-letter-yahoo-2011-9`. This waspish missive of 8 September 2011 is directed at the 'Ladies and Gentlemen of the board' and details:

> our principled demands for sweeping changes in both the Board of Directors (the 'Board') and Company leadership, and outlines the hidden value of Yahoo, which has been severely damaged – but not irreparably – by poor management and governance.

What follows is a classic activist hatchet job – a brick-by-brick demolition of the company's existing strategy. Loeb notes that it is:

> now widely recognized that the Board made a gross error in turning down the $31 per share Microsoft bid in 2008, which would have generated significant returns for Yahoo's shareholders. This mistake is all the more frustrating given Yahoo's current depressed stock price of $13.61 per share.

But Loeb's key criticism is that its board 'destroyed' value for all Yahoo stakeholders by obscuring the value of 'an Iconic American Technology Asset':

> We firmly believe that there is much to be gained from a successful and rapid transition in management, as we are convinced that Yahoo is grossly undervalued. We have followed Yahoo for many years, and our analysis suggests that at a share price of $13.61, with $2.49 per share in tax adjusted net cash, $3.10 per share and $5.24 per share of after-tax values for the Yahoo! Japan and Alibaba Group stakes respectively (Yahoo holdings in Asian technology companies), core Yahoo is left at an implied value of $2.78 per share or 2.2x 2012 EBITDA [earnings before interest, taxes, depreciation, and amortization]. With more effective and focused management, one could realistically envision a re-rating to at least 7.0x 2012 EBITDA, driving a target of over $19.00 per share. When coupled with tax efficient outcomes for its Asian assets, an additional $3.00–4.00 per share stands to be realized.

This paragraph is an argument based on value-investing ideas:

- Loeb sees a discrepancy between the share price and the intrinsic value of the company.

- Loeb reveals that the company is clearly profitable but not profitable enough!

- Loeb zeroes in on key assets held on the balance sheet (the Yahoo stakes in its Japanese business and Chinese Alibaba) that have enormous value when broken away from the main Yahoo business franchise.

- Loeb picks up on the net cash sitting on the balance sheet (worth $2.49 per share).

But he isn't fixated only on the balance sheet – he also recognises that various intangible assets, such as the brand and the technology underpinning the site, have enormous value:

> *It is clear that the Company possesses unique scale and scope as the Internet's premier digital media company. Hidden by Yahoo's senior management drama is a franchise benefitting daily from tremendous investment in resources and new platforms successfully built by Yahoo's corps of talented, committed engineers, product development team and salespeople.*

What emerges from this paragraph is the level of analysis usually undertaken by big private equity companies. Loeb sees tremendous value in the Yahoo brand and as a media leviathan and obviously believes that the company needs new investment to unlock this potential.

As the catalyst for change, Loeb believes that the necessary first step is to change the board, and allow him to introduce new directors who can add value for shareholders – which of course results in the removal of some existing board and executive members:

> *In conclusion, we are eager to present to the Board our candidates and thoughts on the Company's future. We hope that the Board will take our proposals seriously and move towards the leadership overhaul that we are championing. While the decision to undertake Board turnover initially rests with individual directors, ultimately, shareholders like Third Point have other means to effect changes necessary to protect their investment. We are prepared to propose a slate of directors at the Company's annual meeting next year should it become necessary. Such proxy disputes are burdensome, and we sincerely hope that one will not be necessary here. Shareholders have already suffered enough.*

Loeb signs off with a typical call to action:

> *It is time for new leadership at Yahoo. Yahoo's investors, employees, clients and users deserve it. We look forward to having what is great about Yahoo make headlines, encouraged and communicated by new CEO and Board leaders.*

Yahoo's board initially ignored Loeb's demands, largely because he'd been so vocal in demanding changes and releasing the board letter to the media. But he also tried a (slightly) less aggressive approach by approaching Yahoo founder Jerry Yang personally. In a letter dated 14 September (and copied to the wider directors), Loeb notes with regret that his telephone call to Yang had been terminated prematurely (by a fellow board member). He goes on to make the following brutal assessment:

> *As a Founder and major shareholder of the Company, the abysmal record of the current leadership must be heart-rending to you personally, as well as damaging to your net worth. We urge you to do the right thing for all Yahoo shareholders and push for desperately-needed leadership change.*

Noting the results

Yahoo's board tried for many months to fight off Loeb and his proxy shareholding assaults, but eventually caved in (forcing out the CEO Scott Thompson for apparently being misleading about his academic record after what Loeb calls a 'kerfuffle'), and replacing him with Marissa Mayer, a former Google exec. Yahoo also started an aggressive strategic re-alignment, focusing initially on selling a large bit of its 40 per cent stake in Chinese Internet giant Alibaba.

Loeb and investors in Third Point eventually ended up making a decent sum of money from their Yahoo stake – in a second quarter report to those investors in 2012 it emerged that the Yahoo stake was the single strongest investment during the period (going up in value by about 4 per cent over that second quarter).

If you decide to co-invest in a company like Yahoo targeted by shareholder activists don't expect massive, short-term profits. These battles frequently take many months or a couple of years and the uplift in the share price is rarely more than 10–20 per cent.

Meeting a turnaround specialist: Edward Bramson

One of the most successful activists in Europe is Edward Bramson, a suave veteran of many corporate battles and boss of investment outfit Sherborne Investors. Bramson started his corporate buccaneering in 1977 by cofounding New York-based Hillside Capital, one of the first specialist private equity firms in the US. He describes himself as an 'operational turnaround specialist', using many of the techniques developed in the private equity space.

Many shareholder activists within the hedge-fund sector operate using private equity principles. This approach can muddy the waters around these two very distinct strategies. Generally, hedge funds don't have a great record of operating in private equity, and in particular don't seem to have the right operational expertise required to run a business. In particular, hedge funds tend to like to move quickly – get in and out within months – and not interfere too much in how a business is restructured (which is traditionally the preserve of the private equity sector).

Describing the Bramson strategy

Sherborne – Bramson's main vehicle for activism – started in 1986 with a very distinctive strategy: it targets one company at a time. His funds typically look to join the board of directors or engage with the company in a bid to profit from turnaround opportunities, which inevitably leads to speculation that it will ultimately seek to build its stake above 10 per cent. Past successes include taking control of UK telecoms firm Spirent in 2006 after ousting its chairman and two non-executive directors in a boardroom coup.

On Sherborne's website (www.sherborneinvestors.com), the outfit says that it:

> *targets publicly quoted European and US companies that have underperformed the market due to operational, rather than capital structure, issues. We develop a turnaround thesis, acquire a significant equity position, and then obtain a shareholder mandate to effect a change in board composition. Sherborne does not agitate for others to make changes; rather, we assume responsibility for directing or managing a turnaround for the benefit of all shareholders.*

According to Sherborne, the fund aims to:

✔ Release the hidden value in currently unpopular but 'deep value' stocks, making use of long periods of shareholder dissatisfaction.

✔ Acquire a significant minority position of ownership and the support of shareholders.

✔ Work with the firm's existing management on creating and implementing an aggressive turnaround plan.

Only a small (but growing) number of activists like to roll up their sleeves in this way and get involved operationally with the target business. Most activists prefer to nominate some representatives for the board.

Edward Bramson operates two publicly quoted London listed funds called Sherborne fund A (launched in 2010 with £105 million) and fund B (launched in 2012 via a £207 million fund raising). Investors in these funds include hedge-fund legend George Soros and massive institutional investors Invesco Asset Management and Jupiter.

Relating a recent success

Sherborne's biggest target in recent years was the assault on London-based asset-management firm Foreign and Colonial (F&C). Shares in F&C rose by as much as 26 per cent on the back of the attack in 2011. Like many of its peers, the asset-manager's share price had been hit by the dreadful market conditions, with poor performance across its equity funds not helping sentiment towards the firm.

Edward Bramson focused his strategic campaign on F&C's poor mergers and acquisition record, in particular its takeover of REIT Asset Management and Thames River Capital. Sherborne calculated that these two acquisitions alone cost F&C more than £340 million, which compared very unfavourably to the £270 million market capitalisation for F&C.

Bramson eventually forced his way on to the board in 2012, becoming the new chairman. Within a matter of months, F&C was the subject of a comprehensive strategic overhaul, with job losses in support services, and a new strategy of focusing sales on large institutional clients. Its share price shot up and Bramson continued to increase his personal stake in the asset manager. From a recent low of 60 pence in January 2012, F&C's share price had risen to 98 pence by the end of the year.

After shareholder activists gain power, they need to have a plan for change. Outside investors need a catalyst that causes the share price to increase in value. This usually includes a share buy-back, increased dividends, spinning off of noncore units or, very commonly, effectively putting the target company into play for bigger corporate acquisitions. Many successful activist battles end up with a strategic review, corporate restructuring and then a bid from a trade buyer.

Targeting Investment Trusts

A small but hardy band of hedge-fund activists focus their attention on specialist funds that have listed on the stock market – called investment trusts in the UK. Investment trust shares are listed on the stock exchange and trade like any other stock. But because they're closed ended (that is, the amount of money in the fund doesn't change; investors can't add to it or withdraw from it), the shares usually trade at a discount. The activists who target investment trusts are sometimes called *arbs* (after arbitrage opportunities – see Chapter 8), but in reality they use a mix of activism and arbitrage to make money for their investors.

The big opportunity for investors is the discrepancy between the fund's public share price and its net asset value.

The net asset value (NAV) of a listed investment trust is the total value of all assets minus any liabilities, divided by the number of shares in issue. If a fund has total net assets of £100 million (after any debts) and 100 million shares in issue, the NAV of the shares is £1 per share. The NAV is also sometimes called the net book value per share.

In many cases this discrepancy between values (the *discount to net asset value*) can be substantial; that is, the stock market share price can be well below the NAV. This discount can be as much as 20 per cent; for example, if the NAV per share of a fund is £1.00, its current stock market share price is only £0.80. But sometimes this discount can be as much as 40–60 per cent, which means that a fund with NAV of, say, £1.00 per share may in fact be trading at just £0.40 a share on the markets.

Relatively low levels of discount (5–20 per cent) attract so-called arbitrage activity, where hedge funds encourage the fund managers to use any spare cash to buy back the shares at the NAV, thus closing the gap. But very large discounts (over 40 per cent) attract activist campaigns, which usually consist of the hedge-fund manager demanding that the fund be wound up eventually and all assets sold off. In theory, if those assets within the fund reach their NAV, a hefty profit is realised over time.

Investors, especially in closed-end funds such as investment trusts, need to be especially careful about supposed NAVs stated in the reports and accounts. If a fund is forced to wind down and sell its assets in a fire sale, those assets can frequently end up being close to worthless! Sometimes the market is telling the private investor something in a massive discount to NAV!

As an activist, a discount of more than 40 per cent within a listed fund is likely to draw your interest, especially if the discount is in an asset class based in the developed world (the underlying assets are liquid and easy to sell). Although an activist campaign rarely realises a 40 per cent discount, as a rough-and-ready guide you can make around half of that discount (if everything goes to plan!). Sometimes activists merely force the fund manager to do the selling and then buy the shares back from investors.

Anticipating the Future of Shareholder Activism

The future is looking pretty bright for shareholder activists, which is good news because an awful lot of new players appear to be entering this highly specialist investment space. Activists are helped by a number of positive long-term factors, including:

- ✔ Increased merger and acquisition activity sparked by record levels of cash on corporate balance sheets.

- ✔ Increased regulation of the financial services sector hasn't hit hedge funds very hard, giving activists the continued freedom to raise new funds.

- ✔ Relationships between activist hedge funds and target companies are becoming less confrontational and more diplomatic.

Financial services, utilities and technology spaces probably offer the most scope for activist battles in the future.

Activist hedge funds have the wind at their back because of the very public backlash against excessive CEO and board-level pay, which shows no sign of abating. The public anger is good news for activists, who love to point out the lack of value being added by the managers of targeted companies. In particular, America's new financial-reform bill contains a 'say on pay' provision, which allows shareholders in all types of companies to weigh in on executive compensation. The SEC is also trying to make it easier for shareholders to nominate people to boards of directors.

Part IV

Delving Into More Specialist Techniques (with a Little Help)

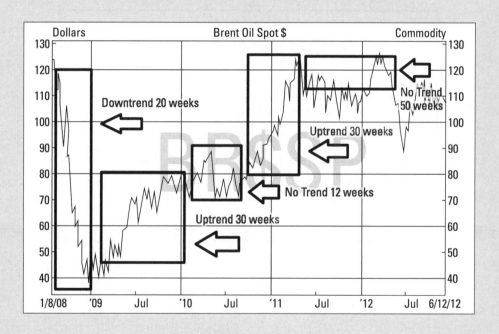

Dollars   Brent Oil Spot $ Commodity

Downtrend 20 weeks

No Trend 50 weeks

Uptrend 30 weeks

No Trend 12 weeks

Uptrend 30 weeks

1/8/08   '09   Jul   '10   Jul   '11   Jul   '12   Jul   6/12/12

web extras

Thinking about investing in the commodities market and want to find out more? Read up on the investment characteristics of commodities at www.dummies.com/extras/managingyourinvestmentportfoliouk.

In this part . . .

✔ New to the commodities market? Swat up on everything to do with investing in commodities and get up to speed with economic cycles and trend following.

✔ Guarantee making impressive returns by reading about investing in emerging markets and taking advantage of special situations such as debt and employing local currency trading.

✔ Learn all about macro-investment and assess the risks involved so you can make informed decisions about whether this approach is for you.

Chapter 13

Advanced Investing in Commodities: Sharks and Rocket Scientists

. . . .

In This Chapter

▶ Explaining contango and backwardation switches

▶ Playing commodities as the new big macro

▶ Going with the flow by using large trends

▶ Capturing trends with CTAs

. . . .

*T*rends are a wonderful feature of nature. Animals flock together and humans often feel more comfortable moving within the crowd, migrating towards a collective target, swimming with the tide. Maybe deep down everybody likes to trust the crowd at times, to believe that surely not everyone can be wrong!

As I describe in Chapter 4, these powerful inclinations pulse strongly through financial markets, which hum with consensus trades (big trends), pushed forward by the sheer might of momentum. Technical analysts spend huge amounts of time and money looking for consistent and repeatable patterns of behaviour that can inform an investment strategy.

As well as in the stock markets, where active traders buy and sell shares on an intraday basis, trend seeking is also present in commodity exchanges where trading activity is every bit as hectic and instantaneous. Hedge funds use this pattern-seeking, consensus-driven behaviour to drive their investment strategies, such as in the work of trend followers, momentum traders and rocket-scientist-type commodity trading advisors (CTAs): this last group is hugely powerful in today's markets and so I devote a whole section of this chapter to what they get up to.

As I explain in Chapter 5, commodity markets are structurally complicated because they're futures markets, where traders buy contracts for future delivery of a physical commodity. In this chapter I investigate investing in commodities in greater depth, covering the big picture economic cycles and trend following. (*Note:* If you're new to commodities markets, be sure to read the commodities sections in Chapter 5 before continuing on in this chapter; there you'll find all the basics that serve as a foundation for the more in-depth discussions I offer here.)

Futures contracts are hugely affected by a wide range of factors, which means that novice investors can lose a huge amount of money by making the mistake of thinking that big movements in the spot price have an inevitable and equivalent effect on futures prices; that is, if spot price A goes up by 10 per cent, the one-month futures contracts go up by the same amount. This world view sounds soothing and elegant, but things don't quite work that way in the noisy real world of commodity markets.

Understanding the Importance of Contango and Backwardation Switches

Contango and backwardation (subjects that I discuss in detail in Chapter 5 as part of my introduction to investing in commodities) can have a huge effect on returns from the commodity futures markets. Many such markets coast along within a big trend favouring contango or backwardation for long periods of time and then suddenly flip around based on some external force or process (such as a supply shock or a recession).

Contango (where a commodity's future spot price is lower than its current price) and *backwardation* (where the future spot price is higher than its current price) trend in very noticeable ways, until . . . they don't! In both cases, the tendency is for the prices to converge; that is, the price of commodities in contango will fall, and the price of those in backwardation will rise. Until the prices converge, investors can profit from arbitrage.

For example, in the massive oil markets, which are rightly popular with many individual investors, the prevailing condition may reflect immediate supply and demand. Crude oil being contango indicates immediately available supply and backwardation indicates an immediate shortage. Anything that threatens the steady flow of oil around the world, such as imminent war, tends to drive the oil market into backwardation.

In commodity markets, backwardation discourages traders and refiners from holding substantial inventories; contango pays them to hold much more stock on hand. Therefore, as a private investor you buy during backwardation phases and sell in contango.

Many analysts and commodity experts blame the inexorable rise of tracker exchange-traded funds (ETFs; see Chapter 16) and massive inflows of retail investor money for the huge switches between backwardation and contango. In a letter dated 23 April 2010 to a Commodity Futures Trading Commission's consultation in the US, oil industry expert Philip Verleger pointed the finger at retail investors, noting that:

> *In recent years, passive investors such as pension funds have allocated a portion of their assets to buying commodity futures to diversify portfolios. This diversification has had the ancillary effect of promoting the accumulation of privately held oil inventories. The rise in these stocks has tended to reduce price variations.*

```
http://comments.cftc.gov/Handlers/PdfHandler.ashx?id=11686
```

This massive increase in the number of ETFs investing in the global oil markets has undoubtedly had an indirect effect on the oil market. As investors pile into oil, the storage of oil dramatically increases and these increased stocks help reduce price fluctuations in response to short-term changes in supply and demand.

But this swarming into commodities as an asset class also profoundly changed the returns to long investments in commodity derivatives. The sheer amount of ETF money swamping the oil futures markets appears to have inadvertently moved the market against ETFs themselves. These investors sought out the returns from backwardation but ended up seeing their returns destroyed by semi-permanent contango!

This huge increase in investor interest (and resulting storage capacity) creates another challenge. The industry has come to rely on this huge storage capacity in order to reduce price volatility, yet for this to persist the industry also needs strong interest from passive investors and . . . contango. But why should investors constantly risk seeing their profits eaten away by contango just to support the oil storage industry? You need backwardation to break out, so you can make future profits!

Playing the Commodity Markets: The New Big Macro

Back in the good old days, commodity markets appeared to be relatively simple affairs. Suppliers such as farmers, miners and oil companies had lots of stuff to sell to large industrial users. By and large, these commodity markets were dominated by *non-profit maximising agents*; that is, the primary business of the buyers and sellers was supplying and buying materials and not making money from the markets.

Flashforward to the 1980s and a new world begins to emerge, echoed in part by films such as *Trading Places*, where vagrant-turned-commodity trader Billy Ray Valentine, played by Eddie Murphy, tries to corner the pork bellies market. By the 1990s these traders had taken centre-stage, dominating the markets to a whole new extent. These specialists made relatively small margins by making sure that the underlying markets were liquid, efficient and easy to trade in.

But as you discover in this section, commodities were beginning to attract a whole new kind of player. Some of these 'investors' tried to corner markets, using the increasingly large commodity futures markets as the cornerstone of their strategy. New-fangled hedge funds also became increasingly powerful, as they spotted inefficiencies within these markets, hunted down arbitrage opportunities and generally turned commodity investments into a new asset class like any other.

Suddenly everyone seemed to be in on the great commodity market scramble, eager to diversify their portfolios into alternative assets. For the right kind of investor armed with huge amounts of leverage, market know-how and computing power to crunch the big trades, opportunity suddenly beckoned on a grand scale. Today, that opportunity is still there.

Cornering a commodity market

One of the simplest ways of making money from commodity markets is to corner the market; that is, buy enough of the commodity so that the price starts to increase because you have a vice-like grip over supplies.

Investors can use a variety of approaches to gain the control necessary to corner a market. Following are two of the most common ways:

- Buying up a large percentage of the commodity, hoarding it to create an artificial shortage, and then selling it at an elevated price. (I provide a couple of examples of this strategy in the following sections.)
- Gaining a near-monopoly of shares in an industry.

Although cornering the market seems like a simple enough endeavour for those with deep pockets, doing so is not without its risks. First, manipulating commodity markets is illegal, and a conviction can result in hefty fines and prison sentences. Second, markets have a mechanism by which trading can be suspended in the event that a commodity's price fluctuates in a suspicious manner. Third, if the cornering investor's intentions are discovered, other investors will actively move to undermine her by making it difficult for her to sell the commodity back. Last, plain old luck (or lack thereof) can cause the ground to shift underfoot – exchange rules change, markets take precipitous turns and so on – destroying the conditions that made the endeavour so attractive in the first place.

Hunting for silver

The first huge modern exercise in market cornering began in 1979, when Texan oil billionaires Bunker and Herbert Hunt tried to hoard silver. They ultimately amassed some 59 million ounces of the precious metal, a massive amount in those days. Their bold gambit seemed to pay off as the price of silver climbed to a high of US$50.35 per ounce in January 1980.

But even the best laid plans of mice and men come to nothing if everyone else in the financial game spots the trick. The price of silver suddenly started to plummet (resulting largely from exchange rule changes regarding the purchase of commodities on margin) and hit just US$10.20 per ounce within two months of their audacious market grab. Their market-cornering exercise failed spectacularly and the brothers ended up owing their creditors a spectacular US$1.5 billion in debts. 'A billion dollars isn't what it used to be,' was the reputed response of Bunker Hunt.

Coughing up if you want cocoa

Thirty years later, another big, bold gamble was underway, masterminded by one of the world's most successful commodity hedge funds. In July 2010, traders at London-based firm Armajaro Holdings Ltd (led by Anthony Ward) noticed a series of weak harvests in Ghana and the Ivory Coast, two of the largest suppliers of cocoa beans to the world's commodity markets.

The fund tried to take control of the world cocoa markets. It bought 240,100 tonnes of physical cocoa worth a grand total of US$1 billion, equal to about 7 per cent of annual global production. This huge portion of production represented the whole of Europe's cocoa needs and enough physical supply to fill five Titanic-sized ships. Their move drove up cocoa prices by 150 per cent in just a few months, with prices at one point hitting 33-year-highs!

Armajaro and its well-paid traders knew the cocoa markets well and traditionally had been one of Europe's top three traders by volume. The firm made no secret of its desire to increase physical delivery of cocoa, saying that it planned 'to develop its physical commodities business by further expanding its sourcing operations to enable it to supply its customers with increasing quantities of traceable commodities'.

Apparently, Armajaro's own customer base (chocolate manufacturers in the main) wanted to know more about the origin of their supply, to make sure that it was traceable and sustainable. Cue Armajaro's eagerness to snap up physical supplies of the stuff.

Armajaro's boss Ward is a notorious 'foodstuffs bull'. He maintains that if investors want a diversified portfolio of assets they should have access to something 'that grows', because world population growth and growing affluence are going to push up foodstuff prices inexorably.

In the end, despite Armajaro's cornering of the cocoa market right before the main confectionary-making season, cocoa markets seeing a 150 per cent increase in cocoa prices and analysts anticipating that cocoa prices would sky rocket even more, things didn't turn out quite as anticipated. Good weather in the Ivory Coast, where 40 per cent of the world's cocoa is grown, produced a bumper crop, easing the markets and sending the price of cocoa back down. By December 2010, Armajaro had sold off almost its entire stake.

Making money from commodity trends

Most ordinary investors have much more humble ambitions than the billionaires and companies I describe in the preceding section. They pile into commodities with two very simple ideas in mind:

- They offer significant diversification benefits.
- They can be used as a way of making investors' own macro bets.

Many hedge funds invest in commodities as a way of playing the global economic cycle (which I describe in Chapter 4 in more detail). In essence, demand for commodities is largely *pro-cyclical*; that is, what's good for economic growth is usually good for commodity prices and especially industrial metal prices.

I talk about macro investing in much greater depth in Chapter 15, but here I explain a simple dual strategy for using commodities as a way of playing the large global trends, powered by the strength (or otherwise) of the global economy.

As I discuss in Chapter 15, many macro-based hedge funds look for distinct trends in commodity prices and then use a massive amount of leverage to gear up their returns from a successful trade.

In the following scenarios, I show how you can make money by playing key macro-economic cycles and central-banking policy interventions.

Scenario 1: Commodities as a growth play

The efforts to push up the price of a commodity (as I explain in the 'Cornering a commodity market' section earlier in this chapter) create obvious short-term trends, powered by the sheer momentum of the buying. Investors like yourself can spot these trends and use them within an investment strategy.

This scenario shows how you can use commodities as a growth play. Using such a strategy lets you exploit the growth taking place in emerging economies around the world:

1. Acceleration in the global growth rate (usually around 3–4 per cent per annum) usually produces faster export growth by Chinese manufacturers, supplying consumers in the key US and European markets.

2. The increase in Chinese industrial output feeds through into an increased demand for copper, iron and other industrial metals.

3. This increased industrial demand causes additional energy imports.

4. As the pace of that industrial demand starts to increase, commodity prices for industrial metals and oil markedly increase, largely because spare, marginal, additional mining and energy capacity that can be turned on very quickly is insufficient.

5. Commodity futures may also benefit from a double win: as spot prices increase, demand to buy additional marginal extra supplies intensifies, pushing down storage levels and resulting in commodity markets moving into backwardation.

6. A macro-influenced investor can thus buy commodity futures, especially short-duration *forwards* (contractual agreements between two parties to buy or sell an asset at some time in the future for an agreed-upon price).

Scenario 2: Precious metals as a recession indicator

Here's how to profit from the reverse scenario, where instead of investing in commodities for growth, you use them (specifically, precious metals) to hedge against a recession:

1. Chinese and emerging-market demand slows down markedly following a credit or banking crisis.

2. Chinese buyers of metals and energy suddenly cut back their usage but are also probably sitting on large storage reserves, which they're keen to run down before buying any new supplies.

3. Commodity prices go into freefall and investors short commodities.

4. Recession creeps into the developed nations, and central banks become desperate to avert a global depression and a massive increase in local unemployment; investors start aggressively shorting shares and buying bonds.

5. Governments increase their spending and start to run up big deficits in order to make up for declining private sector demand, but they quickly hit debt buffers.

6. Central banks wade into action, deploying unusual monetary intervention to forestall contracting demand, increasing monetary supply and generally lubricating credit markets.

7. **Investors become increasingly worried that this monetary pump priming will eventually result in future inflation and as a result they buy the one last 'reserve' asset of choice – gold.**

8. **Gold prices start increasing and silver prices may well increase at an even faster rate, because silver is usually a more leveraged way to play increasing precious metals prices than gold.**

Among industrial metals, copper prices tend to increase fastest as the rate of economic growth increases during a boom.

Energy prices are also *pro-cyclical* (that is, they're positively correlated with the overall economy), but strong evidence suggests that over time oil prices have been trending higher. Plus, oil prices are adversely affected by geopolitical concerns (not normally connected to the global economic cycle) and the oil cartel OPEC exerts enormous influence over them. For these reasons, oil is not as reliable a hedge against recession as is gold and other precious metals.

Examining Other Commodity-Trade Opportunities

Some investors ignore the big macro trends and themes (explained in the preceding section) and focus instead on exploiting complicated market inefficiencies, arbitrage opportunities and discrepancies between similar commodity markets. The key to being successful when making these kinds of investments is uncovering inefficiencies and anticipating in which direction the price of a commodity will move, regardless of what the overall economy is doing.

As examples, I work through two large opportunities for the arbitrage-orientated commodity investor with both markets operating in very liquid, relatively easy-to-trade investment instruments:

✔ The difference between Brent and West Texas Intermediate oil prices.

✔ The crack spread within the oil refining market.

Oiling your profits: Brent versus WTI

The quality of different types of oil varies enormously and you can use these differences in your investments.

West Texas Intermediate oil (known as WTI) is regarded as a sweet crude oil, largely because it's about 0.24 per cent sulphur, a lower concentration than North Sea Brent crude (sulphur level: 0.37 per cent). Most oil companies regard WTI as high-quality oil that's easily refined. Much WTI oil is channelled through storage depots and transfer facilities in Cushing, Oklahoma and this WTI crude trades at a higher price than thicker, more sulphurous Brent crude from the North Sea, which is in turn more expensive to refine into gasoline.

On the whole, for most of the last 50 years WTI traded at a slight premium to Brent oil prices or at the same price, give or take a few cents per barrel.

Not anymore! Figure 13-1 tells a remarkable story. The thick line is the price of WTI while the thin line is the price of Brent. Since 2011, WTI prices have lagged behind Brent oil prices by a huge margin, in some cases as much as US$20 a barrel.

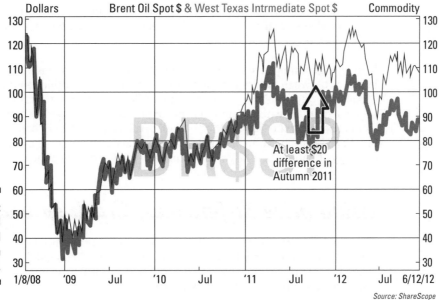

Figure 13-1: Price of WTI compared with Brent oil.

Source: ShareScope

Commentators state different explanations for this consistent discrepancy and no single reason stands out, although lurking in the background is the realisation that WTI should no longer be considered the best reflection for global oil demand (historically WTI's grade of crude is used as a benchmark in oil pricing and is the underlying commodity in oil futures contracts). Other key issues include:

✔ **Major operator Enbridge has experienced supply problems based on pipeline issues.** In 2011, this US-based operator was forced to shut down one of its pipelines after discovering a leak. The pipeline was part of the Lakehead System, which transports up to 670,000 barrels of oil to Midwest refineries, as well as to the Cushing hub.

✔ **The fast-expanding supply of Canadian and Midwest American crude oil (especially from North Dakota) may well be swamping local markets.** This Midwestern oil also can't get down as far as the Gulf Coast; although pipeline capacity exists to the Midwest, no adequate pipeline capacity is available to the Gulf Coast.

✔ **Many Asian buyers are ditching their use of WTI and opting instead for Brent crude as a standard.** This North Sea oil grade is a closer match to the region's light, sweet crude.

✔ **OPEC has expressed concern that WTI may be an inaccurate benchmark.** OPEC is another major player in the world's oil supply and prices. Its oil prices are lower than the WTI and Brent prices because its oil, which comes from various Middle Eastern and Central and South American countries, has an even higher sulphur content. But OPEC is able to exert disproportionate influence (at the margins) on oil markets because it can effectively push prices by controlling the supply of oil on global spot markets (that is, decreasing or increasing supply to push oil prices up or down.

Many hedge funds have been attempting to make money from this difference in prices between different regions for oil. If oil is oversupplied in the Midwest of America (and can't be moved around easily), the plan is to transport it to regional markets where demand is much stronger. The cost of shipping crude from Cushing in the Midwest to the Gulf Coast is about US$10 barrel by truck and US$6 barrel by train. If a hedge fund can access enough cheap transport capacity, it can make a tidy margin on each load of oil transported.

Using price differences: Crack spread

Many hedge funds focus their attention on a price differential called the *crack spread* (which doesn't refer to the rampant increase in illegal drug usage in the US!). This is a key energy price difference within the energy markets that's closely monitored by many hedge funds.

Pity the poor oil refiners. They're caught between two markets: the raw materials they need to purchase (mostly in the form of unrefined oil) and the finished products they sell (petrol, diesel and so on). The price of that unrefined crude oil moves up and down for all sorts of reasons, nearly all out of the refiners' control. Yet their end product of refined gasoline, petrol or diesel tends to be much more stable in price.

That difference in the pricing is the *crack spread*: the margin that refiners realise when they buy crude oil while simultaneously selling the products into an increasingly competitive market. The purchase of a crack spread is the opposite of the crack spread hedge (selling the crack spread). It entails selling crude oil and buying products. Refiners are naturally long the crack spread because they continuously buy crude and sell products. At times, however, they do the opposite – buying products and selling crude – and thus find purchasing a crack spread a useful strategy.

Market traders including hedge funds have been trading crack spreads on US-based exchanges for more than a decade, using heating oil, gasoline and crude oil futures. In recent years, the use of crack spreads has grown enormously as a result of dramatic price fluctuations caused by extreme weather events such as hurricanes or political oil crises.

Various US-based futures exchanges facilitate crack-spread trading by treating each spread trade as a single transaction. All refiners use these exchanges and develop a crack-spread futures market strategy based on their own output patterns . . . and available cash!

A long crack call (buying a crack call option) or a short crack put (selling a crack put option) is defined as the assignment of futures positions, which, at exercise, involves buying one underlying heating oil or gasoline futures contract and selling one underlying crude oil contract.

If the refiner's supply and sales commitments are substantial and if it's forced to make an unplanned entry into the spot market, prices may move against it. To protect itself from increasing product prices and decreasing crude oil prices, the refinery uses a short hedge against crude and a long hedge against products, which is the same as purchasing the crack spread. You can mimic this strategy to exploit this situation.

Crack spreads can move up and down incredibly quickly, because lots of different variables affect them, including seasonality. Heating oil, for example, tends to move to a premium over gasoline in winter and early spring, but generally loses ground to trade at a discount in the summer driving season. Spreads also vary based on a refinery's equipment, product mix and target market.

Figure 13-2 illustrates how the spread changed markedly during just one year. The chart shows recent trends in a single product crack spread: the difference between the US Gulf Coast conventional gasoline spot price (the solid black line) and the Louisiana Light Sweet crude spot price (the dotted line). Crack spreads can be positive (the light shaded region) or negative (the dark shaded region), depending on relative product prices.

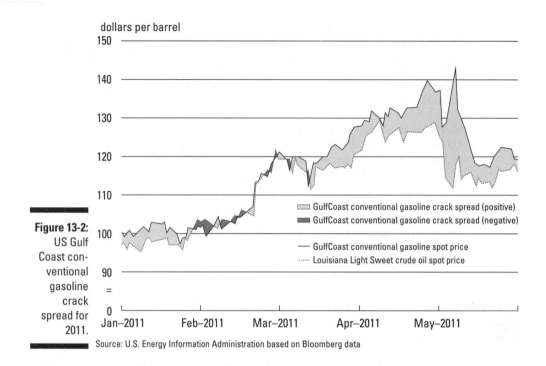

Source: U.S. Energy Information Administration based on Bloomberg data

Figure 13-2:
US Gulf
Coast con-
ventional
gasoline
crack
spread for
2011.

Trending Big – When Appropriate

When reading about the world of commodity markets, you may be concerned that these global electronic marketplaces aren't quite as efficient as they're cracked up to be. After all, as I discuss in Chapter 6 on market efficiency, if markets were constantly inefficient, and offering up profit-making opportunities on a regular basis, the masses of hedge funds, institutions and private investors would surely notice, move in, swamp the opportunity and then move off again. In other words, if an inefficiency is big enough, everyone would be tempted to make money from it, and within a few days/weeks/months that opportunity vanishes.

But not all market inefficiencies are necessarily a profitable opportunity. Take my discussion of the spread between Brent and WTI oil from the earlier section 'Oiling your profits: Brent versus WTI'. If you have access to huge amounts of money to buy transport companies, you can profit from this difference between Brent and WTI prices. But the vast majority of hedge funds don't have that kind of capital or expertise – thus this market inefficiency isn't easy to arbitrage away!

Equally, although the hugely powerful hedge-fund computing systems spot loads of market anomalies, many of these opportunities disappear within just a few days. Sometimes an opportunity lasts for only a few minutes before vanishing.

Markets are largely efficient and investors have to work incredibly hard to make an extra profit. Most of the time they must be willing to take on more risk or be more patient over the long term. And yet, markets do sometimes work in odd ways that offer up opportunities. For example, if you know that oil markets are going to trend continually towards contango (check out the earlier section 'Understanding the Importance of Contango and Backwardation Switches') you can short one-month oil futures.

What's even better is that these opportunities appear to be persistent, observable and can be invested in long or short. Crucially, they're also built on a profound psychological insight, which is that although every crisis is different, the way people react to them is often very similar!

Scratch away the shiny surface of most professional investment strategies and you discover the same underlying mix of greed, hope, fear and despair. If you accept this ever-present reality you can work out how people are going to react, and then predict what may happen next by analysing historical price patterns.

The premise of this psychological view of investing is that price patterns provide insights into the behaviour of investors in different scenarios. Clearly, therefore, trends are crucially important, with powerful up and down trends a frequent and observable trait of financial markets.

Tracing the emergence of trend-seeking hedge funds

Trends are powerful and persistent. A 1993 study conclusively shows that relative winners tend to continue as relative winners for up to one year, whereas recent relative losers tend to continue their losing streaks.

Trend-following strategies are therefore also referred to as *momentum strategies*, because they're based on this assumption of well-performing indices continuing to do so in the near future. Hence, this strategy relies on backward-looking signals rather than forecasts of the future.

Many of today's most successful hedge funds built their entire investment strategy around the following facts:

- ✔ Investors react predictably to external stimuli.
- ✔ Their reaction forms a trend.
- ✔ This trend frequently develops upwards or downwards momentum.
- ✔ The momentum can extend over time and develop into a major trend, lasting long enough for astute investors to make significant sums of money.

Most investors who follow trends look to get in on a trend that's already emerging, though some look to forecast trends before they arise.

Analysing a trend in action

To help understand how trends form – and how you as an investor can use them – I take a look at the oil commodity markets. Like many commodity markets, oil futures markets move through relatively long periods when they're non-trending, and choppy, as well as periods where they're working within a relatively long-term trend (upwards or downwards).

The chart in Figure 13-3 shows the spot price of Brent oil from August 2008 to December 2012. Over this period the price slightly declined from a peak of about US$125 a barrel (at the beginning of the period) to US$110 (at the end of the period). But over the intervening four years oil prices zoomed down and up in an extremely volatile fashion. Crucially, you can see noticeable periods where oil trended up or down for a reasonably long period of time, usually many weeks.

Figure 13-3 shows these trends inside the thick black boxes. For instance, a 20-week period appears at the beginning of this period where oil trended downwards. That was quickly followed by a longer 30-week period of rising prices, which was stopped dead in its tracks with a further period of 12 weeks where no trend is discernible.

You can spot evident trends that last for many weeks (the longest one is 30 weeks). Trends go up and down, but for the smart hedge fund with access to gearing, the direction of the trend doesn't matter. What's important is that investors in oil are behaving in a predictable way that hedge funds can capture within a trading strategy. A trend-seeking hedge fund can profit from rising *and* falling markets: a trade's profitability is determined by the trend's size and breadth, not its direction.

Hundreds of hedge funds have built strategies on this sort of trend following, in particular based around futures markets. These more complicated options-based markets offer up the opportunity to look not only for trends in the spot price, but also trends in the pricing of futures contracts for forward deliveries.

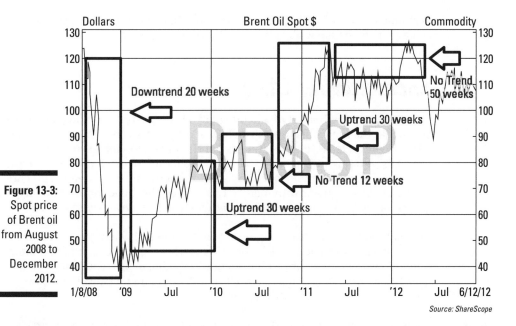

Figure 13-3:
Spot price
of Brent oil
from August
2008 to
December
2012.

Source: ShareScope

Many futures traders looking for trends go long a futures contract each month for which the trailing 12-month return is above cash returns and short if the trailing12-month return is below cash returns.

As this section shows, momentum is a powerful force within the markets and describes the way certain assets keep increasing in value, driven up by key fundamental measures such as profits growth that seem to be accelerating. Therefore, momentum-based investors rely on predictive fundamental analysis of the kind I explore in Chapter 9. Although both momentum investing and trend following focus on an asset's movement, a crucial difference does exist: in *momentum-based investing*, investors make their investment decisions on the assumption that a trend, once begun, will continue (a security that is moving up – or down – will continue to do so, for example) and will take long or short positions based on this assumption. In *trend following*, investors look at the share price, trade as necessary to profit from the price's rise or fall, and then close the position and sit tight until the next big trend comes along.

Reviewing the Remorseless Rise of Commodity Trading Advisors

Trend-seeking is now a core strategy for many of the world's largest hedge funds, especially those professing to be commodity trading advisors (CTAs).

In simple terms, a CTA fund is a hedge fund that uses futures contracts to achieve its investment objective of following a big trend.

Encountering CTAs

If you open up the bonnet of a hedge fund's trading strategy, you usually discover that the fund's managers run lots of different strategies incorporating futures contracts, options on futures contracts and foreign exchange (FX) forwards. Although CTAs were initially commodity-focused, they now invest across all futures markets including shares, bonds and FX; spreads and carry trades are also popular with many CTAs. (Given this huge range of underlying assets, many CTA funds prefer to call themselves *managed-futures funds*.)

The main bulk of CTAs are long-term trend followers: when a market shows a clear uptrend, CTAs are usually long this market. In essence, they're momentum followers (see the preceding section) tracking a big trend, although they may end up following a huge number of individual markets, which means they can pick up lots of varying trends.

Whatever the particular fund strategy, the fundamental source of returns is usually based around long-term *secular shifts* (that is, time frames lasting usually at least a few years) in capital flows (that is, trends). Hence, trend-following CTA funds make most of their money when markets are volatile and fear of financial instability is in the air.

CTAs only deal in futures contracts that are traded on exchanges. This preference for futures based contracts is because very little counterparty risk applies with these options and these derivatives-based structures are also the most liquid traded instruments in the financial markets.

CTA fund trading time frames can be short term (10 days or less), medium term (11 to 30 days) or long term (more than 30 days), although long-term trend followers may well hold a position for six months to a year or more.

Most CTA funds tend to fall into one of two main categories:

- ✔ **Discretionary:** In this strategy, traders hope to forecast prices by analysing supply and demand factors and other market information. These traders tend to focus mainly on commodities.

- ✔ **Systematic:** These strategies typically use computer programs to conduct quantitative analysis in an effort to exploit price trends. They look across hundreds of different markets and asset classes including shares, bonds, FX and commodities.

Totting up the CTA numbers

CTAs have grown enormously popular in recent years, especially after the global financial crisis of 2008 – hundreds of individual CTA funds exist, some with tens of billions of dollars under management. Researchers at BarclaysHedge say that assets under management in the CTA futures space grew from US$0.31 billion in 1980 to US$320 billion by the third quarter of 2011.

Lots of different specialist strategies reside within the CTA category, but BarclaysHedge confirms that systematic trading is the most common strategy within the CTA universe, representing US$269.33 billion in assets under management (AUM; the value of the assets that an investment company manages for its investors). In contrast, discretionary traders managed US$27.57 billion as of the third quarter of 2011.

Make sure the commodity trading advisor you select shares your trading philosophy and goals. For example, not every CTA is a long-term trend seeker. Short-term traders often try to profit from brief reversals of the long-term trend or trading off the news and events of the day or week. By contrast, fundamental traders (see 'Analysing a trend in action' earlier in this chapter) use the traditional supply and demand for a commodity as a predictor of its future price. Spread traders exploit differentials between markets such as the crack spread opportunity (check out the earlier section 'Using price differences: Crack spread') or between different delivery months of the same commodity.

Remaining disciplined for success

CTA investing is all about being disciplined, methodical and unemotional about trading. As one CTA says, 'if it's not in the data, don't bother torturing it; move on and find the next big trend'. Yet after a strategy is statistically proved to be profitable, that trend can then be converted into a mathematical formula and used in calculation systems designed to spot general trends.

These emotionless systems search for specific things on a regular basis. Many CTA funds base their systems on simple momentum indicators, such as price moving average or price channel breakout models. However, the complication is that these models can cover over 100 markets for hugely different durations – from just a few seconds to many months.

Systematic trend followers don't care about contradictory fundamentals. They make long and short trades if their models tell them to! CTAs can make money on the downside, by being short.

Volatility is hugely important for nearly all trend followers regardless of strategy – many fund managers size positions and place stops based on the underlying level of market volatility.

CTAs have what's called a *large optionality component*. A position for a CTA is really a call on the trend continuing: a trend follower loses money when a trend reverses. This focus on trends means that managers have to juggle months of small losses (trends that don't materialise) alongside periods of large gains (trends captured), plus the occasional large drawdown when a trend suddenly stops or turns violently the wrong way.

Periods of stock-market meltdowns, debt crises and the like often result in large gains for CTA funds: this turbulence usually starts a new trend. Most CTAs also wait for confirmation that a trend is over before exiting.

Discussing whether CTA funds work in practice

CTA funds have become hugely popular because – unlike many once-popular alternative assets – they produce bumper results and make investors money . . . some of the time!

Providing uncorrelated returns

Analyses of past returns suggest that CTA funds largely provide a fairly constant stream of positive returns uncorrelated to traditional asset classes such as shares and fixed income. In fact, a variety of studies show that CTA funds have low-to-negative correlations to traditional asset classes over the last ten years.

Analysis of data firm Morningstar's Diversified Futures index (comprising many varying individual fund strategies) suggests that CTA funds were –0.22 correlated to the MSCI World equity index; that is, they tend to increase in value when equity markets start falling.

A US Center for International Securities and Derivatives Markets study in 2006 shows that discretionary and systematic CTAs (which I define earlier in 'Encountering CTAs') historically exhibit relatively low correlations *between one another*. Therefore, if you can put together a mixed bag of very good CTA managers at least you don't have to worry too much about them all falling in value at the same time!

Supplying absolute gains

Uncorrelated returns are fine and dandy, but as an investor you really care about *positive, absolute gains*: does the fund make a return in most years?

Various industry studies state that most CTA funds delivered impressive returns in the last few decades. For instance, one 2009 study finds that CTA strategies generated positive returns in 12 of the 15 worst months for shares since 1987. Another survey that looked at CTA fund performance during market panics reveals that CTA funds returned 43 per cent on average in the 'tech wreck' from 2000 to 2002 while US shares dropped 45 per cent. During the credit crisis from 2007 to early 2009, CTA funds returned almost 20 per cent compared to a 50 per cent decline for shares.

According to Morningstar, from 1 February 1992 to 31 January 2012 the MSCI World equity index produced a cumulative return of 264 per cent (6.7 per cent per year) compared with 464 per cent for the Morningstar Futures index (the equivalent of 9 per cent per year).

Numerous studies suggest that investing in CTAs is only for you if you're willing to take a long-term view. Returns in CTA funds appear to come in short bursts, with often extended periods of sideways movement. In particular, CTA funds typically underperform equity markets during bull runs (such as 1997–1999, 2003–2007 and 2009–2010).

Hearing opposing views

Most academic economists, however, aren't convinced by the positive industry studies. Many researchers point out that they don't always include the impact of fees on total returns to outside shareholders – all costs including trading fees can typically total 4–5 per cent per year!

A study by economists at Yale included fees in their calculations and concluded that average CTA funds didn't add any meaningful value for investors in 1994–2007. Even though the average CTA fund beat returns from holding Treasury bills by more than 5 per cent per year, that out-performance fell to a tiny 0.85 per cent per year *after* fees were included!

The biggest negative for CTA returns is their volatility. Although expected returns for most trend-following CTA funds are in the mid-teens in percentage terms, drawdowns can be similarly sized. A short-term investment in a CTA fund can be painful, particularly if you make it right before a major drawdown.

In addition, one of the biggest flaws in indices that track the returns from CTA funds is that these funds are rarely publically traded – which means that no official pricing exists and so valuation is difficult.

Many analysts also worry that recent poor returns (2011–2012) suggest that the magic may be fading from CTAs as a strategy. Part of the problem seems to be one of size: as the number of CTAs has grown, more and more money is chasing a similar set of trading ideas. Perhaps too much money is chasing too few opportunities.

Winton Capital

Winton Capital is a medium-term trend-following fund. It trades a portfolio of over 100 international futures, options and forward contracts. These consist of stock indices, bonds, short-term interest rates, currencies, precious and base metals, grains, livestock, energy and agricultural products.

Set up by theoretical physicist David Harding in 1997, Winton boasts 170 employees, 92 of whom have PhDs or MAs, many in theoretical physics, maths and statistics. Winton's offices don't feel like typical investment trading floors but more like a post-graduate study area with whiteboards full of diagrams, equations and notes.

Harding himself is a pioneer of trend following in Europe. In 1987 he co-founded Adam, Harding & Lueck (AHL), a quantitative fund manager, which was later acquired by the Man Group. Winton's own track record is hugely impressive – over ten years starting in 2000 the Winton Futures Fund has never had a losing year and enjoyed an annualised compound annual rate of return of 19.7 per cent since inception.

Catching a successful CTA in action: Winton Capital

If you're looking to understand how CTAs work their computing-driven magic, start with an outfit such as Winton Capital. This London-based hedge fund currently manages US$15 billion, making it the world's number 2 in CTA funds.

At the core of the Winton approach is a hardnosed respect for numbers and 'big' data – like many of its competitors, the firm is constantly on the lookout for big new trends backed up by an exhaustive analysis of data sources. Its main strategy is based on using price action and computers to identify clear trends and then trading those trends for profit, regardless of the overall direction of markets. This systematic focus means that emotion is largely removed from the financial equation – which in turn helps its traders make profits when wider markets are busily panicking.

Harding labels Winton an expert at global statistical financial analysis; that is, the outfit's analysts like to harvest and clean up huge amounts of data which they then use to trade across different asset classes. But this obsession with data doesn't mean that the firm's principal managers aren't interested in emotions entirely – like most CTA funds, many of its most powerful insights are based on understanding key behavioural trends.

Winton makes a great deal of money out of volatility. Its research suggests that the volatility is in fact not something to worry about – a very different message from most academic economists, who think that volatility is enormously destructive for most private investors.

For Winton Capital, the key challenge in the future is to hunt down constantly new sources of diversified, non-correlated returns; that is, to find new asset classes, markets and trades that can make its traders money even if they ignore the big global trends. Winton's constant search for alternative sources of returns is based on a worry that global markets are becoming increasingly intertwined and correlated – Winton's more recent response to this correlation is to take a more conservative approach and target lower levels of portfolio volatility.

Winton's expected return models are a mix of fundamental and technical indicators used within its Base System. This system weights the 1,000 stocks from the MSCI World index according to forecasted volatility. The system is exclusively momentum-based.

As of summer 2012, the core Winton investment focus is to be long (buy) 'safe' government bonds from the US, the UK, Germany and Japan.

Winton is careful to remind investors that CTA strategies don't always produce a positive return: the firm calculates that two down years occur in every 15 years.

Spotting the wrong kind of markets for CTAs

The most successful CTA funds can boast double-digit annual returns for much of the first decade of this century, but that doesn't mean they haven't had more than their fair share of bad years. In particular, 2011 and 2012 proved to be torrid years for many CTA funds.

Outfits such as BlueTrend (a US$11 billion Geneva-based fund) and Winton Capital (from the preceding section) experienced rotten autumn 2012s, with losses of as much as 5 per cent in one month. Pinpointing what went wrong for these hedge-fund goliaths is difficult, but many experts believe that these funds were hit by the 'wrong' kind of volatility!

Although most CTAs benefit from intense financial and political volatility, unorthodox monetary policies can wrong-foot some of them. In particular, a risk on/risk off (RoRo) environment (in which investors regularly move back and forth between risky shares and less risky sovereign debt based on central bank policy decisions) causes havoc for trend followers. Trends quickly reverse causing CTAs painful losses. Plus, prolonged volatility often causes the CTAs' computers automatically to reduce their leverage, meaning that even when they make money, it's far less than it should be!

Many analysts note that a future bonds crisis may spell doom for the trend followers. CTA hedge funds made huge profits from a decades' long bond (upwards) trend, because trend followers benefit in times of crisis when investors flock to bonds as a safe haven, inflating already rising prices. (Futures broker Attain Capital suggests that bond positions account for almost 25 per cent of a typical trend-following model's returns since 1990.) The concern is what happens when bonds suddenly start to sell off because they've increased too much in value. As an investor, you need to ask whether you think that CTA funds can ride the next downward leg in bond prices and continue to bring you profit.

Chapter 14

Investing in Emerging-Market Equities and Currencies

*T*he remorseless rise of hedge funds has occurred in an era of unprecedented globalisation, but this is no coincidence. Over the last 40 years the financial system has spread its tentacles all over the planet, and trading for many sectors, such as bonds, is now truly international. Many institutional investors don't think twice about buying US shares one day and selling Chinese renminbi or Australian shares the next.

This globalisation favours the hedge-fund community, and many leading practitioners come from developing-world countries such as India and China. The international bias is reinforced by the huge choice available at the global-market levels, allowing an innovative manager the opportunity of worldwide reach at the touch of a button. The growing enthusiasm for developing-country markets is also driven by the simple fact that emerging markets, such as China, Brazil and India, are growing much faster than their developed-world counterparts.

This powerful economic progress has produced more than two decades of astonishing returns in the stock and bond markets. The rush into these emerging markets is great news for you, as an advanced private investor, especially if you're willing to put in the research to find the best opportunities. You can copy much of what the emerging market hedge-fund community is doing, which is why in this chapter I examine its core strategies to see what works. I describe investing in emerging markets, taking advantage of special situations such as debt and employing local currency trading so that you can get in on the impressive returns.

Investigating Emerging Markets

Emerging markets (EMs) are countries that are in the process of developing economically. They typically have per-capita incomes at the lower to middle end of the world range, and are in the process of moving from a *closed market economy* (one that is not open to business from other countries) to an open market economy.

But a wide variety of different countries and opportunities lie behind this rather bland definition. A broad classification of EMs includes China and Russia, two of the world's economic powerhouses, as well as highly developed South Korea and fast-growing but still relatively poor Colombia. The link between all EMs, however, is that they have in the last few decades embarked on rapid economic development and reform programmes and thus emerged onto the global financial scene.

Although only around 20 per cent of the world's nations are considered EMs, these countries constitute approximately 80 per cent of the global population. In fact, according to hardcore enthusiasts, EM states may well account for an astonishing 50 per cent of world gross domestic product (GDP) in the next ten years. If that happens, investors in developed countries have a great deal of catching up to do, because most private and institutional investors in the UK and US have a little under 10 per cent of their assets in EMs of one shape or another.

EMs have replaced developed-world small caps and technology stocks as the planet's favourite growth assets. (For more, flip to Chapter 9 where I describe those growth investors with a passion for companies, markets and countries where profits seem to be constantly trending upwards.)

But something else is also afoot that's absolutely fascinating. These fast-growing, developing countries are becoming increasingly popular with investors worried about the financial imbalances in the West. Countries such as Russia and China appear to have better balance sheets and stronger, more robust economies than many once-successful developed-world economies such as Spain or France. EM shares and bonds are certainly still viewed as volatile, but their perceived riskiness has declined in recent years. The situation sparked a massive surge of interest in EM currencies and bonds, which helps the hedge-fund community with its openness to investing in different asset classes.

Identifying EMs for your investment

To discover which countries comprise the EM asset class, check out the equity-market index that many mainstream and hedge-fund managers use as a benchmark. The MSCI Emerging Markets Index was founded in 1988 and is now tracked by hundreds of different funds. Collectively the country stock markets included in this index moved from about 1 per cent of the global equity opportunity in 1988 to 14 per cent in 2010.

These EM countries have changed incredibly over the last decade. Many of them used to be net importers of capital, but today many of their governments are international investors themselves, through the creation of sovereign (government) wealth funds where the state saves up extra revenues for the future.

The 'mainstreaming' of EM among western investors hasn't been entirely pain-free. EM stocks in particular can be very volatile in terms of pricing – shooting up and down in value as investors switch risk on and off.

Table 14-1 looks at MSCI Emerging Markets Index data from November 2012. Over the previous 12 months, many EM regions fell in value, with emerging Eastern European markets in places such as Hungary and Romania being especially badly hit. That's also true for the last three and five years. But look at the far right-hand column in the table showing annualised returns over the last ten years: these figures indicate that EM stocks overall have returned an average gain of 10 per cent per year for the last ten years.

Table 14-1	The EM Story in Numbers (Using US Dollars and as at 15 November 2012)			
Annualised Historical Returns (%)				
MSCI Index	*1 Year*	*3 Years*	*5 Years*	*10 Years*
BRIC (Brazil, Russia, India, China)	−5.180	−5.950	−9.180	16.370
EM (Emerging Markets)	0.530	0.410	−5.080	12.790
EM Asia	3.570	2.050	−4.720	11.050
EM Eastern Europe	−7.110	−4.070	−12.600	10.240
EM Europe & Middle East	−1.990	−1.550	−9.280	10.410
EM Far East	3.760	2.820	−4.150	10.440
EM Latin America	−7.260	−4.130	−4.540	19.160

Source: MSCI and iShares

Table 14-2 digs a little deeper into these equity-market returns and highlights the massive volatility on a year-by-year basis. In a good year, such as 2009, EM stocks can increase by 78 per cent in value and even in an average year returns of 20 or even 30 per cent are possible.

These statistics serve as a reminder that investors drop EM stocks when worries about a global recession increase sharply. When the global markets hit a turbulent patch in 2008, EM stocks declined by a whopping 53 per cent overall.

Table 14-2	Annual Returns from the MSCI EM Index
Year-by-Year Returns	*Index Returns (%)*
2011	−18.42
2010	18.88
2009	78.51
2008	−53.33
2007	39.39
2006	32.17
2005	34.00
2004	25.55

Source: MSCI

That volatility in EMs also shows up in the constituents of the index. In Table 14-3 you can see that countries such as Russia and India now comprise only around 6 per cent of the global index. In good years, when the bulls were rampant, these countries comprised as much as 10–15 per cent of the index.

Table 14-3	Allocation of the MSCI EM Index (Ten Largest Countries as at 15 November 2012)
Country	*Percentage of Fund*
China	17.84
South Korea	15.17
Brazil	12.38
Taiwan	10.72
South Africa	7.62
India	6.83
Russia	5.77
Mexico	5.05
Malaysia	3.77
Indonesia	2.85
Total	88.00

Source: iShares at http://us.ishares.com/product_info/fund/
overview/EEM.htm

Like all growth markets EM markets are volatile, which is where hedge funds come in handy because they aim to mitigate that risk. Using a hedge-fund approach you can cut the volatility by more than half without giving up half the returns.

Looking at hedge funds and EM

Hedge funds have become more and more active in EMs over the last few decades, with a vast range of different strategies, including focusing on traditional shares (going long equities probably accounts for as much as 90 per cent of the funds in this space), event-driven investing (exploiting price inefficiencies following a merger, a bankruptcy, the release of an earnings report or other corporate event) and global macro and fixed-income arbitrage (in which investors make trades based on an analysis of trends in the global economy and exploit arbitrate opportunities in bonds, respectively).

Crucially, hedge funds can offer exposure to sophisticated EM investments, including commodities, property, currencies and derivatives.

The love of 'growth' stocks in countries as diverse as Brazil, India and Indonesia hasn't stopped hedge funds employing innovative strategies such as:

- ✔ Using leverage to increase return potential significantly.

- ✔ Pushing trades out across asset classes based on a macro strategy; this strategy can help avoid potential liquidity traps that are quite common in smaller, less mature EMs.

- ✔ Shorting to help to increase profits. Many EM equities can become fearsomely expensive, which opens up possibilities to sell the weaker companies. Managers can also draw on the growing range of derivatives that now exist to help protect the portfolio or to leverage it.

Many EMs and their government-appointed regulators don't allow short-selling! Plus, some smaller countries have a distinct lack of futures or other derivative products with which to hedge risk.

Investing in the EMs has some unique risks, including a lack of transparency at the company level (which can make evaluating investment opportunities difficult). You also need to be careful about liquidity in some markets, especially when western investors all start to sell simultaneously during a market scare!

Joining an expanding space

EM investment funds began to emerge in the mid-1980s when the International Finance Corporation (IFC) set up the first mutual fund that invested solely in securities from EMs, with seed capital of around US$50 million. Since then the

EM fund community has grown exponentially, with hedge funds experiencing some of the fastest inflows of money.

According to Hedge Fund Research, in 2012 EM funds had approximately US$121 billion in assets under management. Investors have stampeded into EM equity-driven hedge funds largely because of impressive returns. Before the global financial crisis in 2008, many EM hedge funds were delivering returns in excess of 25 per cent annually, well above the hedge-fund industry average in the developed world.

Many investors pulled money out of EM funds in the crisis, but by 2010 the market was growing again. By summer 2012 the number of EM hedge funds had reached an all-time high with 1,073 funds (14 per cent of all hedge funds globally).

This recent inflow of money is perhaps powered by the realisation that Asian economies may be in the process of slowing down and investors want to make money from local equities *falling* in value. EM returns may be hit by deterioration in the sovereign debt crisis among developed countries (their main customers), a rise in inflation, bad loans, corruption and strengthening currencies. If the cynics are right, investors need a hedge-fund manager to play both short and long the local markets.

An example EM hedge fund

One of the most successful recent EM-based hedge funds is GAM Talentum Emerging Long/Short fund, managed by Enrico Camera and Iain Cartmill. This US$70.1 million fund invests largely in shares, with one-, three- and five-year annualised returns of about 9 per cent (based on 2012 returns). Importantly, these solid numbers don't seem to have come about from excessive risk-taking, with the fund's worst drawdown or peak-to-trough fall at less than 7 per cent versus a sector average of more than 40 per cent. In fact, in 2008 the fund gained 8.7 per cent while the MSCI Emerging Market Index lost more than half its value.

The fund's managers say that the secret is to focus on mining information about up-and-coming earnings revisions, echoing many developed-world peers who closely monitor earnings estimates to find companies that may pull a positive surprise. Check out Chapter 3 for a more detailed discussion of this strategy. The managers go long on companies deemed to have a competitive edge and whose valuations and prospects they believe have been underestimated.

A *Financial Times* report in spring 2011 noted that the fund's managers 'believed analysts weren't appreciating the upside that AVI, a South African consumer staples and healthcare products retailer, was likely to experience as a result of the company's new plant investments coupled with the country's rising disposable income. Within a year, the stock had doubled. On the short side, the fund bets against companies that are likely to be hit by competitive and macro headwinds.'

The sad track record of local funds

Although more than 800 funds run by local managers exist in Asia, few are very big or have long track records. HSBC Global Asset Management reckons that, of around 70 local hedge funds in India in 2007, only 10 or so survived through to 2012. After a period of considerable gains in the first half of the last decade, many of these local hedge funds were caught in a nasty liquidity trap, losing on average 80–90 per cent of their value.

Remembering the risks of an EM-focused strategy

EM hedge funds may be popular, but they still represent only 5 per cent of the hedge-fund universe, with a tiny handful of EM funds boasting more than US$1 billion in assets. Crucially, many investors still insist that the EM opportunity is based on *beta* (the measure of a security's volatility or systemic risk); that is, in reality you're not really taking a noncommittal bet on EMs but betting that these local equity markets are going to carry on increasing in value.

Playing Emerging Markets in Alternative Ways: Special Situations

Although most EM hedge funds focus on shares in one shape or another, a small but growing band choose to focus on what's traditionally called *special-situation* opportunities in the equity and bond spaces. I take a quick look at some examples in this section, focusing in particular on how these investors look at fixed income securities or debt.

A growing number of managers are targeting EM debt as a new strategy. This area has become a rich seam for investors in recent years, outperforming every asset class this century to date with 10.75 per cent annual returns and volatility of just 9.5 per cent. Many hedge funds bought into Argentinean state debt (at very low price levels) hoping to force the government to repay its international debt. Bizarrely, many of these distressed debt managers have also started buying debt from supposedly developed countries such as Greece, Portugal, Italy and Ireland, which many hedge funds increasingly regard as EMs!

In addition, many local bond markets are now surprisingly sophisticated: hedge funds can not only buy local currency and dollar-denominated EM bonds, but also play spreads over Treasuries (essentially wagering on the performance of US Treasury bills, Treasury notes, Treasury bonds and Treasury Inflation Protected Securities [TIPS]) or run trades that target EM currencies versus the dollar and euro.

Other hedge funds concentrate more on local private companies or shares. For instance, large Brazilian hedge fund Permal has built a big portfolio of short-term private-equity positions in local companies. Others, such as UK-based fund-management group Ashmore, have effectively married private equity with shareholder activism. Ashmore's managers look to 'take control of an often complex and difficult situation, and aim to create value through an event or series of actions which transforms the company'. According to Ashmore, 'this investment theme has historically achieved very strong returns' in the 100 plus transactions with which it's been involved (source: Ashmore's website at `http://www.ashmoregroup.com`).

What's helped many specialist managers is that practical factors in the local markets seem to be moving in their favour; that is, sovereign (government) dollar bond issuance hasn't kept up with demand and local corporations are issuing more and more bonds. In fact, most hedge-fund managers think that companies rather than governments will increasingly issue future bonds: the US$80 billion in new sovereign bonds issued by developing countries in 2011 was eclipsed by the US$210 billion of corporate issuance.

This growth in bond issues is a deliberate strategy by national governments to improve local capital markets. States are increasingly looking to stimulate the growth of institutional savings markets, and eventually reduce risks to external shocks by having a largely local market dominated by local investors.

As EM governments issue more bonds, investing in local currency debt is an increasingly popular choice as opposed to investing in government debt issued by EM states that's denominated in dollars. Crucially, local currency debt can be a natural hedge against dollar weakness.

The last decade has witnessed a massive improvement in sovereign risk levels! Many EM states have sound balance sheets, with relatively low levels of borrowing. Also of help is that the economic links between EMs are often weak – China's economy for instance is increasingly being driven by local consumer demand. Therefore, many EM states may continue to thrive even if the US or UK is mired in a deep recession.

Local EM bonds may have become less risky, but don't underestimate the dangers. The reason for growing developed-world interest in this specialist space is because of its own challenges: unfunded pension liabilities, global liquidity and the relative unattractiveness of developed-world asset classes.

Opportunities in China

Investing in Asia generally and especially China can be a difficult business, even for hedge funds with departments full of researchers, lawyers and traders. Asian markets and particularly the onshore, mainland Chinese equity and debt markets can be opaque, difficult to trade in and subject to governmental interference. Chinese shares have had a horrid time since the global financial crisis, pushed lower by not only slower national growth, but also political uncertainty and a distinct lack of enthusiasm on the part of most local investors for risky stuff like shares.

But some hedge funds still managed to push and build a solid record in these difficult markets. One good example is Pacific Alliance Asia Opportunity Fund, which has a track record that stretches back to October 2006; a version of the fund also trades shares on the London Stock exchange under the ticker PAX.LN. Like most investors in the region it had a brilliant 2007 (up 60 per cent), a bad 2008 (down 18 per cent, which is well below the average losses for the region) and then a steady few years including an 11 per cent gain in 2010 and a 7 per cent increase in 2012 (see http://pax-fund.com/shareholder-communications/monthly-reports for the data).

This fund is typical of a growing number of Asian-based hedge funds in that it uses a number of different strategies to try to grind out a positive return in all markets. In its October 2012 newsletter to investors, for instance, the fund reports that it has 51 per cent of its money invested in something called 'bridge funding', with another 28 per cent in 'distressed and secondary market (for private equity deals) structures'. Last but by no means least, 7 per cent is invested in event-driven strategies and arbitrage opportunities.

This fund's money is increasingly moving into areas based on two distinct core theories. The first idea is to retreat to fundamentals-driven, deep-value investing (that is, spotting bargain opportunities that may exist on the public exchanges or in private company markets). The second idea is ploughing money into assisting businesses fund their expansion and growth via bridge funding. This category can include everything from helping property developers fund their next project to working with fast-growing companies to finance their projects outside the conventional banking system. This idea of replacing local banks and funding organisations with hedge-fund money is a huge growth market with potentially large returns for many hedge funds.

Converting Your Money: Emerging Markets and Currency Trading

One of the most exciting areas of growth for hedge funds in the developing world is local currency trading. In fact, foreign exchange (FX) can be seen as a separate asset class to external EM debt (which I discuss in the preceding section), with more explicit exposure to currency and interest-rate movement, and instruments ranging from local treasury bonds to *currency forwards* (which lock in the future price at which currency can sell) and interest-rate swaps (in which one interest rate is swapped for another, using a specified amount of principal). I talk about FX investing at the global level in Chapter 5.

In this section I discuss some approaches that hedge funds use in regards to EM currencies, such as the Balassa–Samuelson theory (based on the idea of convergence between EM and developed-world currencies), carry trades and purchasing-power parity.

Introducing the Balassa–Samuelson theory

Many hedge-fund managers in the FX space focus on the higher-interest rates on offer from local, developing markets – a familiar feature for those involved in strategies that seek to take advantage of the forward rate bias, which rewards investors willing to take on EM risk for substantial positive returns over time. (For more on this strategy, flip to Chapter 5.)

But many more hedge-fund managers are drawn to an even bigger opportunity: the convergence of *real exchange rates* (that is, the purchasing power of one currency relative to another), which is based on something called the *Balassa–Samuelson theory*. In simple terms, this theory suggests that growing local economies positively impact productivity rates, which results in those local markets becoming wealthier, with a knock-on effect on local FX rates! For more details, see the nearby sidebar 'Examining the Balassa–Samuelson theory'.

Examining the Balassa–Samuelson theory

The Balassa–Samuelson theory says that local, developing market currencies are essentially moving in only one direction – upwards – as they 'appreciate' in value in relation to developed-world currencies. In most economic models, differences in labour productivity between developing and developed economies drive inflation adjusted exchange-rate appreciation, so that a 1 per cent difference in productivity rates in favour of an EM relative to an Organisation for Economic Co-operation and Development (OECD) country leads to a higher real exchange rate relative to the OECD country by 1 per cent.

In other words, this theory suggests that relatively high productivity growth in the tradable export sector of most EM states results in higher wages paid to those workers. These labour market transformations (for instance, skilled workers become scarce with an inevitable increase in their wages) lead to a rise in the price of domestic (non-tradable) prices and thus real exchange rate appreciation for the developing country. Furthermore, because most EM economies now have inflation targets (both explicit and implicit), most of this real appreciation comes via adjusted current value and steady (incremental) appreciation rather than inflation.

If you think that this academic theory works – as many hedge funds do – consider buying local EM currencies because they're going to increase in value over time compared to developed-world currencies.

You may be wondering whether this neat-sounding strategy works in the real world of messy economies. The short answer seems to be an unambiguous 'yes'! Research by economists suggests that a robust and stable positive relationship does exist between real income per capita (driven by productivity growth) and the real exchange rate. But some important caveats remain about this convergence-trading theory:

- ✔ This trade doesn't work as well if it's based on a credit boom or if the rate of economic growth is excessively above its 'natural', or expected, rate as warranted by the underlying rate of return on capital and labour.

- ✔ This effectiveness of the trade seems to wax and wane over time. According to one study, the Balassa–Samuelson theory, which suggests that a positive correlation exists between growing local economies, productivity rates and FX rates, was less applicable during the 1970s and early 1980s than it is today. In previous decades the correlation seemed to fade because of heavy exchange-rate management by local, developing-world governments. Less prosperous countries artificially elevated exchange rates higher than the underlying economic fundamentals would typically warrant. In essence, currencies were overvalued relative to income, and this resulted in periodic currency crises.

- ✔ This theory varies greatly on a country-by-country basis. Some nations such as South Korea appear to have experienced currency appreciation exactly as expected, but others such as Argentina experienced stagnation and then a decline in the convergence process.

Carrying on trading

Not all currency trades that hedge funds use are based on convergence (as with the Balassa–Samuelson theory in the preceding section). A much bigger set of strategies is based around some form of carry trade – an idea I also mention in Chapter 5.

All carry trades are based on a simple premise: those assets that offer the highest returns to investment in general attract the most capital. Countries are no different and in the world of FX, the carry trade is an easy way to take advantage of this basic economic principle.

Carry trades involve investors buying a currency that offers a high interest rate while selling a currency that offers a low interest rate. They're profitable because an investor is able to earn the difference in interest – the *spread* – between the two currencies. Carry trades work because of the constant movement of capital in and out of countries, with interest rates the chief driver of money flows into an economy. If a country's economy is doing well (high growth, high productivity, low unemployment, rising incomes and so on), it offers investors in it a higher return on investment.

A carry trade is a long-term strategy. Before entering into one, you have to be willing to commit to a time-horizon of at least six months.

Seeing the carry trade in action

Assume that the New Zealand dollar (NZD) offers an interest rate of 5.25 per cent, while the Norwegian krona (NOK) offers a rate of 0.50 per cent. To execute the carry trade, you buy the NZD and sell the NOK. In doing so, you earn a profit of 4.75 per cent (5.25 per cent in interest earned minus 0.50 per cent in interest paid), as long as the exchange rate between these two currencies doesn't change.

So the basics of this trade are as follows:

- **Long NZD position:** You earn 5.25 per cent.
- **Short NOK position:** You pay 0.50 per cent.
- **Spot rate holds constant:** Your profit is 4.75 per cent, or 475 basis points.

To help understand the mechanisms powering this trade, take a step back and examine how a carry trade may be run using local bank deposits and loans in the two countries.

Picture a fairly sullen investor in Norway, grinding his teeth at an interest rate of 0.50 per cent per year on his local bank deposit. He rings up his FX broker and asks what rate New Zealand banks are paying on their local dollar deposit accounts. He gasps in horror as he discovers that the lucky Kiwis are getting 5.25 per cent.

Seeing that interest rates are much higher with the New Zealand bank, the Norwegian investor is suddenly motivated to find a way to get some money into a NZD account! Now imagine that the investor can somehow trade his deposit of NOK paying 0.50 per cent for a deposit of NZD paying 5.25 per cent. Effectively, he 'sells' his NOK deposit, so that he can 'buy' an NZD deposit. After this transaction he owns an NZD deposit that pays 5.25 per cent in interest per year, 4.75 per cent more than the rate on offer from his NOK account: score!

With millions of people doing this transaction at a national level, capital flows out of Norway and into New Zealand as investors take their krona and trade them for New Zealand dollars. New Zealand attracts more capital because of the higher rates it offers. This inflow of capital thus increases the value of the currency.

Understanding risk aversion

If the carry-trade strategy sounds relatively simple, that's because it is. When it works, it works like clockwork. But, unsurprisingly, occasionally the carry trade breaks down . . . and when that happens investors lose a great deal of money. The main challenge is that when investors start to worry aggressively about risk at the global level – called *risk aversion* – they tend to pull money from carry-trade strategies. The cause of this extra risk can be anything from a Middle East oil crisis to a panic about government defaults. But whatever the cause, the reaction is usually very straightforward – anything regarded as risky, such as carry trades, falls over!

In order to work properly, the carry trade requires investors to be confident enough to take on the risk of investing in the higher-interest rate currency in a typical FX pair. When investors are risk averse they usually prefer to put their money in safe-haven currencies that pay lower interest rates; that is, the exact opposite of the carry trade.

For example, in the summer of 1998 the Japanese yen appreciated against the US dollar by over 20 per cent in the span of two months, mainly as a result of the Russian debt crisis and the Long-Term Capital Management (LTCM) hedge-fund bailout amounting to more than US$3.6 billion. Similarly, just after the 11 September 2001 terrorist attacks, the Swiss franc rose by more than 7 per cent against the US dollar over a ten-day period.

Country trade balances (the difference between imports and exports) can also affect the profitability of a carry trade.

Measuring investor risk aversion with a single number is difficult. One method you can use to get a broad idea of the risk aversion levels is to look at the different yields that bonds pay. The wider the difference (the spread) between bonds of different credit ratings, the higher the investor risk aversion:

- ✓ **Low risk aversion:** Carry trades are most profitable.
- ✓ **High risk aversion:** Carry trades are least profitable.

Getting down to fundamentals: Purchasing-power parity

Long-term focused investors often use ideas derived from fundamentals economic data to see whether a currency is fairly valued relative to its peers, and in particular whether FX rates adequately reflect local inflation rates. At the core of this fundamentals-driven strategy is an economic theory called *purchasing-power parity* (PPP).

This theory suggests that the exchange rate between two currencies (and thus two countries) is in equilibrium when their domestic purchasing powers (at that rate of exchange) are equivalent. Put simply, a bundle of goods should cost the same in two countries such as Canada and the US when you look at the exchange rate between those two countries.

The key insight of this theory is that price differentials for the same goods in different countries are unsustainable in the long run because market forces equalise prices between countries, forcing the exchange rate between the two currencies to play catch-up. The market forces this readjustment through the great motor of free trade in goods and services between nations, which inevitably impacts and equalises prices between the two countries.

An offshoot of the purchasing-power parity concept, *relative purchase-power parity* predicts the relationship between the inflation rate and the currency exchange rate between two countries. In essence, the theory suggests that, as a country's inflation rate rises, the value of its currency falls.

Watching PPP in action: Anyone for a whiskey?

To understand why and how the PPP theory can be so powerful, consider an example focusing on two countries with a long border and a shared love of free markets: the US and its northern neighbour, Canada. Suppose that US$1 is currently selling for C$2 on the exchange-rate market.

Imagine a busy trade in whiskey between these two countries. In the US, a bottle of whiskey sells for US$40 while in Canada it sells for C$100. At the exchange rate (US$1 = C$2) the bottle costs US$40 in the US, but the equivalent of US$50 if bought in Canada (C$100 ÷ US$2 = US$50). Clearly an advantage exists to buying the whiskey in the US, and so Canadian consumers are better off travelling to the States to purchase their hooch. If they decide to do so, you'd expect to see a number of changes begin to happen, almost overnight, if free trade exists between the two countries:

1. Canadian consumers snap up US dollars in order to buy the whiskey in the US.

2. Lots of US dollars being bought causes the US dollar to become valuable relative to the Canadian dollar.

3. The demand for whiskey bottles sold in Canada decreases, and so the price local retailers charge starts to go down.

4. The demand for whiskey bottles sold in the US increases, and so the price retailers charge goes up.

Eventually these varying factors should cause the exchange rates to converge, meaning that prices in the two countries begin to change so that PPP is established. If the Canadian dollar declines in value to US$1 = C$2.50, the price of a whiskey bottle in Canada goes down to US$40 (US$40 × C$2.5 = C$100).

This example demonstrates that in the long run having different prices in the US and Canada isn't sustainable, because an individual or company can gain an arbitrage profit by buying the good cheaply in one market and selling it for a higher price in the other market.

Many investors use the PPP theory to drive an FX strategy, betting that the relationship between two currencies is going to change over time as the PPP theory drives a readjustment. All sorts of indices chart the theory, the most easily accessible of which is that provided by *The Economist*. Many hedge funds run a long-term PPP-driven strategy betting that some countries have an overvalued currency (they probably short these currencies) while some currencies are woefully undervalued (they probably long these ones).

Perusing the perils of PPP

This PPP strategy doesn't always work out quite as planned. The world doesn't have completely free trade and thus local bottlenecks in terms of prices can remain for many years because of import and export restrictions. In addition, moving goods across borders costs money to arbitrage away the opportunities.

Sometimes the cost of travel between two countries, combined with the existence of a large amount of trade in perishable goods, means that prices between countries don't move as expected. After all, even if the price of local salads is markedly different between two countries, no one would bother with the effort of moving fresh lettuce around the world; the salad may even go off after a few days and still cost a fortune to transport.

Chapter 15

Investing Macro Style: Seeing the Big Picture

. . . .

. . . .

*T*he economic rates that I discuss in Chapter 4 – interest rates, gross domestic product (GDP) growth rates and inflation rates – have an enormous influence on the way that modern financial markets operate. These rates tend to ebb and flow, usually causing (or as part of) regional or global economic cycles. This big-picture scenario is called *macro-economics*, and it looks at all the disparate economic factors as a way to understand the behaviour of the economy as a whole. Therefore, macro-economic strategies are ones in which investment approaches in shares, bonds, commodities and foreign exchanges (FX) are determined by key macro-economic signals.

In this chapter I provide an introduction to the macro-investment approach, take a closer look at bonds (which, as tools used by central banks to direct their economies, react fairly predictably to macro-economic trends), lay out the risks involved and discuss some of the macro hedge funds that you may want to emulate.

Checking out Macro-Economic Basics

To understand how interest rates, GDP growth rates and inflation rates interact with each other, consider a simple example. In periods of economic optimism, economies experience strong GDP growth, with rates increasing 3–10 per cent per year: the lower rates represent long-term trend rates for leading developed-world economies, such as the UK and US, whereas the latter double-digit returns aren't uncommon in many developing countries. But as these growth rates increase, economies 'heat up' and capacity constraints emerge.

In fast-expanding economies you'd reasonably expect bottlenecks to multiply in sectors such as construction, housing, energy and food. Those bottlenecks involve rapid increases in local prices and wages, which in turn push up inflation rates. Unfortunately, high inflation rates (especially those above 10 per cent per year) end up having a huge negative impact on the local economy, with central bankers usually quick to intervene by increasing interest rates to control local price rises.

Eventually, interest rates can hit such high levels that growth rates collapse, construction stops and businesses stop investing. Local economic growth peaks (along with interest rates) and then starts to fall sharply, plunging the local economy into a recession. As this recession bites, interest rates also start to fall sharply as do inflation rates. A trough is reached, and central bankers try to encourage a renewal of growth, with very low interest rates and government fiscal expansion through heavy state spending. With luck the economy picks up.

This cycle of growth, recession and recovery is repeated time and time again at both the global and national level.

Thinking about the impact on investments

What's crucial for investors to understand is how the cycle impacts or even in some sense synchronises with local bond, equity, commodity and FX markets. In other words, what effect does a sudden switch in economic activity have on the price of a local equity or on FX rates? Are local equity markets entirely synchronised with the growth rate or is a lag of some sort involved as local investors react to changes in growth?

Many academics and hedge funds have explored the idea of interconnectedness and synchronicity between macro-economic cycles and financial markets. In simple terms, they want to see whether using key macro-economic signals can help you work out how different shares or financial markets are going to respond to changes in the economy. Research firm Parala is one such company fusing academic thinking about economic cycles with investment strategies that look to switch between different asset classes (shares, bonds and commodities) or equity sectors. The charts in Figures 15-1 to 15-3 show how these myriad economic and business processes are interconnected and why as an investor you need to think about the big picture.

Figure 15-1 shows the ebb and flow of the US-based ISM index and the Reuters CRB Commodity index. Although the two indices aren't perfectly synchronised, you can clearly see the relationship between the two signals. (The ISM index monitors new orders and production among US manufacturers and the CRB Commodity index looks at the price of a range of futures-based commodity prices including oil and foodstuffs.)

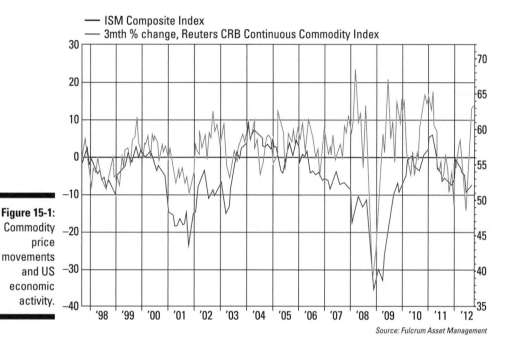

— ISM Composite Index
— 3mth % change, Reuters CRB Continuous Commodity Index

Figure 15-1: Commodity price movements and US economic activity.

Source: Fulcrum Asset Management

The key message from Figure 15-1 is the close relationship between US manufacturing output (as measured by the ISM) and commodity price indices; that is, as US industrial output increases, you expect an increase in the price of commodities.

This relationship is confirmed by Figure 15-2, which looks at another industrial confidence indicator: the US Purchasing Managers Index (PMI) and the S&P GSCI Commodity Futures index (a rival to the CRB index). Again, the relationship is close but not synchronised.

An increase in manufacturing orders and industrial confidence in the core US market is likely to result in a sharp increase in the price of commodity futures.

Figure 15-3 looks at the relationship between the ISM index again and the benchmark equity index, the S&P 500. Again, a clear relationship exists between industrial growth and equity prices; that is, the price of shares is heavily influenced by wider macro-economic factors.

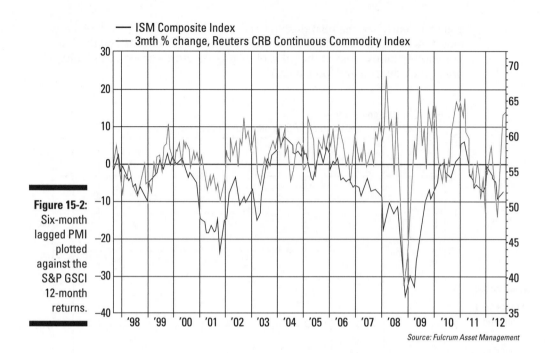

Figure 15-2: Six-month lagged PMI plotted against the S&P GSCI 12-month returns.

Source: Fulcrum Asset Management

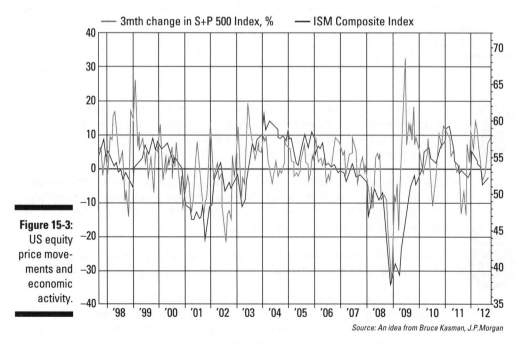

Figure 15-3: US equity price movements and economic activity.

Source: An idea from Bruce Kasman, J.P.Morgan

Many analysts believe that equity markets are indeed closely correlated with changes in industrial and GDP growth, but that this relationship usually involves equity investors pushing up share prices *ahead* of a growth upturn; that is, they attempt to price in a recovery in share prices at least six months before an actual upturn confirmed by data such as the ISM corporate index.

Analysts such as Parala take the thinking about the connectedness of macro-economic signals to different asset classes and apply it to individual equity sectors and even individual stocks. According to Parala, *pro-cyclical* sectors, such as technology or durable goods, outperform the broad market during macro-economic expansions, whereas *counter-cyclicals*, such as staples or precious metals, insure investors against recessions. Parala also believes that:

> *While a broad-based labelling of sectors and securities as being 'pro' or 'counter' with business cycles is somewhat useful in portfolio formation, a more precise identification of the underlying statistical and economic relations has the potential of generating much greater outperformance and lower attendant portfolio risk.*

This type of research shows that, above all, despite their best intentions investors are slow to react to corporate news and developments in the macro-economy. Some analysts think that this slow response is because of a reluctance to take aggressive positions because of the career risk involved; that is, few fund managers have ever been fired for failing to predict a recession! As a result, many fund managers hold on to their losers at the beginning of a downturn and then oversell their winners as the recession bottoms out.

Parala and other macro-based researchers want to identify a small but reliable set of macro-economic indicators that can help you build a robust portfolio of shares, bonds and commodities. They then build these into a series of multi-asset class Dow Jones indices: see these indices in action at `http://www.djindexes.com/macroallocation`.

Like many of its peers, the Parala analysis is constantly changing largely because risk factors change a great deal and can be highly dynamic. Macro-economic variables also vary over time. In other words, these signals can be useful but they don't always work.

Using macro risk to consider your investments: The Investor Dashboard

An alternative way of pulling together disparate trends and cycles is to look through the prism of risk. Table 15-1 shows the Investor Dashboard that's available online every month at `www.portfolioreviewonline.com`. It was developed with an ex-hedge-fund manager called Nick Bullman, who runs a research-based consultancy called Check-Risk focused on risk.

The key for Check-Risk (and its long list of pension-fund clients) is that investors need to avoid the major blowouts in risk, when volatility spikes upwards and shares in particular sustain major losses. According to Check-Risk, no single indicator can spot these sudden moves in the market, just a series of behavioural measures, as well as macro-economic indicators, technical measures and volatility indices.

According to Check-Risk, you need to look at the full range of measures *in the whole* and then monitor the *quantum* of change, indicating both the speed and size of the change, in each measure over time.

That thinking lies behind Table 15-1, which looks at a range of measures for the month starting May 2011 but with a particular focus on changes in the measures of risk. In essence the investor needs to skim along each line to look at the colour of the risk assessment; that is, the traffic light signals. A series of reds indicates that risk is building within the economic and financial system, whereas lots of greens tells you that markets are confident and buoyant.

If you use tables like the Investor Dashboard, do so regularly and make only small changes to your portfolio. Don't overtrade based on a change in one simple measure. Instead, as more indicators flash red (indicating more volatility and an economic slowdown), start to think about minimising portfolio risk, taking profits, increasing cash and possibly buying secure assets such as US Treasury government securities.

Table 15-1			Investor Risk Dashboard for 1 May 2011				
	Price	*1 Month Percentage Change*	*ACC/ DEC**	*Better/ Worse*	*Direction Change?*	*Status*	*Risk Assessment*
Behavioural Risk Factors							
Periphery Europe Sovereign CDS	609.87	20.68%	ACC	↘	No	Severe	Red
Sovereign UK CDS	57.53	10.21%	ACC	↘	Yes	Moderate	Amber
FTSE Volatility (VFTSE)	15.05	−2.39%	DEC	↘	No	Severe	Red
FTSE Insider Buying and Selling	2.46:1	3.35:1	DEC	↘	No	Benign	Green
Nationwide Consumer Confidence	44	15.78%	ACC	↘	Yes	Moderate	Amber
FTSE Volume Ratio (UKX/Volume)	8.32	27.21%	ACC	↘	Yes	Moderate	Amber
Real Risk Factors							
London Interbank Spread OIS	0.27	50%	ACC	↘	Yes	Moderate	Amber
US TED Spread	23.75	−3.14%	DEC	↘	Yes	Mod/Sev	Red
Gold	1563.7	7.31%	ACC	↘	No	Severe	Red
WTI Crude Oil	111.74	2.70%	ACC	↘	No	Mod/Sev	Red
FTSE Dividend Index Future	198.8	0.45%	DEC	↘	No	Severe	Red
Baltic Dry Index	1269	−17.05%	ACC	↘	Yes	Mod/Sec	Red
Other Factors							
Gold/Silver Ratio	36.79	−0.35%	DEC	↘	No	Severe	Red
FTSE 100 20 / 200 day moving average	Above	1.17% (20 DMA)	NR	↘	Yes	Moderate	Amber
Robert Shiller CAPE for S&P 500	24.23	1.04%	ACC	↘	Yes	Mod/Sev	Red

* ACC = Accelerating; DEC = Decelerating

Understanding the Importance of Bonds

Implementing an investment strategy using macro-economic signals, even one based around risk as I describe in the earlier section 'Using macro risk to consider your investments: The Investor Dashboard', is relatively easy – at least in theory:

1. **Buy shares if you think the economy is booming and growth rates are heading upwards, and then stock up on commodities as inflation intensifies.**

2. **Sell stocks and commodities as growth stalls and start buying bonds, especially government gilts.**

3. **Start buying shares again as the recession bottoms out, on the expectation that growth is going to resume.**

I detail this asset-allocation cycle in Chapter 5. But the earlier section 'Thinking about the impact on investments' suggests that perfect synchronicity doesn't exist between markets and economic signals and that many managers are slow in responding to clear signals about, say, risk. Also, equity markets try to get ahead of any move upwards in the economy; that is, they're probably about six months ahead of any firm data indicating an economic recovery.

In reality, a great deal of informational noise – much of it contradictory and potentially misleading – surrounds risk, macro signals and financial assets. Equities in particular can be very volatile and sometimes share prices are moved by factors that have nothing to do with interest, inflation or GDP growth rates, or economic/business cycles. For instance, investors sometimes get worried about legislation and its impact on a particular sector or they get excited by the prospect of a massive increase in merger and acquisition (M&A) activity.

For these reasons, many institutional investors prefer to use bonds as a better indicator of wider macro signals and risk measures, rather than shares. Bonds and especially government securities tend to react very quickly to the macro-economic signals and risk measures I discuss in this chapter.

Bonds are largely regarded as being lower-risk investments than shares, which is why they're so popular with big institutions such as pension funds and central banks. Huge numbers of bonds have been issued, which means that bond markets are extremely liquid (lots of buyers, sellers and securities), deep and global. Bonds are also hugely popular with hedge funds because trading costs are low and transparency high.

Bond investors are very influenced by macro signals, reacting in a fairly synchronised way to measures that suggest a downturn is on its way or inflation is about to increase. Macro-economic signals that indicate a recession are usually positive for bond pricing whereas inflation is bad news for bond prices.

Here's a very simplistic explanation for this tendency: central banks attempt to keep their economies on an even keel, and they use macro-economic indicators to plan economic policy. When the economy begins to stall, central banks will buy bonds as a way to inject cash into the economy. In so doing, interest rates will fall, bond prices will increase (because of the increased demand) and more businesses and people will begin to buy and invest. Conversely, when central banks need to remove cash from the economy to control rising inflation, they will sell bonds, which increases interest rates, reduces demand and pushes down prices, thus reducing inflation.

For these reasons bonds are an important component for macro-economic investing: First, they're the proverbial canary in the coal mine: by watching what's happening in the bond market, you can get an early indicator of what's going on in the market as a whole – info that you can use when designing your strategy. Second, they form a key part of a diversified investment portfolio.

Bonding with bond basics

Bonds are fairly simple to understand:

- ✔ Bonds are essentially an IOU by an issuer (a government or large corporation) who borrows money from you.

- ✔ The IOU consists of a promise to repay you the principal at some point in the future (at maturity, when the bond is redeemed) and along the way you also receive a regular income called a *coupon*.

- ✔ This coupon gives you a yield (the coupon interest rate against the asking price for the bond), which you can then compare to the yields from other bonds.

Bond investors are relatively simple folk. They care enormously about capital preservation (getting their money back) and aren't hugely worried about making an enormous capital gain (unlike equity investors who tend to be very focused on capital gains). They want the certainty of getting repaid in the future and being rewarded with a decent, sensible income along the way that's sufficient to cover the risks of lending.

Seeing the risks for bond investors

The global bond markets are truly massive, with trading levels and deal sizes that tower above equity markets. Many hedge funds prefer to trade in bonds precisely because of this huge scale and depth as well as the relatively lower levels of risk. But investing in bonds isn't risk-free:

- ✔ **Inflation** is bad news for bond investors (although bonds that pay a yield linked to inflation indices do offer much more protection). For the most part your interest coupon is fixed to maturity, and so any increase in inflation rates means that you're getting less real income (that is, after the impact of inflation). Most bonds perform terribly in a high-inflation environment.

- ✔ **Credit risk** is a large concern for investors (flip to the later section 'Determining credit risk' for more).

More precisely, bond investors worry about the following issues:

- ✔ Will the bond holder get repaid: that is, what's the default risk at maturity? (Check out the later section 'Measuring the Risk of Bond Default'.)

- ✔ How does the coupon yield compare to other rates from other issuers: that is, are bond investors being adequately rewarded for taking on the risk of default?

- ✔ Is the yield comfortably above current inflation rates?

- ✔ How senior is their specific claim if the worst happens and the issuer defaults: that is, what security exists for one bond against any assets?

- ✔ Do they pay the original issue price (*at par*, as it's called), a premium or is the bond priced below its issue price (which tends to indicate that some concern exists that investors may not be repaid in full)?

Bonds don't always trade at the issue (par) price. Worries about the different levels of risk that comes with different issuers can massively affect prices. If you think a default is even remotely possible, you bid down the price to below par. If you think that the risk level is low and the income yield wonderfully high, you bid up the price above par.

Bond investors worry terrifically about *balance-sheet* risk, meaning that they minutely inspect an issuer's assets and liabilities and the accompanying cash flows. They look for any indication of insufficient cash income to pay the regular income coupons. They also worry that balance-sheet stress indicates future credit risk.

All these worries often push bond investors towards a determined *diversification strategy*. They consciously make sure that they have a mix of different risk levels, yields and issuers. As worries about macro levels of risk increase, they may for instance sell any bonds regarded as a tad risky (corporate bonds, emerging-market bonds) and focus instead on government securities. Equally, if a sudden financial shock looks imminent, many bond investors switch into short-duration government securities as an alternative to holding cash in the banking system; that is, they run their cash operations by investing in gilts that mature in the next few months.

By contrast, if worries about systemic financial meltdown start to fade away, bond investors look to diversify by investing in riskier assets such as corporate bonds or even bonds issued by emerging-market governments and large corporations (see the next section).

Emerging from the shadows: Developing-nation bonds

In Chapter 14, I note that more and more hedge funds are beginning to focus on emerging markets. This growing international diversification is echoed by bond investors: emerging-market bonds have grown massively in popularity over the last decade! Many investors seem to have overcome worries about developing-world countries defaulting on their debts and now view emerging markets as potentially stronger than their developed-world peers.

This new-found confidence in emerging markets can't hide the fact that many developing countries still have weak national balance sheets. Although many of these governments don't owe as much as the US or UK governments, the corporate sector is still heavily in debt in many nations.

One novel take on this challenge comes from a London-based hedge fund called Stratton Street, which has set a Wealthy Nations Bond fund working in partnership with private bank EFG. This fund is trying to capitalise on a specific opportunity based on value considerations: it focuses its investment selection criteria only on bonds from countries where overall levels of indebtedness are low and yields relatively high. The fund uses a scoring system called WONDA (see the nearby sidebar 'Wealthy Nations Bond scoring system') that produces a hierarchy of 'favoured nations'.

TECHNICAL STUFF

Wealthy Nations Bond scoring system

The WONDA scoring system boasts a number of overlays to help work out a nation's score. These measures are built around a nation's balance sheet and its net foreign asset position: that is, the analysts look at the total domestic liabilities and assets and compare them with the foreign, external balance sheet. The fund's researchers are looking to see if a country owns a great many assets internationally that may be much bigger than its domestic debts.

The system also looks at the relative value of the bonds on the market (are the bonds good value when compared to other issuers) as well as key macro-economic indicators. The resulting scoring system eventually produces a graph which looks at the net foreign assets of selected countries (in green; those with net liabilities are in red) versus the total GDP.

TIP

The overlays used by the WONDA system produce a bias towards oil-rich states. Countries such as Qatar and the United Arab Emirates are clearly not going to have problems paying down their debt – their net foreign debt position is incredibly low and they have oodles of foreign assets.

Russia is another example of this relative-value-based overlay built on macro-economic analysis. Mention Russian top-tier debt (that is, the loans it will pay off first in the event of default) and most investors think you're crazy, but according to Stratton Street, Russia has low overall total levels of debt and the government has explicitly said that it will back the debt of its largest state-owned companies. That doesn't necessarily apply all the way down the pecking order to smaller entities, but Stratton believe that the elevated yields on offer more than compensate for the extra (in their opinion, low) risk with investment grade debt.

TIP

The Stratton Street fund pays close to 6 per cent per year in income (at least 300 basis points above most UK gilts or bonds). (*Note:* Basis points, which are equal to 1/100th of 1 per cent, are used to note the degree of change in interest rates and financial instruments.)

Measuring the Risk of Bond Default

Bond investors worry about risk and in particular the chance of issuers defaulting on their bonds (which usually means that bond investors don't get their money back). Therefore, concerns about default (plus future inflation rates) have a huge impact on bond pricing.

In fact, many bond investors are more paranoid than virtually any other kind of investor and are reluctant to take on extra risks. Unlike most equity investors, who accept risks such as shares going up and down and companies stopping and restarting dividends in return for potential extra returns, bonds are supposed to be safer and less volatile in terms of price – which also helps explain why returns on bonds have been more modest over the last few decades.

Unsurprisingly, therefore, investors in bonds require reliable ways of measuring risk.

Determining credit risk

Credit-risk measurement is available through the research of a number of different credit rating agencies – namely S&P, Moody's and Fitch. Each of the agencies has its own specific measures and methodology, but all produce ratings that tend to cluster together and roughly mean the same thing. Table 15-2 compares the ratings as they move from the highest grade (safest), which is usually AAA, through to the lowest grade, which is a company in default (usually marked C or D).

These ratings can change over time. For example, the government of South Korea found itself downgraded from AA– to BBB– in just a few years.

Central to this dynamic process is regular research. Here's S&P's research process in some detail:

1. **Issuer requests a rating prior to sale or registration of a debt issue.**

2. **S&P analysts conduct basic research, including meeting issuers to review in detail the key operating and financial plans, management policies and other credit factors that impact the rating.**

3. **Analysts present findings to S&P rating committee of five to seven expert voting members.**

4. **Rating committee decides rating.**

5. **Issuer notified and has the opportunity to appeal prior to the rating publication.**

6. **Rating published.**

7. **S&P monitors issuers for at least one year from date of publication; issuers can elect to pay S&P to continue surveillance thereafter.**

Table 15-2	Differences between Bond Credit Ratings from Different Agencies		
	Moody's[1]	**S&P[2]**	**Fitch IBCA[2]**
Investment grade			
Highest grade	Aaa	AAA	AAA
High quality (very strong)	Aa	AA	AA
Upper medium grade (strong)	A	A	A
Not investment grade			
Lower medium grade	Ba	BB	BB
Low grade (speculative)	B	B	B
Poor quality and may default	Caa	CCC	CCC
Very speculative	Ca	CC	CC
No interest being paid or bankruptcy	C	D	C
In default	C	D	D

[1]The ratings from Aa to Ca by Moody's can be modified by adding 1, 2 or 3 to show relative stature of the company

[2]The ratings from AA to CC by S&P and Fitch may be modified by adding a plus or minus sign to show the relative strength within the band

Insuring with CDSs

The credit ratings that I describe in the preceding section aren't the only measures for assessing the risk of default. Many investors, especially in the institutional space, also use credit-risk measures based on swaps, which in turn price in the likelihood of default. These financial instruments are known as *credit default swap* (CDS) spreads and were first introduced in 1997. They're essentially an agreement between two parties (based on bonds) to insure the face value of the assets (their original value at issue) if anything goes wrong, such as a default: this arrangement is called the *reference obligation*.

On a very simplified level, swaps are a form of insurance in which the seller offers protection against default to a buyer who wants to insure against the risk of a debtor going bust. That insurance or protection comes with a fee attached to it – when the buyer pays that fee the CDS compensates the seller if a credit event (a default, for instance) hits the borrower.

Credit default swaps are quoted in the market as an annualised percentage spread, over LIBOR, known as the CDS spread. For example, the CDS spread quoted for a bond issued by XYZ company may be 100 basis points (bps). If the CDS buyer wants to protect a US$10 million investment in an XYZ bond, the buyer has to pay the CDS seller an annual fee of US$100,000 (typically paid quarterly).

Table 15-3 (from UK-based financial services firm Catley Lakeman) shows the current range for CDS spreads associated with the largest UK-based banks as well as debts issued by leading developed-world governments. This wealth of information reveals that some banks (and governments) are seen as more trustworthy in terms of their bonds than others, but remember that the cost of this insurance can change radically over time.

As you read this table, keep these points in mind:

- ✔ **Five Year:** The averaged CDS spread over a period of five years, shown in basis points.

- ✔ **Year End 2011:** The CDS spread at the end of 2011, in basis points.

- ✔ **Tier 1 Capital %:** A measure of the bank's financial strength, determined by the bank's core capital (capital from shares and disclosed capital). A capital ratio of 6 per cent or higher is considered well-capitalised.

- ✔ **Rating:** The credit rating S&P assigned to this entity (refer to the preceding section for definitions of the different ratings).

Table 15-3	CDS spreads as at 22 November 2012			
	Five Year	*Year End 2011*	*Tier 1 Capital %*	*Rating*
Bank				
Banco Santander	306.818	353.043	11.01	A
Barclays	158.728	196.701	12.9	A
BNP	161.005	257.937	11.6	A+
Citigroup	148.32	285.49	13.55	A
Credit Suisse	124.57	147.594	18.1	A
HSBC	93.729	142.01	11.5	AA
Lloyds TSB	168.335	341.685	12.5	A
Rabobank	82.411	122.164	17	AA

(continued)

Table 15-3 (continued)

	Five Year	Year End 2011	Tier 1 Capital %	Rating
RBS	187.3	345.508	13	A
Royal Bank of Canada	58.073	101.668	13.3	AA
Soc Gen	191.172	338.978	10.7	A+
Governments				
Argentina	2765.883	921.98		
Brazil	104.503	161.587		
France	88.119	222.296		
Germany	29.995	NA		
Ireland	183.323	726.13		
Norway	19.224	44.281		
Russia	146.947	275.122		
South Africa	164.67	202.067		
Spain	318.515	393.516		
Turkey	143.67	287.087		
United Kingdom	30.34	97.5		
United States	35.68	NA		

Many hedge funds look at the direction or dynamic of the CDS spread and then bet that it will change markedly over time. Loads of hedge funds made a lot of money betting that the CDS spread for Greek sovereign debts would continue to increase while the CDS spreads for state-backed banks in the UK would fall back, when the UK government promised not to let those high-street banks go bust.

Making use of bond correlation

Bonds tend to be highly correlated with each other. If bond investors start selling government gilts, they probably start selling corporate bonds as well. Keep this tendency in mind as you plan your investment strategy.

Table 15-4 shows the correlation between returns from holding different bond-rating categories ranging from ultra safe government AAA securities to corporate sub-investment grade bonds (BBB or less).

Table 15-4   Correlation between Gilts and Corporate Bonds

Bond Rating Category	Average Monthly Correlation with Gilts (%)
AAA	93
AA	90
A	83
BBB	79
Total Investment Grade	90

Bond investors are willing to be opinionated and in effect boss around governments, countries and large corporations. If they start to think that they may not get their money back or that yields are too low for the risk levels, they simply *short* a bond, pushing the price down and interest rates up. Governments can huff and puff about these aggressive bond investors who are willing to black-mark states and companies, but they can't do very much to stop them following a breakdown in trust.

Meeting Macro Hedge Funds

I don't play the game by a particular set of rules; I look for changes in the rules of the game.

George Soros, legendary macro hedge-fund manager

Although many investors obsess about risky assets such as shares, hedge-fund managers are on the whole a fairly dispassionate bunch. They're happy to go long or short any asset class, bonds or shares. Their core concern is to use any asset class to make money in any kind of market.

One particular breed of hedge-fund manager takes this dispassionate, multi-asset class world view and moves it on to a whole new level. Macro-fund managers think across asset classes, and start with a top-down analysis that's inexorably linked to an understanding of how macro-economic factors affect individual markets. In essence, they may start with an analysis of inflation or interest rates in different countries (they're a fairly global bunch) and then work out a strategy that involves trading everything from bonds and FX to shares to express that macro view.

You can see their approach as top-down thinking but applied to different individual markets using a bottom-up analysis. In other words, they use macro factors and examine the individual dynamics of a market or security to look for an investment opportunity.

Macro managers can go long or short, and use leverage to improve their returns. Unlike conventional managers with portfolios full of different, diversified stocks (or bonds), macro managers take concentrated positions – ideally with limited downside but huge potential upside. Their trades usually fall into one of two major categories:

- ✔ **Directional:** Capturing a trend, no matter how fleeting.
- ✔ **Relative value:** One currency, for instance, may be undervalued compared to another.

Many macro funds are also high-frequency traders, responding to news flow such as employment and GDP figures to make a large number of small bets on interest rates and stock and bond prices.

Whichever strategy they use, these macro hedge funds tend to employ a fairly limited number of trading instruments:

- ✔ **FX trading** is usually based around the relative value or strength of one currency versus another. Currency pairs are a staple of the macro trade, and these pairs trades can be executed in markets that are extremely liquid and trade 24 hours a day, 6 days a week, usually based around the interbank market. The leverage involved can amount to as much as 100 times. Favourite ideas include the carry trade and a focus on emerging-market currencies appreciating (see Chapter 14).
- ✔ **Interest rate trading** usually involves global sovereign (government) debt, with lashings of leverage. Strategies include outright directional movements on government debt through to relative value trading in which a portfolio manager trades one debt instrument relative to another.
- ✔ **Equity index trading** is based on a benchmark index such as the S&P 500 and involves everything from simple ordinary shares to index options.

Macro-fund managers are usually looking for long-term shifts in capital flows, that is, big trends. Therefore they take a world view with a medium- to long-term perspective. They also tend to concentrate more on fixed-income products such as bonds and currency markets than on equity or commodity markets.

Judging macro investing's success as a strategy

Macro hedge funds have boomed over the last few decades. Back in the 1990s, just a few well-known pioneers focused on this top-down, macro-economic driven thinking, including George Soros. But their notorious successes encouraged other investors to move into the sector, and within a decade macro investing had become mainstream.

Until fairly recently these macro hedge-fund managers managed to produce some pretty impressive numbers. Over the ten years to September 2010, the Dow Jones Credit Suisse Global Macro Index (an index focused on macro hedge-fund managers only) posted an annualised return of more than 12 per cent, compared to a –0.2 per cent annualised return for the MSCI World Equity Index.

The single biggest reason for these impressive numbers is that macro hedge funds benefit hugely from increased volatility in currencies, interest rates, commodities and equity markets.

Also, the macro strategy has a low correlation to shares. With a low correlation, the assets are neither positively correlated (always move in the same direction) nor negatively correlated (always move in opposite directions). By including assets with low correlation, hedge fund managers can both reduce risk for the portfolio as a whole and invest more aggressively. But a third really important factor is that macro as a strategy performs well when markets are driven by overall macro-economic themes rather than by individual bottom-up fundamental analysis. And that's precisely what happened in the last decade, as markets globalised and everyone became a macro-economic expert!

Macro hedge funds are in their element in a world where currencies freely float, countries encourage free trade, and capital import and export restrictions are relaxed. These unfixed FX regimes are likely to be volatile, and trading is also helped along by innovative new options-based financial structures, such as swaps and derivatives.

Watching macro investing in action

Macro hedge-fund investors think big! They're global in scope, willing to use different asset classes whenever appropriate and, crucially, likely to be internally organised in a very different way compared to rival strategies. Most successful macro funds are run as funds of funds, where risk capital is spread out among different styles, markets and countries but all under one roof with a centralised risk control function.

Macro hedge-fund managers have another peculiar focus: as traders they like to get in early to catch a key trend or investment idea and then tend to exit before a market finally turns; that is, shoots up or down in value by a substantial margin.

Other unique characteristics for macro hedge-fund traders include:

✔ Their portfolios are usually very liquid and their funds generally offer investors redemption terms that reflect this liquidity.

✔ They tend to make most of their money when volatility (in FX, bonds or shares) increases; that is, they tend to perform well during times of increased risk and uncertainty.

✔ They may have dozens of individual positions, but in reality tend to relate to just a few big themes or ideas.

Introducing the major players and their investments

> *Macro investing is all about a 'smart idea, grounded on exhaustive research, followed by a big bet'.*
>
> Julian Robertson, macro hedge-fund manager, `http://` `www.businessweek.com/1996/14/b34691.htm`

> *Our mandate is to find the 200 best companies in the world and invest in them, and find the 200 worst companies in the world and go short on them. If the 200 best don't do better than the 200 worst, you should probably be in another business.*
>
> Julian Robertson, `http://www.investopedia.com/` `university/greatest/julianrobertson.asp`

The best-known global macro funds include George Soros's Quantum Fund, as well as Moore Capital, Caxton Associates, Brevan Howard and Tudor Investment Corporation. The long-term historical record suggests that many of these funds have delivered astonishing returns. For instance, Soros's Quantum Fund returned 30 per cent per year between 1968 and 2000 while Paul Tudor Jones turned in five back-to-back 100 per cent+ years early in his career.

These big numbers have been powered by some even bigger macro investment calls! Back in 1987, for instance, Jones successfully predicted and traded on the collapse of the developed-world stock markets. Five years later, in September 1992, Soros forced the British government to pull the British pound from the European Exchange Rate Mechanism, and in the process famously made US$1 billion.

Soros suggests that a huge trade deficit is frequently accompanied by the government spending more, as well as tight monetary policy (higher interest rates to stem borrowing). If that's the case, a country's currency may rise in value, as the US (dollar) did in the period 1981–1984 as global investors flooded into the US attracted by its tight monetary policy.

But not all macro trades have been quite so successful. Back in 1994 for instance many managers incurred large losses when they made huge, unhedged bets that European interest rates would decline, causing bonds to rise. What happened was that the Federal Reserve *raised* interest rates in the US, pushing up euro interest rates!

Describing recent macro hedge-fund trades

Over the last few years the types of successful trades made by this elite group of managers has been hugely varied. Many managers made a huge amount of money back in 2008/9 betting against Greek debt and then reversed their trade in the next few years by buying into Greek bonds after it became clear that the Eurozone would bail out the government.

Other managers made money in more exotic trades, such as buying dated eurobonds issued by the Ivory Coast government. After a brutal civil war, massive civil unrest and a missed interest payment, these African sovereign bonds collapsed in value (to close to 30 cents on the dollar). Mainstream investors thought the country was about to go bust and sold their state bonds, but some hedge funds concluded that this was short-sighted and that the government would be keen to restart issuing debt when the internal fighting stopped. They were, eventually, right and bond values did bounce back, powering huge profits for some adventurous macro hedge investors.

Macro hedge funds are fairly circumspect about detailing the inner workings of their investment strategies (as you'd expect), which means that you only tend to hear about the big successes (after the fact) and not the long tail of strategies that make no money or lose everything! But you can get a glimpse of the sheer range of strategies and ideas from an article in hedge-fund trade publication, *Funds Europe*. At www.funds-europe.com/latest-news/9673-macro-hedge-fund-strategies-success-in-april you can see a quick summary of typical macro hedge-fund trades during the month of April 2011.

Overall, all the macro funds tracked by this publication showed a profit of 3.36 per cent in the month – much the best return in over two years. The publication reports on data from Hedge Fund Research that points to a number of key trades, including:

- ✔ Short US dollar positioning.

- ✔ Long commodities, particularly silver, natural gas and oil.

- ✔ Strongest equity exposure to stocks in technology and healthcare based on improved earnings and a more positive consumer outlook.

- ✔ Asian-focused hedge funds experienced steady gains.

Copying macro hedge-fund trades

To help you see whether you can get a little of the macro hedge-fund action, in this section I describe some trades and traders.

Panicking over the euro

In January 2011, an online blogger reported an encounter with a senior trader at one of the world's largest macro hedge funds (the full blog is at `http://simonkerrhfblog.blogspot.co.uk/2011/01/global-macro-trading-examples-of-set.html`). Though anything blogged is to be taken with a touch of salt, this is a rare and convincing glimpse into how macro hedge-fund managers make money. The article looked at one simple idea and how a big macro trade was implemented. The trade focused on the relationship between two currencies (the dollar and the euro) in 2010.

As I discuss in Chapter 14, a number of key economic drivers are available to benchmark FX rates such as those between the euro and the dollar. Valuations are supported by key fundamentals such as the PPP theory, popularised by the Big Mac Index. Interest rate differentials are also crucially important, as is the policy environment; that is, what the central bankers may do next to stabilise or 'protect' a currency.

As the blogger notes, 'great macro trades have [usually] been set up by governments attempting to talk down markets when their policy objectives clash with what the markets discount as sustainable'.

Here are the crucial aspects of the blog. The year 2010 proved to be a classic trade in the FX markets. The rate between the euro and the dollar varied substantially between a high of US$1.18 to the euro and a low of US$1.45. Then, suddenly, the Greek crisis came along and everyone panicked about the possible demise of the euro! But then an equally unexpected event arrived (unexpected except by most hedge-fund traders): the US economy slowed down. This was swiftly followed by yet more quantitative easing by the US Federal Reserve, which served to disillusion dollar investors.

But Europe can always be relied upon to have the last word, as worries about Greece started spreading to Portugal and then Spain.

For hedge-fund investors, a series of notable turning points and moments of revelation often occur that aren't widely reported and certainly not seized on by most ordinary institutional or private investors at the time. In this 2010 situation, the blog reveals that these turning points and revelations included the following:

✔ A close look at the macro-economic data and market reports would have showed very high levels of dollar short positions 'just before the [US] monthly employment report for July 2010 released on the 6 August 2010'.

✔ Pattern recognition became crucial for hedge-fund traders, and in particular:

the break in the multi-quarter uptrend for the Euro (versus the Dollar) that occurred in December 2009. The Greek debt crisis powered the multi-month fall in the Euro which lasted into the middle of 2010. The break in trend of itself is often a good entry point for a trade but also [the hedge fund manager must also] identify the second and third high quality entry points.

✔ Many hedge-fund managers focused on assessing market sentiment, especially by tracking WWW search traffic. The particular fund discussed in the blog 'monitored the occurrence of the phrase "quantitative easing" on the web in August, September and October to ascertain the degree of dominance in the minds of investors'. The blogger notes that, 'global macro trading is often about assessing the persistence of action by the various actors in the market drama'.

✔ Managers also looked for a trigger. In particular, many traders looked at how the S&P 500 equity index moved in a very different direction to US FX rates: 'over the first few trading days of August the S&P was flat whilst the euro was still appreciating against the dollar'. This divergence between two well-known signals was hugely important and a great clue about market behaviour: 'a correlation break that lasts for one-to-two days . . . can indicate a movement to follow that lasts for 2–3 months'.

Briefing on Brevan Howard

One of the leading macro fund managers in London is Brevan Howard, now the largest hedge-fund manager in Europe and run by the legendary Alan Howard. A very experienced trader and notorious investment pessimist, Howard has dedicated much of his professional career to making sure that he's always minimising his risk. In fact he's such a cautious type that he reputedly refuses to deposit cash at investment banks overnight, preferring the reliability of short duration US government Treasury Bills.

That innate attention to detail around 'safety' extends to Brevan Howard's assorted trading strategies across the business, with risk managers ruthlessly enforcing a house view that when an investment strategy doesn't pay off, traders cut their position quickly to reduce downside risk. Traders within Brevan Howard are also provided with written agendas directing them to steer clear of certain markets to minimise risk.

Brevan Howard has built up an enviable record in recent years, turning in solid positive numbers for much of the last decade. Apart from the firm's innate caution, working out what the fund has been up to is difficult, although newspaper reports suggest that the various Brevan Howard funds did make significant gains betting against Greek bonds back in 2008 and 2009. Other more recent reports from 2011 and 2012 suggest that the managers have increased exposure to gold..

Looking for really big bets in the future

Like it or not, the decisions of central bankers and politicians move markets. Many investors are sufficiently spooked by this omnipotent power that they engage in a dangerous game of Risk On Risk Off (nicknamed RoRo). When central bankers loosen monetary policies, risk is back on and everyone seems to flock to shares. But sometimes the ineptitude of politicians (such as their failure to solve the Eurozone crisis with determined, united action) causes a market panic, and suddenly investors move into a risk off phase, dumping risky equities in favour of so-called safe assets such as bonds.

This RoRo trade is dangerous because it encourages people to over-trade and work out a way of second-guessing the markets and the political elite. Crucially, it also means that investors somehow have to develop powers of clairvoyance about the future. In that respect, private investors have the same problem as most hedge funds: no one knows what's going to happen next and particularly not how key political decisions may affect the global economy.

Maybe, though, that lack of knowledge isn't so much an impediment as a way of levelling the playing field between hedge funds and individuals. Perhaps the diligent and quick-witted can look at the same big trends (the macro signals) and work out their own tactical short-term trading strategy.

If that's the case, what big moves should you be looking for that may profoundly change the global financial markets? Five big trends suggest themselves, all fairly self-explanatory, and each with its own, fairly obvious investment implication:

- ✔ **The return of inflation:** At some point the big western economies will recover sufficiently for prices to start rising. Construction may boom, and wages start increasing. More to the point, central bankers may try to convert all their monetary intervention into new money supply, adding oil to the fire. When that happens, you may see inflation measures such as the retail price and consumer price indices shoot up. That would be an obvious sell signal for all conventional (non-indexed linked) bonds.

✔ **Japanese chaos:** The Japanese government is running up a huge budget deficit in order to kick-start its economy. This fiscal and monetary pump priming has resulted in a massive expansion of the Japanese state debt, to more than 200 per cent of GDP. At the moment that deficit is being funded by Japanese savers but as soon as Japan starts running up a current account deficit – and no more new local Japanese bond buyers emerge – its government has to start thinking about funding its requirements from external investors. These investors are presumably going to want higher interest rates, which would cripple local budgets. That would prompt a possible run on Japanese state bonds and a sudden sharp decline in the value of the Japanese yen relative to the dollar.

✔ **Recovery in the US housing market:** Eventually the US housing market will bottom out, with prices in key regions stabilising and then even increasing. If and when this happens, the result may be in a boost for US consumer confidence, renewed levels of personal borrowing and more new home-construction starts. That would be good news for US house-building shares, good news for China as the US consumer starts spending again and good news for the US dollar.

✔ **China rising:** As China continues to expand its consumer economy, local inflation rates must remain at elevated levels. Eventually Chinese consumers are going to choose to spend more of their money on local consumer goods and interest rates will start to rise: good news for local Chinese shares and the renminbi currency.

✔ **Panic about the US's dominant economic status:** The US housing market may recover but many investors remain hugely worried about the government's vast debts and massive deficit. The combined willpower of the US political elite may work out a way to combat this massive debt mountain, but a chance remains that debts will continue to rise and the dollar start to weaken. Investors may choose to switch many of their US Treasury Bill and Bond holdings offshore, putting yet more downward pressure on the US dollar and encouraging a panic about the dollar's strength. This currency depreciation may push local inflation rates up and cause a sudden increase in interest rates. A massive bonds sell off would then occur and the US recession lurch into a deep recession.

Part V
Tools of the Trade: Useful Instruments

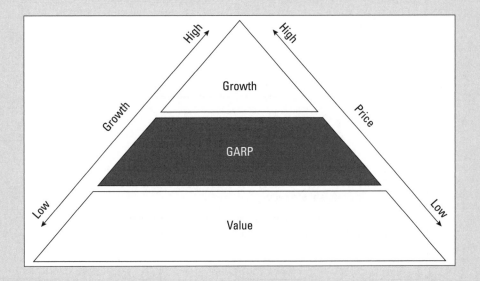

Part IV

Tools of the Trade:
Useful Instruments

In this part . . .

✔ Want to hear about the next big investing idea? Read on to find out about ETFs and how these funds can cut costs and simplify your investment strategy.

✔ Learn about spread-betting techniques and CFDs and be confident about the pros and cons of both practices.

Chapter 16

Following Indices: Exchange-Traded Funds and Other Trackers

- -

In This Chapter

▶ Tracking a major index with an ETF

▶ Varying the ETF theme with further funds

▶ Increasing returns with other tracker structures

▶ Getting technical with traded options

- -

*T*o implement your investment strategy you need a tool, most often an individual share or bond. A great many hugely successful professional and private investors have made fortunes by fairly consistently picking the right stock or bond. But of course this approach entails some pretty big risks (see Chapter 2 for more on risk). To minimise the risks, you can invest in an index-tracking fund (what I call in this chapter *exchange-traded products* or ETPs), the most common form being an exchange-traded fund (ETF).

In this chapter I investigate this next big investing idea, which is as easy as investing in an ordinary share but with less risk. I describe the nature of ETFs, helping you understand why these funds cut costs and simplify investing. I also introduce a few variant structures – including traded options – and how you can use them to get as involved as you like in the world of ETPs.

Entering the World of Exchange-Traded Funds

Investing by picking an individual company or bond introduces specific risks. Perhaps some of your individual bets go wrong, exposing your limited ability to stock-pick individual shares successfully. Or assume that something peculiar happens, such as you buy shares in UK oil giant BP because you think that oil prices are going to rise. They do, but then – theoretically, of course! – a sudden and catastrophic oil blowout occurs at one of their rigs and reveals systematic management incompetence. Your BP shares fall in value even though your broader bet on oil prices was correct. Such problems are called *idiosyncratic risk* (which doesn't suggest that you're an idiot!).

Thankfully a better way exists of implementing your broader strategic objectives for your portfolio without taking the risk of betting on an individual company or relying on your stock-picking skills. This method involves investing in an index that captures a particular set of companies, bonds or prices. For example, instead of investing in just BP, you invest in a sector index that tracks the fortunes of the world's leading oil companies.

Or you can simply decide that a better, more diversified choice is to invest in a broader market index such as the FTSE 100 for large British firms or the S&P 500 for big US stocks. By investing in an index, you don't have to laboriously buy every stock within that index (500 for the S&P 500 and 100 for the FTSE 100); you simply make use of an exchange-traded fund (ETF).

These trackers come in all shapes and sizes but the essential idea is that you don't buy an individual stock, but invest instead in a broad index that captures your key strategic objective.

Tracking indices

Stock market indices have long dominated the world of shares. Every hour or so the factual news radio stations report on how the benchmark S&P 500 or FTSE 100 indices are performing. Investors are trained to think about investing using an index, and ETFs make doing so easier than ever. You just pick up your phone or, alternatively, log onto the Internet, tap in the symbol of the fund you want to buy and click! You've just bought exposure to the S&P 500 or FTSE 100 index. You can then sit tight holding these shares for the next 5 or 50 years or sell them 5 minutes later. The choice is yours, and the ease of trading exceptional. Plus, the underlying costs of these funds are incredibly low.

Most fund managers charge 0.05–0.50 per cent per year for managing an ETF, whereas a manager who actively manages that portfolio of stocks can easily charge more than 1 per cent per year. The cost is lower because managing an ETF is really only one step up from operating a computer. The fund manager simply makes sure that the composition of the fund tracks the composition of the index. With a little bit of help from a software program and trading technology, this process can be virtually automated. Hence no need to pay for a Porsche-driving fund manager!

Investing in the S&P 500 index with SPY

To help you understand the beauty and simplicity of an ETF, I look at a very successful example: investing in the S&P 500 index, the world's leading blue chip equity index.

You decide that this benchmark index gives you the right exposure to the world's leading profit-making companies. You consider investing in the big stocks within the index (outfits such as Apple and Exxon), but decide that you want more diversification and no risk of picking the wrong stocks.

Therefore you have to choose a fund, because dozens of S&P 500 trackers are available, issued by a multitude of large banks and fund-management groups. You decide (for right or wrong) to invest in the biggest of all. This ETF has the ticker SPY, is listed on the New York Stock Exchange and is managed by huge fund-management company State Street. For a quick snapshot of this huge fund, visit www.spdrs.com/product/fund.seam?ticker=SPY#.

This S&P 500 tracking fund has a number of key characteristics, including (at the time of writing):

✔ Market capitalisation of US$103 billion.

✔ A charged total expense ratio (TER) of 0.10 per cent.

✔ A dividend (paid quarterly) derived from the companies that it invests in; the yield was 1.90 per cent in late August 2012.

✔ Shares in the fund are listed on the US stock market.

✔ Market price of the last reported trade on the exchange was US$141.79 per share.

SPY invests in the constituents of the S&P 500. Table 16-1 shows the top ten holdings within the fund, with familiar names such as Apple, Exxon and Microsoft topping the list. Needless to say, another 490 stocks reside in addition to these top ten holdings. The table details the weight of each company the fund holds; for example, shares in Apple comprise 4.80 per cent of the total value of the SPY fund.

Table 16-1	Top Fund Holdings in SPY Index Tracker as of 21 August 2012
Name	*Weight (%)*
Apple Inc	4.80
Exxon Mobil Corp	3.20
Microsoft Corp	1.80
International Business Mach	1.79
Chevron Corp New	1.73
General Electric Co	1.73
AT&T Inc	1.68
Johnson & Johnson	1.46
Procter & Gamble Co	1.43
Wells Fargo & Co	1.43

For comparison, Table 16-2 looks at the S&P 500 index being tracked by the SPY fund. Almost instantly you can spot that the companies in the index mirror the companies in the fund.

This fund tracks the index and the aim of the exercise is to make that replication as close to perfect as possible. In fact, the fund website shows that over the last year the correlation between the SPY tracker and the S&P 500 is exactly 1, which means that they move as one, going up and down together in response to market events.

Table 16-2	Top Companies within the S&P 500 Index as of 21 August 2012
Name	*Weight (%)*
Apple Inc	4.85
Exxon Mobil Corp	3.21
International Business Mach	1.80
Microsoft Corp	1.79
Chevron Corp New	1.73
General Electric Co	1.73
AT&T Inc	1.69
Johnson & Johnson	1.45
Procter & Gamble Co	1.43
Wells Fargo & Co New	1.41

Market capitalisation indices

By and large, the most popular, liquid stocks are priced 'right' – that is, their prices reflect all current market information – on a day-to-day basis. Based on the current state of knowledge, for instance, Apple shares are probably accurately priced at current levels, although that may change if some news comes out suggesting that they should go up or down in value.

In essence, Apple's share price is efficient (that is, Apple stock trades at its fair value based on current market events and conditions) and its market capitalisation is derived by multiplying the number of shares in issue (at the time of writing, that's just under 1 billion shares) by the current share price (which is currently US$668 per share). This simple equation suggests a market capitalisation of US$627 billion for the world's leading IT company. Whether you think that figure constitutes good value or not is up to you, but if you add up the market capitalisations for all the companies in the S&P 500 you end up with a rather big number that reveals the total market capitalisation for all 500 companies in this index: currently, US$12.9 trillion.

Of that total market capitalisation for the S&P 500, 4.85 per cent – $627 billion – is (not coincidentally!) Apple's market capitalisation.

S&P (the index provider) decides on the exact weighting in the index by using market capitalisation – a simple notion that relates to the efficient market theory (which I discuss in Chapter 8). Market-capitalisation-based indices are by far the most common form of index construction (for details, see the nearby sidebar 'Market capitalisation indices'). A few other ways of building an index also exist, as you encounter in the later section 'Seeking synthetic trackers'.

Understanding the SPY tracking structure

The managers of the SPY ETF use a lot of computing power to make sure that they constantly track the S&P index via their fund, plus an active trading desk (where they can execute buying and selling transactions). For example, if the price of Apple declines by 10 per cent in value on one day, bringing its weighting within the index down from 4.85 per cent (as in Table 16-2) to 4.37 per cent, State Street's fund managers sell their holdings of Apple shares to make up the difference.

The key to this particular index fund is that the managers are *physically replicating* the index. So, if a particular share is in the index, the fund managers make sure that those physical shares are also in the fund; that is, they buy the underlying assets, be they stocks, bonds or silver nuggets. You can read more about physical tracking funds in the next section.

Considering physical replication trackers

That physical tracking is the norm in the US market, and the concept of holding the underlying, physical assets is simple to understand, even though the details of how it works – which you fortunately don't need to concern yourself with – are a bit more complicated.

In essence, you're buying into a fund that copies the index by buying the stocks (or bonds for that matter) within your chosen index. As that index changes in composition on a daily basis, so do the holdings of the fund. All this for 0.10 per cent in charges: bargain!

In general, tracking major developed-world markets such as the S&P 500 is best done on a long-term buy-and-hold basis using physically replicating ETFs; they're cheap and do exactly what they claim.

Physical replication is fine and dandy if you're tracking a broad, liquid, well-known index such as the S&P 500, where tens of thousands of professional institutions operate on a real-time basis.

But some indices aren't as liquid or efficient. In the following sections, I look at the complications and errors that can occur with specialised indices. (***Note:*** Although these types of issues can happen with all indices, it's a bigger problem with more specialised indices.)

Complications related to specialised indices

Unlike general indices, specialised indices may track, for instance, Indian shares or a specialised sector of the US mainstream equity space such as small-cap US stocks that pay a high yield. Within these specialised indices all manner of complications arise, including:

- ✔ A small number of underlying stocks.

- ✔ More illiquid stocks, with wider bid–offer spreads.

- ✔ An illiquid market that hampers the fund manager's ability to buy the underlying stocks.

- ✔ Varying tax treatment of dividends, depending on the tax jurisdiction (check out the later section 'Thinking about tax for total returns').

So physically tracking a specialist index can be a tad more complicated than tracking the S&P 500. This needn't prevent a fund provider from setting up an ETF, but their management costs may be a little higher.

Index tracking errors

Tracking errors can also emerge, which involve a discrepancy between the returns from the underlying index against the returns from the fund. Tracking errors can amount to as much as 1.5 per cent a year. They may emerge for a whole bunch of reasons, not least those bigger management fees, and their effects can be drastic. You may think that your ETF is tracking an index and should return 5 per cent this year, but in fact the fund returns only 3.5 per cent. So the tracking error is 1.5 per cent. For more on tracking errors, check out the later section 'Knowing the risks'.

Seeking synthetic trackers

The risks of physical-replicating ETFs that I describe in the preceding section have caused people to create an alternative fund, called the *synthetic tracker fund*. In essence, this features just one crucial change from a physical replicating fund. A synthetic tracker fund following the S&P 500 does everything the same as the conventional index tracker in the earlier section 'Considering physical replication trackers', but its core holdings aren't the stocks inside the index but instead what's essentially an IOU.

The issuer may be a large investment bank that already holds all those stocks within the S&P 500 as part of its normal trading portfolio. The bank's trading desk simply issues an IOU to the fund, which says that they promise to pay out on the return from investing in the index. As collateral they issue what's called a *swap* (a kind of complicated IOU wrapped up within a contract), which is that promise measured against the return from the index as well as collateral to back-up the promise. That collateral can come in many different shapes and sizes and be whatever stock they hold within their portfolio at the time.

Imagine that a synthetic tracker is following the S&P 500 over the next year. The ETF fund starts with a market capitalisation of US$100 million when the S&P 500 index is at 1,400. One year later the index has gone up 10 per cent and the index level is now 1,540. The fund should now be valued at $110 million.

Behind the scenes the value of the swap and the associated collateral backing up this return has simply increased from a total of $100 million (probably comprising $90 million in collateral and a $10 million swap contract) to $110 million ($99 million in collateral and $11 million swap contract). The beauty of this synthetic tracking is that no tracking error whatsoever need exist and the issuer can also underwrite to pay out the total net return including dividends (after tax has been accounted for). Costs may also be substantially lower as a result and crucially this synthetic swap is very efficient in dealing with less liquid markets.

Less developed markets and alternative asset classes are best tracked using synthetic ETPs.

The downside of a synthetic tracker is immediately obvious: as the investor, you're taking a risk with that IOU. In essence you're gambling on the credit worthiness of the bank issuer, which introduces the concept of *counterparty risk*, the risk that the counterparty (in this case the bank) will not live up to its contractual obligations. The bank does its very best to mitigate that risk for you by offering up that collateral, and regulators probably force the bank and the issuer to limit that exposure to the swap contract to 10 per cent (at most) of the value of the fund.

But you can't get away from the fact that you're taking a risk. As an investor you need to balance the potential reward of lower tracking errors, access to new markets and lower expenses against the counterparty risk.

Knowing the risks

The debate between physical and synthetic tracking has become heated in recent years and many investors have what can seem like an irrational distrust of synthetic ETFs. Pros and cons exist for both forms of tracking: you simply need to understand the risks and make a considered judgement. To help you weigh up whether ETFs are for you, check out Table 16-3.

Table 16-3	Advantages and Disadvantages of ETFs
Advantages	*Disadvantages*
Cheap	Substantial trading costs: that is, dealing charges and bid-offer spread (the latter can be over 1 per cent)
Liquid and easy to trade – continuous pricing during the day	Can trade at a discount or premium to net asset value, which can eat into your gains if you buy at a premium, for example, that disappears by the time you're ready to sell
Can be shorted and leveraged to increase returns	Short track record of many funds, making it difficult to evaluate whether the fund has been historically successful
Huge choice and access to a wide range of indices; that is, you can diversify broadly	Unsuccessful ETFs can quickly shut down
Ability to invest in a whole market through one fund	Not all ETFs are that cheap – some specialist ETFs charge close to 1 per cent, which is still much lower than most ordinary mutual funds
	A tracking error can emerge; that is, a difference between the change in the value of the fund and that of the index

The following sections outline other risks associated with ETFs.

High tracking errors in physical replication tracking ETFs

For physical tracking funds, the most obvious risk is the tracking error that I mention in the earlier section 'Considering physical replication trackers'. When the ETF manager holds the basket of shares (or assets) that comprises the asset, notice that he doesn't promise to pay the actual return on the underlying index! He merely promises to try to track the index and sometimes a discrepancy opens up between the fund return and the index return. Most listed funds such as ETFs manage to keep that tracking error to the absolute minimum, but be aware that some listed funds and many unit-trust index trackers produce hefty errors amounting to more than 1 per cent or even 2 per cent per year.

You also need to keep a beady eye on dividend payments and how they affect tracking errors. An ETF typically pays out dividends received from the underlying shares it holds on a quarterly basis, but the underlying stocks pay dividends throughout the quarter. Therefore, these funds may hold cash – cash that could be better deployed in an actual investment, making you a potential capital gain – for various time periods throughout the quarter, even though the underlying benchmark index isn't composed of cash.

Market risks affecting the ETF's sector

Another factor to watch out for is *market risk* – that the sector or market the ETF is tracking drops based on a variety of factors such as economic conditions and global events, investor sentiment and sector-specific factors. In a big sell-off, investors typically sell all shares regardless of structure – and so, being very liquid, ETFs can suffer disproportionately. When panicking, investors are likely to sell first an ETF share they can get rid of in real time via their broker instead of a unit-trust fund for which they have to wait to the end of the day to establish a proper pricing level.

'Hidden' costs in expensive or exotic ETFs

You also need to be careful of expensive ETFs and even more exotic indices. The reality is that not all ETFs are created equal. Market-leading ETFs may quote wonderfully low expense ratios in their blurb, but a more detailed analysis of the market may reveal huge variations in costs.

A study by the US-based American Association of Individual Investors (AAII) identified expense ratios for 281 of the 299 funds in the US market in 2006. Of these 281 funds, 35 had an expense ratio of between 0–0.22 per cent; 130, 0.21–0.5 per cent; and 96, 0.51–0.75 per cent. More alarmingly, 14 funds had expense ratios above 0.75 per cent – which is an awfully high charge for what should be a simple exercise in tracking a major market.

Risks associated with stocklending

If you invest in a physical tracker you can probably be confident that your counterparty risk is very low; after all, your fund manager owns the big basket of shares you're tracking. But you do need to be aware of a risk based around the activity of stocklending. Those physical baskets of liquid assets represent a real opportunity for ETF specialists (such as, in this section, iShares), and *stocklending* is when they lend out the share and bond certificates for limited periods of time to external organisations who want to borrow them.

The borrowers are likely to be hedge funds or bank-trading desks with a particular view on a company (bearish or bullish) and want to make a quick profit by speculating on stocks and bonds they don't own. The borrower of stocks and bonds in an iShares ETF portfolio obviously has to pay a fee for the duration of the loan. It also lodges collateral, which in nearly all cases amounts to more than 100 per cent of the value of the loan and, in some isolated cases, can amount to as much as 145 per cent of the value of the loan.

iShares openly discloses on its websites how it manages the stocklending programme (look under the Securities Lending tab on each fund page at www. ishares.com). For instance, its FTSE 250 ETF at the beginning of December 2011 lent out 91 per cent of its shares by value of the fund.

iShare's investors can also download a spreadsheet that shows the collateral it receives in return – Table 16-4 shows the collateral offered up by borrowers using shares from the FTSE 100 index. In December 2012 that collateral in the FTSE 100 tracker included shares in American tobacco group Philip Morris, giant consulting group Accenture and asset manager Invesco. As you can see, average collateralisation is about 112 per cent of the value of the shares loaned. In addition, fund custodians want some diversified risk for lending out more speculative FTSE 100 large-cap stocks. In return, over the last year, the fund earned 0.01 per cent in fees, 60 per cent of which finds its way back into the fund via a lower total expense ratio (TER).

Table 16-4   Stocklending Activity for iShares FTSE 100 ETF (at 15 December 2012)

Security Name	Security Country	Security Weight (%)
Philip Morris International	United States	9.692
Accenture PLC – CL A	United States	7.331
Mastercard Inc – Class A	United States	6.873
Invesco Ltd	United States	5.314
Stanley Black & Decker Inc	United States	4.006

The risk with stocklending is that, if markets freeze up and borrowers start a scramble for liquidity, passive fund managers (those who invest according to a predetermined strategy) operating extensive stocklending programmes can find themselves in trouble, not least in liquidity terms as they try to unwind their collateral portfolios. But outfits such as iShares are very careful about the collateral they accept in return for lending out their fund portfolios, and in many cases they make a deliberate effort to over-collateralise the risk exposure.

The extreme concern is that volatile markets impact massively on the value of that collateral. Stocklending is monitored on a daily basis but sudden moves in value can happen so quickly that the fund custodians are unable to adjust the collateral backing fully, leaving investors in the fund potentially losing all their capital.

ETFs that track indices that nobody uses

Remember to be wary about the index that's being tracked. As competition intensifies in the ETP sector generally and in ETFs specifically, more suppliers are turning to highly specialised indices, which is no problem unless disreputable indices end up emerging.

In recent years, for instance, research firms have launched all manner of complex indices that track hedge-fund strategies – clever stuff perhaps, but not really the same as tracking the bog standard FTSE 100. If you aren't careful you can end up tracking an index no one uses or cares about or that has no real economic value.

Getting in on the action

If you're wondering who's using these new-fangled ETFs, the answer is everyone! The ETF revolution is truly global – new providers are springing up in almost every part of the developed world and ETFs are even threatening to invade the developing world with launches in places as varied as Botswana and Taiwan.

Gauging just how successful this index-tracking revolution has become is fairly straightforward, because many of the leading ETF issuers such as iShares and Deutsche Bank (through its DB X trackers unit) closely monitor the market, attempting to spot key trends and generally keeping a watchful eye on liquidity on exchange.

Booming ETFs!

At the end of June 2011, analysts at Deutsche estimated that the global index-tracking industry had reached assets under management of US$1.4 trillion globally, with 22 per cent (€216.4 billion) concentrated in European-listed funds. Over the most recent ten-year period, the European ETF industry grew (in measuring assets) 13-fold (13.2x), the US ETF market grew over 6-fold (6.5x) and the Asian ETF market grew over 2-fold (2.6x). These numbers represent extraordinary growth because ETFs were virtually nonexistent in Europe at the beginning of the twenty-first century and even in the US they were a tiny niche. Now ETFs are arguably the fastest growing part of the whole global asset-management business.

At the end of December 2011, the Deutsche analysts reckoned that over 3,210 exchange-traded products (funds and notes) of some sort existed globally.

The numbers in the nearby sidebar 'Booming ETFs!' prove that ETFs are mainstream and global. Yet most investors are probably more interested in understanding which asset classes and markets are capturing these huge new investment inflows into ETFs. Table 16-5 from BlackRock (parent of iShares) provides an idea of the key markets favoured by investors using ETFs. Unsurprisingly shares of all shapes and sizes dominate the market, although inflows into bonds as well as commodity funds have increased markedly over the last few years.

Table 16-5   Markets ETFs Invest In (end November 2011 or Most Recent Period Available

Exposure as at November 2011 in US$ Billion	AUM (Assets under Management	Market Share (%)	Year-to-date Change in AUM (%)
Shares	1067	69	0.4
North America	556	36	4.6
Emerging Markets	204	13	−14.3
Europe	114	7	−5.8
Asia Pacific	79	5	−3.8
Global excluding US	66	4	3.2
Global equity	48	3	89

Exposure as at November 2011 in US$ Billion	AUM (Assets under Management	Market Share (%)	Year-to-date Change in AUM (%)
Fixed Income	251	16	21.1
Commodities	196	13	5.7
Alternative	4	0	−1.2
Currency	8	1	27.8

Source: BlackRock Investment Institute, Bloomberg

Answering queries: An ETF FAQ

In this section I provide answers to a few common questions that investors often pose as regards ETPs:

- ✔ **What is the difference between an exchange-traded fund and a unit trust?** This is perhaps the basic issue for many private investors. Most of the index-tracking funds on offer are shares-based funds that are 'listed' on an exchange, and thus the acronym used to describe them starts with an E, as in exchange. That means you have to buy and sell an ETF through a stockbroker, who can deal in real time – although a bid–offer spread also exists between the asking and selling price. Many investors don't have accounts with stockbrokers but use an adviser who may not even have access to a dealing platform. In this case, you probably have to use an index-tracking unit-trust fund or an open-ended investment company (OEIC) where the fund is structured in almost exactly the same way as an ETF but with dealing on a daily basis (see the later section 'Trusting in units' for more).

- ✔ **Is knowing the difference between the various acronyms (ETP, ETF, ETN and so on) important?** Absolutely! Nearly all the most popular structures for stock exchange listed funds come under the umbrella description of ETPs, with the main difference being between the products structured as funds – ETFs – and the rest. The latter includes notes (ETNs), certificates and exchange-traded commodities (ETCs). Don't think of these as being right or wrong, just different. For instance, ETNs are probably the only way of accessing many alternative assets, whereas most investors invest in ETFs. See the later section 'Introducing Other Trackers – ETFs and Beyond' for more on these other structures.

- ✔ **Which is better – physical or synthetic tracking?** In a synthetic ETF, the issuer tracks a major index but that return is in effect a form of IOU. In a physical fund, the managers own the share. Nothing's right or wrong about each, you just need to understand the different risks (see the earlier section 'Seeking synthetic trackers').

✔ **Is counterparty risk a big problem?** ETNs and certificates have an obvious risk – they're IOUs by a large financial institution, a form of securitised derivative. But that risk can be overstated and blind investors to their opportunity.

Two of the major ETF players in the UK are Lyxor and Deutsche DBX, owned in turn by national banking giants SG and Deutsche Bank. Both offer a huge range of funds, many at very low expense ratios – investors who ignore this range of funds must be concerned that the French and German governments would let these national champions go bust. Although possible, this eventuality is unlikely – and even if they did go bust, an additional set of protections is in place (including collateral) to protect the investor.

The Financial Services Compensation Scheme (UK) doesn't cover listed products (funds, notes and certificates). If you invest in ETFs, ETNs or ETCs, you do so at your own risk – the government isn't going to bail you out! Note that no such protection exists in the US.

✔ **Stocklending activity – how much goes on and who benefits?** In the earlier section 'Risks associated with stocklending', I explain that stocklending is a perfectly acceptable practice (many actively managed funds also engage in securities lending) and involves the stocks and bonds in a portfolio being lent out to a third party. Concerns include:

  – What happens if the borrower of shares in the fund goes bust?

  – How easy will it be to grab back and *sell* any collateral offered up by that borrower?

But remember that stocklending is carefully managed and monitored. You need to make your own decision as to whether you're happy with the procedures and collateral on offer.

✔ **How liquid is the ETF?** ETFs have become insanely popular in Europe, with trading volumes exploding in recent years. But that liquidity can also be a curse as markets stress or liquidity seizes up. Market makers may choose to expand the bid–offer spread on lightly traded ETFs to unacceptable levels – these spikes in bid–offer spreads can also move around on an intraday trading basis. These excessive spreads also point to a bigger challenge – ETPs of all shapes and sizes are emerging in Europe, but that listing activity isn't always translated into action on exchanges. Many European ETFs, for instance, boast low Average Daily Volume (ADV; the number of shares traded each day) figures and at times unattractive bid–ask spreads, which can nibble away at (or completely devour) your returns.

Liquidity issues also show up in the difference between the asking and selling price: the bid–offer spread. In theory, this should be a matter of a few basis points at most; that is, a few hundredth of a percentage point. But in many ETFs, bid–offer spreads can shoot up to 1 per cent or more, resulting in higher costs. (The *bid*, or *offer*, *price* is the price a buyer is willing to pay for a security, and the *ask price* is the amount the seller is willing to accept. The bid–offer spread is the gap between the two.)

✔ **Are ETFs the most tax-efficient route for my investment?** In general, ETFs offer tax advantages over mutual funds because of the way they are structured and classified. Although exceptions do apply, you pay capital gains taxes on ETFs only after you sell your entire investment, unlike mutual funds, which incur taxes whenever the assets in the fund are sold.

The tricky part is that many ETFs invest in foreign bonds and shares where the home government imposes a withholding tax – the US government, for instance, can claim as much as 30 per cent of any income paid out on its domestic shares and bonds. In the UK, dividends from non-UK dividends are subject to corporate taxes. Therefore, many ETFs sold to UK residents are issued in Ireland, where the withholding taxes can be reclaimed by the fund manager, allowing the investor in the UK to receive their dividend income gross.

As a result, many investors needlessly worry about ETFs where the ultimate holding company appears to be based in Dublin, the Republic of Ireland. Their concern is that, although Ireland is covered by EU fund rules, the structure of the fund may be looked upon as opaque and something of a tax dodge.

In reality, these offshore tax homes are a complicated way to deal with underlying fund administration problems based around tax on dividends and capital gains (a subject I discuss later in 'Thinking about tax for total returns').

Each fund and asset class varies enormously and so investigate fully the tax status of your ETF.

Introducing Other Trackers – ETFs and Beyond

The investment world has tinkered and adapted the basic ETF model (that I describe in the earlier section 'Entering the World of Exchange-Traded Funds'), producing a number of structures built around the simple idea of index tracking via a fund.

Trusting in units

The mass-market variation of the index fund is the *mutual* or *unit trust*, an open-ended vehicle that's priced daily and can issue new units on a daily basis if it so chooses as more investors buy in.

Unit trusts are typically run by large fund-management groups such as Fidelity, Scottish Widows, Legal and General, and HSBC in the UK and Vanguard in the US. No discrepancy should exist between the underlying value of the units and the price quoted to your adviser or dealer. Any dividends that come from holding the shares in the portfolio are distributed as a yield, paid on a regular interval, to unit holders.

Noting ETNs

In essence, an *ETN* (exchange-traded note) is simply a tracker (like an ETF) but where the IOU from the issuer is very explicit.

Many synthetic ETFs feature quite a complex structure of swaps and collateral, which the ETN replaces with a simple IOU. The bank promises to make the payment and your IOU becomes in effect another form of bank debt. If the bank that issues the IOU goes bust, you lose your money.

The advantage of an ETN is that it's simple, easy to structure and can be built quickly. These attributes help keep costs to the minimum and allow an issuer to respond very quickly to changing markets. They also help the issuer design a product that tracks a more complex, more opaque market that can't be replicated using a traditional structure. This innovative structure means that ETNs are especially useful in tracking things such as commodities or replicating hedge-fund strategies.

The counterparty risk of investing in an ETN is very high because you're effectively buying into a bond issued by the bank, and an unsecured one to boot! If the bank goes bust you may not get your money back – which is precisely what happened to many investors in Lehman's ETNs.

Investing in commodities

Exchange-traded commodities (ETCs) do what they say on the tin – track a physical *spot commodity* market price (one traded with the expectation of actual delivery) or a *composite commodity index* (a grouping of assets that represent a particular market sector). In effect, they're close to the synthetic ETF structure (from the earlier section 'Seeking synthetic trackers') in that the fund managers (ETF Securities in the UK) buy swaps with a counterparty, which in turn guarantees to pay out the returns of the underlying index.

With many commodities-based funds, the underlying index isn't comprised of shares, but lots of individual 'futures' based contracts which track a spot price for the delivery of a commodity at some point in the future.

Thinking about tax for total returns

Dividends present issues for many ETPs. The problem, especially for international index funds, is that different tax jurisdictions treat dividends in different ways. Some countries such as the US impose withholding taxes and apply a charge at source. Other countries have an entirely different framework and tax the investor who receives the dividend payment. This complexity introduces the concept of net and gross dividends.

More fundamentally, those humble dividend payments matter hugely to total returns, regardless of whether they're taxed at source or not. Many long-term studies of returns over the last 100 years reveal that dividends account for 30–90(!) per cent of the total returns from investing in risky shares, which in short confirms the importance of dividends. But what matters even more than the dividends is that you choose to reinvest them in the underlying stock or index.

When you combine the compounding effect of dividend reinvestment with a constantly increasing dividend yield (hopefully the absolute payout increases with inflation), you discover that dividends can be the *primary* source of total returns over the long term.

Some index trackers don't pay a dividend at all because their underlying asset class, such as commodity futures, isn't one that yields a dividend. Some share markets such as Japan also yield a very low dividend.

But most mainstream share markets and all bond markets pay out an income and effectively you have two options:

- ✔ Take those regular dividend payments (usually quarterly or half yearly) as a payout and then reinvest directly via a broker or deploy the cash elsewhere.
- ✔ Find a tracker fund that follows the *total return* from an index.

A total return index (both the index and the ETF) fund rolls up the regular dividend payments into the index level; that is, it doesn't pay out the yield but reinvests it. This can be especially useful for investors in emerging markets where tax regimes vary enormously and loads of currency and capital control issues exist. It can also be useful for the forgetful investor in mainstream markets who wants someone else to worry about constantly reinvesting the dividend.

Total return indices tend to be tracked by synthetic index funds, simply because the mechanics of dividend tracking and reinvestment can be time-consuming and expensive. Best to use an IOU from investment banks where that counterparty promises to pay the total return including dividends; that is, the bank does all the complicated number crunching to include the dividend payment. The bank probably has a huge inhouse tax team who are better able to work their way through complex dividend tax regimes.

When you look at an index, investigate whether the total return is net of dividends and withholding tax (the most common form) or gross (the tax hasn't been deducted).

Searching for value stocks: Fundamental trackers

Fundamental indices aren't developed by religious extremists but are indices that pick up on the idea of dividends but broaden their focus to so-called value stocks generally. In Chapter 9 I look at the debate between value and growth, and without repeating the key challenges, clearly some investors don't believe that the market always puts a sensible price on certain unloved stocks. In particular, value investors believe that an investment strategy that constructs an index entirely around its market capitalisation isn't necessarily the greatest idea, because it rewards stocks whose share price is growing fast and not the company with a sound balance sheet or solid, sustainable profits growth.

Some value investors prefer to invest in an index whose constituents are decided not by the manic mood swings of the market but by their fundamental value, using measures such as the dividend yield (higher yielding stocks are a bigger percentage of the index) or a combination of fundamental factors including the book value of the companies.

Taking an active approach to managing indices

In recent years a strange form of tracker fund has emerged on the scene. These low-cost funds still track an index like any other ETF or ETN, but the index itself is based on the active decisions of a fund manager or economist/strategist. These indices can change in composition quite quickly because the rules governing them can be quite flexible.

Many traditional ETF investors believe that these actively managed indices are a sham and just another way of packaging up active fund manager's decisions, inside a cheap index tracking fund. But they're undoubtedly popular in areas such as bonds and in multi-asset class portfolios.

Putting Other Tracker Structures to Work: Geared Derivatives

The talk of ETNs, ETCs and so on in the preceding section reminds you that when investment-bank structurers are let loose on a bunch of initials, confusion reigns! The natural reaction of many investors is to steer away from all this complication and stick to the easy-to-understand stuff. But that can be a mistake, because these more innovative structures are incredibly useful for more advanced, sophisticated users who are willing and able to take the time to understand the risks and rewards.

For instance, many hedge funds are very active in trading ETCs and ETNs. Plus a great many adventurous private investors use more complicated structures than the humble ETC or ETN. Sitting beyond the classic 1:1 tracker (also called *delta one* in the trade) – where you get £1 of extra return for every £1 increase in the value of the underlying index (less any costs) – is a complex world of leveraged financial products called *geared derivatives*. These options-based structures are enormously powerful in the right hands, and even cautious, conservative UK and European investors may find themselves tempted to use the odd bullish turbo or bearish covered warrant that I discuss in this section (they aren't available in the US).

Long-term buy-and-hold investors should stay well away from covered warrants, turbos and leveraged trackers. Although cautious, tactically inclined investors can use covered warrants to hedge parts of their share portfolio in a trending downwards market, only ever use a small percentage of your available assets and operate strict stop loss procedures, wherein you place orders to sell an asset when it reaches a certain price. Both of these manoeuvres can limit your losses.

Using covered warrants

If you want to avoid the risky exotic structures of the sort I cover in Chapter 17 (the most common being spread betting), you can employ a safer option where your risk is fixed to your initial investment, using listed options that come in different shapes and sizes. Perhaps the most popular is *covered warrants*, which are derivative-based financial products listed on the London Stock Exchange.

Covered warrants give the buyer the right, but not the obligation, to buy (call) or sell (put) an asset such as a share at a predetermined price (strike price) on a predetermined date (expiry date). Covered warrants are easy to use and you can trade them through any stockbroker. They enable you to set up a risky strategy that amplifies the movement of the underlying asset.

Your maximum loss being limited to the initial amount invested doesn't mean that these options-based structures aren't still highly risky. At expiry, if the price of the underlying asset is below the strike price for a call, the covered warrant expires worthless and all your capital is lost.

The main attraction of trading covered warrants is the gearing they provide. As a covered warrant investor, you're required to invest only a fraction of the price it would cost to purchase the underlying asset directly. Because covered warrants are geared instruments, they amplify the returns the underlying security provides in relation to the amount invested.

You invest £1,000 in a firm's covered warrant, which is equal to an exposure of £10,000 invested directly in the same stock. A 10-times geared covered warrant moves 10 times faster than the underlying. For a call, if the underlying value increases by 1 per cent, the warrant's value increases approximately 10 per cent. Of course, the reverse also applies: a 1 per cent decrease in the underlying causes a 10 per cent loss of the warrant's value.

Each covered warrant features the following:

- A fixed lifespan set when it's first issued that's determined by its expiry date.

- The expiry date is the last day on which the covered warrant can be traded. For example, a June call issued in February would continue to be tradable until a set day in June of that year (usually the third Friday of the month).

- Short- to longer-term covered warrants are available with 3-, 12- or 24-month durations.

If you're looking to hedge your portfolio or have a 3- to 12-month view on an asset, use traded options on big blue chip stocks (flip to the later section 'Chewing Over Traded Options') or a covered warrant. If you do so, make sure that you think through your strategy and how you plan to take profits and cut losses – and risk only a small percentage of your portfolio!

Short-dated covered warrants (less than 1 month to expiry) tend to be highly volatile and the most risky. Less experienced investors should stick to covered warrants with at least 6 months remaining to expiry, to realise their investment objectives.

When you choose to hold covered warrants to expiry, their cash value is automatically paid out into your broker account with no action required on your behalf.

Powering up for turbos

Recent years have seen the emergence of *turbos*, another form of geared, derivatives-based listed products that track major indices (as well as individual stocks). This stock-market-listed structure offers geared exposure to the upward or downward trends of an underlying asset, but at a fraction of the cost of purchasing the asset itself, even though they move on an equal basis. As a result, small price movements translate into higher percentage changes. You can choose to buy a long turbo if you think markets are about to rise or a short one if you believe markets are set to fall in price.

Like its close brother the covered warrant (see the preceding section), a turbo has a limited life period (usually less than six months) and is listed on the London Stock Exchange; the only UK issuer is French bank SG.

If a company's share price is £1.00 and you anticipate a rise, you buy a long turbo at, say, 15 pence. If the firm's share price rises by 10 pence, the price of your turbo increases by the same amount, providing a greater return in percentage terms because you bought the turbo at a fraction of the underlying share's cost. The turbo (which boasts leverage of at least six times the underlying return) increases by 66 per cent compared to only a 10 per cent increase in the price of the share (10% × 6.5 times leverage).

You can lose your entire capital if your investment strategy is wrong; that is, the turbo expires worthless. To guard against that, turbos have an in-built knock-out barrier, which limits the downside risk to your initial investment in the event that the market goes against your view. The level is pre-determined at the issue of the turbo.

If you have a strong very short-term view about the markets (measured in the next 1 to 10 weeks) and want to use leverage to boost your profits (if you're correct), a turbo makes more sense than a covered warrant (which is better for a short/medium-term view for up to 12 months). Use the turbo alongside short duration traded options (flip to the later section 'Chewing Over Traded Options').

If your view is incredibly short term, say over a matter of just a few days or a few weeks at most, think about using the leveraged trackers that I discuss in the next section (but be constantly on guard for increased volatility within the markets).

Multiplying returns with leveraged trackers

Covered warrants and turbos (see the two preceding sections) don't exist in the US market, where instead investors use an arguably simpler structure for tracking key markets: *leveraged trackers* that multiply your returns from tracking an index by two or three times the initial return. They're an incredibly simple-to-understand structure but with devilishly complex payout profiles.

If you want to track the S&P 500 index and gear up your exposure, you search for a leveraged S&P 500 tracker. Loads are available, some offering as much as three times the *daily* change in the index: in other words, the issuer looks at the daily change of the S&P 500 and adjusts the value of the tracker (at the end of the day) so that it changes by three times that daily change. So if the index moves by 2 per cent, you can expect the tracker to increase by 6 per cent in value.

You can buy two and three times leveraged trackers and five times trackers may appear in the future! They offer exposure on the upside (long/bullish) and downside (short/bearish) and can track all sorts of major indices.

Think about using a leveraged tracker when you believe that a distinct short-term trend is at work, preferably over a few days or weeks, with the market or share heading decisively in one direction.

If markets trend in one way for a long period of time, in a relatively steady fashion, a leveraged tracker can make you lots of money. But (and this is a big but) markets don't always trend in predictable ways. They can be volatile and move all over the place in a very unpredictable fashion.

Table 16-6 depicts an underlying imaginary index called the Globo Index. Over five days you can see two different scenarios at work.

Table 16-6   Different Outcomes for a Leveraged Tracker

Scenario 1: Bullish trend

	Day 1	Day 2	Day 3	Day 4	Day 5
Start level	100				
Globo Index	102	105.06	109.2624	114.7255	115.8728
Change (%)	2	3	4	5	1
3x leveraged					
Start level	100				
End of day level	106	115.54	129.4	148.81	153
Daily increase (%)	6	9	12	15	3

Scenario 2: Range-bound but volatile					
	Day 1	Day 2	Day 3	Day 4	Day 5
Start level	100				
Globo Index	102	105	99.75	101.75	99.7
Change (%)	2	3	−5	2	−2
3x leveraged					
Start level	100				
End of day level	106	115.54	98.29	104.1874	97.93
Daily increase (%)	6	9	−15	6	−6

Scenario 1: Understanding the effect of compounding

In Scenario 1, bullish markets are trending upwards. You buy a 3x long leveraged tracker providing three times the daily gains of the Globo.

The index starts at a level of 100 at 8:30 a.m. on day one and finishes the week 15.8 per cent higher. The 3x leveraged tracker ends the week with a 54 per cent gain, not the 45 per cent profit you may first think if you were to add up the week's gains in the unleveraged tracker (2 + 3 + 4 + 5 + 1 = 15) and multiply by 3). The 54 per cent gain is the result of compounding, whereby lots of small daily changes keep 'compounding up' on top of each other. Bear in mind that this fund tracks the daily returns and that the trend upwards has been fairly volatile. Obviously a 3x leveraged *short* would perform in almost exactly the opposite way and lose you 54 per cent of your money.

Scenario 2: Going pear-shaped

Scenario 2 in Table 16-6 shows what happens if the index essentially goes nowhere and finishes the week near to where it starts; it's range-bound but very volatile along the way! A straight 1:1 tracker ends at a price of 99.7 (in line with the index, assuming no tracking error) but your 3x long leveraged tracker ends at 97.93, a loss of over 2 per cent. The discrepancy is caused by volatile prices and leverage amplifying that variance.

Leveraged trackers are for short-term investment strategies *only*: never use them for a long-term punt on the direction of a market. Always operate them with strict stop losses and with only a small part of your portfolio.

Chewing Over Traded Options

Traded options is a form of options-based derivative that gives you the chance to gear up your returns from investing in a financial asset. Although complex at times, traded options deserve their own section because of their flexibility and the opportunities they offer sophisticated investors. In this section I describe some of the concepts and terms you need to know.

A traded (or listed) option relates to an underlying ordinary share, such as in Exxon or BP. The option refers to the underlying quantity of ordinary shares to which your option applies. Most UK equity options contracts deal in 1,000 shares whereas US options are usually in 100 shares. An option is always priced in points or, as many refer to them, *ticks*. The point value is then multiplied by how many shares the option is on.

Putting and calling options

Options come in two main forms, especially for equity-based options:

- ✔ **Call options** give the holder the right, but not the obligation, to buy a fixed number of shares of the underlying stock at a fixed price within a fixed period of time. In general, a call option rises in value when the asset on which it's optioned (an ordinary share) increases in value.

- ✔ **Put options** give the holder the right, but not the obligation, to sell a fixed number of shares of the underlying stock at a fixed price within a fixed period of time. Put options *generally* rise in value when the underlying asset falls in price.

Accepting that options can be complicated

The pricing of options is a relatively complicated task, with lots of Greek terms and complex equations. But as an investor you need to understand just three simple but hugely important facts of options life:

- ✔ **They're a wasting asset; in other words, their value is dependent upon the time scale over which they're held.** All options expire at some stage in the future, and so they have value only for a set period of time. *Wasting asset* indicates that the price can decrease or waste away the closer it gets to its expiration date.

Whatever you do, don't sit tight holding a bunch of options over many months expecting those assets to retain their value regardless of the time over which they're held.

✔ **No simple linear relationship exists between the change in price of the underlying asset and the price of the option.** Imagine that BP shares go up by 30 per cent over a three-month period and you're forecasting – based on a licked thumb in the air and good luck – a 3:1 ratio between the ordinary share price and the option. In these circumstances don't expect the options to rise by 90 per cent in value. Options pricing is complex and the time over which you hold them really, really matters!

✔ **Options are hugely impacted by volatility.** If markets are very volatile, issuers of options are worried that their geared options may be extremely volatile in terms of pricing. That means they increase the value they charge for their options contracts. If by contrast volatility is low, pricing may fall.

Seeing the basic option terms in practice

Although options trading uses many complicated terms, the basics are relatively simple. Three terms matter more than anything else:

✔ **Premium:** The value of an option and what the buyer pays or the seller receives.

✔ **Strike price:** The price at which the underlying product will be exchanged.

✔ **Expiry:** The date the option expires.

Luckily the same terminology applies to call and put options. Imagine that you're about to buy an HSBC (ordinary shares priced at £5.57) September £5.40 call, priced at £0.24. In this case the premium price is 24 pence and the strike price is £5.40. The expiry is the 3rd week of September (most options expire on the 3rd Friday of the month).

By contrast, a Royal Dutch Shell (ordinary shares priced at £23.09) September £23.00 *put*, priced at £0.345, means that the premium for this option is £0.345 with a strike price of £23.00. The expiry is again the 3rd week of September.

Appreciating the pretty options chain

On any one day literally hundreds of different calls and put options are available on a traded or listed options market, all with vastly different prices per contract. To make sense of them, markets construct an *equity options chain*. This table contains all these different prices, durations and choices on one simple screen – like everyone else, options traders want to be able to see the whole range of individual contracts on one screen!

These options chain tables can contain many different features, including:

✔ Different months for different series of options, for puts and calls.

✔ Options issued, mainly for the very largest companies, on the FTSE 100 or S&P 500.

✔ Option strike price.

✔ Prices of the underlying ordinary shares.

Pricing options

The two crucial elements in the pricing of an option are intrinsic and time values:

✔ **Intrinsic value** is the amount of money an option is worth if it were exercised and turned into shares today. Therefore, it's the difference between the underlying security and the option's strike price.

Using the HSBC September £5.40 call as an example, if the underlying HSBC shares trade at any price above £5.40 the call option is worth at least the difference: the intrinsic value. So if the stock trades at £6.00, the option is priced at a minimum of 60 pence, because if the option gives the holder the right to buy shares at £5.40, he can immediately sell the shares in the cash market for a profit of £0.36 (60 pence less the call option price of 24 pence).

If HSBC ordinary shares are trading for as little as £5.00, do the options have any intrinsic value? No! Nobody is going to buy the option (the right to buy shares at £5.40) when the shares can be bought in the cash market for £5.00.

✔ **Time value** is the amount by which the premium (price) of an option exceeds its intrinsic value (assuming it has any intrinsic value). If a BT June £1.50 call is trading at 45 pence with the stock at £1.75, the option has a time value of 20 pence and an intrinsic value of 25 pence.

If the BT June £1.80 call is valued at 10 pence with the stock price at £1.70, obviously no intrinsic value exists in the options and the 10 pence premium is all time value. If BT stock is trading at £2.00, the £2.25 call option with 1 month to expiry may well be trading at 5 pence, but the £2.25 call with nine months till expiry is priced at 25 pence.

The longer the option has till expiry the more time value it has and there-fore the higher its price.

Being in the money (or not)

The next set of crucial terms is based around the concept of being 'in the money' or not. Three different terms describe call and put options. To help explain how each works, I use the imaginary HSBC traded options pricing from the earlier section 'Seeing the basic option terms in practice' (the current share price is £5.57):

- **In the money:** For a call option, the strike price is below the underlying asset's market price; for a put option, the strike price is above the underlying asset's market price. Example: The HSBC share price is greater than the £5.40 option level and so the contract has an intrinsic value (share price – the option strike price). If the share price is £6.00, the intrinsic value is 60 pence (6 – 5.40).

- **Out of the money:** Some options are priced in such a way that they would have no real value if they were cashed in or redeemed at that moment of time; that is, they are worthless at that moment in time or 'out of the money'. So in our case if the shares in HSBC are less than £5.40 they are out of the money because the premium value consists of only future time value and therefore has zero intrinsic value.

- **At the money:** When the strike price and market price are identical. Example: The HSBC share price is at £5.40 and has no intrinsic value.

Only in-the-money options have an intrinsic value; at-the-money calls/puts and out-of-the-money calls/puts have only time value.

Other phrases used in this context include *just in the money* (to describe an option with a tiny amount of intrinsic value) and *deep in the money* (where the option has oodles of intrinsic value).

Understanding the contracts behind options

The key term you encounter as regards the contract structure behind options is *the right but not the obligation*, as in 'an option gives the holder the right but not obligation to buy a set number of shares at a set price on or before a set period of time'. In simple terms, this phrase indicates that you don't plan to take physical ownership of the underlying shares, but are just buying the right to buy or sell some shares.

Options are contract-driven financial products and the vast majority of those options aren't converted into the real, physical underlying shares.

Chapter 17

Taking a Punt on the Financial Markets

*B*etting on financial markets has boomed in the last decade. Many British companies, such as IG Index, lead the world with a whole heap of new innovations and cutting-edge websites. Without doubt, these big spread-betting firms make the job of betting on financial indices incredibly easy and relatively painless. Adding to the attraction, these bets on the direction of major markets are tax-free in the UK, which makes a big difference compared to traditional structures where lucky investors pay tax on capital gains. *Note:* This tax-friendly regime for spread betting exists in the UK for a reason: spread betting on financial markets is precisely what it says – betting, not investing, and a 2012 overhaul of UK gambling tax eliminated capital gains and stamp taxes for gambling winnings. In the US, however, gambling winnings are fully taxable and must be reported on tax returns.

Before you toss your portfolio headfirst into the spread-betting pool, heed these two warnings: one, spread betting is gambling, which means a very good chance exists that you're going to lose money most of the time. In fact, you can end up losing a lot unless you're careful and diligent, which means understanding exactly what you're getting into. Two, spread betting in financial markets is illegal in the US. Although some countries that ban spread betting allow their residents to set up online accounts with UK spread-betting companies, the US isn't one of them, courtesy of the 2006 Unlawful Internet Gambling Enforcement Act.

Which is why you need this chapter. Here I lead you through some spread-betting techniques and approaches, and the closely related alternative of CFDs, as well as the pros and cons of both practices.

Introducing Spread-Bet Basics

Spread betting is a specific type of gambling in which you win not by picking a winner or loser, per se, but by correctly identifying whether the actual outcome is higher or lower than the stated range (the *spread*). Today, spread betting is the biggest and most common form of financial betting. Quite simply, you bet on a financial market with a spread of prices and returns based on the likely direction of that market. For example, suppose that the bid for a stock is £100 and the ask is £103, but you think the stock price will go below £100. In that case you would wager, say, £2 for every pound below £103 that the stock falls. If the price falls to £97, you win £6; if the price increases to £109, you lose £18. Of course, how you actually place your bets and garner your profits and losses is a bit more complicated; I cover the details in the following sections.

Understanding how a spread bet works

When you place a spread bet you have three decisions to make:

- ✔ What you want to bet on.
- ✔ The size of the bet.
- ✔ Whether you want to pay for a *stop loss* (to limit the amount you may lose if things go wrong; check out the later section 'Dealing with the downsides').

To place a spread bet, you ring up your broker who gives you two numbers: the *bid price* (at which you'll sell) and the *offer price* (at which you can buy, sometimes called the *ask price*).

The *bid* is always the lower of these two numbers and the difference between these two numbers is known as the *spread* (so no prizes for guessing where the term *spread betting* comes from!).

Imagine that you've bought a share or are trading in a financial index; here's how you make money using spread betting. The change in the price of the financial asset (the share or index) is measured in *points*: for shares 1 point = 1 pence and for indices 1 point usually equals £1.

You can place a bet of any value against every point change in the underlying financial asset; say, £1 or £100 per point. To close a *buy* bet, you sell at the current bid price whereas to close a *sell* bet you buy at the current offer price. The profit you make is the points difference between the opening bet and the closing bet times the value of your bet per point (that is, £1 or £100).

Meeting the concept of margin

Spread betting is traded on *margin*, which means that when you open a trade you need to place a deposit of only a percentage of the position's total value.

If a position moves against you, you may have to pay additional money over the initial deposit called a *margin call*. The spread-betting company requests this payment if your open positions are running at a loss. My advice is not to open positions that require all your available funds as an initial deposit.

To understand margins, imagine that shares in BP are trading at 450 pence per share. If you buy 1,000 shares it costs you £4,500 plus dealing charges; but with a buy spread bet by contrast you pay only £4.50 for £10 a point.

If the share price rises to 455 pence, you make a profit of £50 on the actual shares (1,000 × 0.05). But with a spread bet you also make a profit of £50 (50 points × £1).

In order to buy the actual shares in the traditional manner, however, you have to pay the full value of £4,500 before commission or stamp duty. With a spread bet, the deposit requirement (often called the *margin requirement* or *notional trading requirement*) is based on the value of the trade. This margin requirement differs between different underlying assets and different spread-betting companies. With some spread-betting companies, the margin require-ment for a stock such as BP may be 10 per cent, with the amount to pay upfront calculated as follows:

(£ per point × total number of points) × 10 per cent

That is:

£10 × 450 points = 4,500 × 10 per cent = £450.

Spread-betting companies accept your cash as a deposit or offer you a credit account where you have a set level of credit. Avoid credit accounts unless you're incredibly confident and experienced and have an excellent track record. Betting using credit is a mug's game, in my humble opinion.

Working a long/buy trade

You make a long trade as follows. Imagine that shares in oil giant BP are currently trading at 430–430.5 pence. As the investor, you consider two scenarios:

✔ **The shares are going to *rise* in price:** In this scenario, you decide to put down a bet at 430.5 at £10 a point.

✔ **The shares are going to *fall* in price:** In this scenario, you decide to put down a bet at 430 at £10 a point.

If BP's shares rise in value to 435–435.5 pence a share, your first scenario obviously succeeds. You close your position with a sell bet at 435 and make a profit of £45 (4.5 points × £10). With BP shares up, the second scenario makes a loss: if you sell out at 435, you make a loss of £50 (5 points × £10).

Trying a short/sell trade

If you decide to go short, you expect the share price to drop in value, so you sell at the bid price with the intention of buying at a later date when the stock is cheaper.

Imagine that BP shares are being offered at a spread of 450–451 pence and you think that price will fall very soon. You decide to sell at the bid price of 450 pence and you bet £5 per penny on that downward movement. A week later BP's shares do fall in price and you're offered 430–431 pence. You close your position by buying at the offer price of 430 pence. Your profit is worked out as follows:

450 − 430 = 20 × £5 = £100

But you've left your position open for five working days (a week) and so you need to calculate your rollover costs and deduct these from your profit. To do so, you take the total trade consideration and multiply it by the overnight financing rate (2.5 per cent + the London Inter Bank Offered Rate (LIBOR) (the average interest rate for lending): I call that 1 per cent for this example. You divide this by 365 and multiply by the number of days you held the position (5).

So if in total you placed an order worth £450, your calculation is:

£450 × 3.5 per cent = £15.75 / 365 × 5 = £0.21

Therefore, your total profit is £100 − £0.21 = £99.79.

Making money on the way down as well as on the way up

You think that the FTSE 100 benchmark index is going to fall in price. Your wager on a falling market involves placing a down bet (known as a *short* on the FTSE 100) based against an initial level of 6,000 points settlement – what the loser pays the winner – at £5 per point.

If all goes to plan and the index falls, you make a profit. If the index falls 100 points to 5,900, you cash in by contacting your broker and closing the position (buying back the contract sold earlier). Based on a bet size of £5 per point (though this amount is usually negotiable), your profit is 100 points × £5, which is £500.

If the market goes the wrong way and increases in value to 6,050, you owe the spread-betting firm £250 (50 points × £5).

Spread Betting in Action

Now you get to place yourself in the position of an advanced investor looking to put your money where your mouth is and get down and dirty with spread betting. This section is practical and covers such essentials as deciding on time frames and strategies, physically placing your bet, protecting yourself against the downsides and ensuring that you're fully aware of the advantages and disadvantages.

Placing your bets, please

Here I describe how you go about placing a bet that the FTSE 100 is going to rise in value. Most spread-betters use an online platform (you can use a telephone service if you prefer, but I think the Internet service is less expensive). Typically, you log on to the system with the aim of buying that index when it reaches a certain price and then follow these steps:

1. **Find an Order button of some sort on the website where you're given a range of options.** Because in this example you reckon that the FTSE is going to rise, you click the Buy button.

2. **Work out what your stake is.** Most trading systems default to £1 but you can probably bet as much per point as funds allow, usually with a minimum of £1.

3. **Gulp as you realise that you've started trading!** When the market hits this value, your trade is automatically executed, although orders aren't usually guaranteed.

4. **Set your stop-loss level – or enter a relative number of points (stops) away from your opening level at which you want to be stopped out.** For example, 100 points (stops) below the level at which the buy order is executed and your position is closed if the market falls 100 points from your opening level. Check out the later section 'Dealing with the downsides' for more details.

5. **Enter a limit sell order as well, but in the opposite direction.** I discuss limit orders later in 'Working out your time frame and strategy'.

6. **Submit the order and confirm.**

With these six steps, your order is complete. When executed, you usually receive an email confirming your action.

Perusing some practical issues

You need to think about a few basic features when operating a spread-betting account:

- **Tight-dealing spreads:** The tighter the spread, the more money you can make. With a major index, look for one offering 2 or maybe 4 basis points. (Wider spreads result in higher asking prices and lower bid prices, which means you pay more when you buy and get less when you sell.)

  As a rule, the longer the period of the bet, the wider the spread and the more the broker is charging you to trade.

- **Spreads:** They're generally lowest for bets that remain open only until the end of the trading day. (Spreads fluctuate during the trading day, and they tend to be low when the market is relatively calm. When the spread is low, you can simultaneously buy and sell positions with the intent of closing both when the spread is at its maximum level, thereby limiting risk and maximising your chances of earning a profit.)

- **Margin calls:** If you can find a broker who offers low margin requirements that's a huge plus (flip to the earlier section 'Meeting the concept of margin' for details). Many brokers typically offer 2–10 per cent, although margins on foreign currency trading can be as low as 0.75–2 per cent.

- **Other factors to watch out for:** A minimum bet size of just 50 pence on selected markets; the ability to negotiate the bet size; £1 is usually the minimum trade amount, but the maximum can be much larger, perhaps £1,000 or even £3,000 a point.

Working out your time frame and strategy

All spread-betting firms offer you the opportunity to enter orders ahead of time. These different orders can include:

- **A market order:** Buys or sells at the current price.

- **A limit order:** Sells above the market or buys below: for example, if the FTSE is trading at 5,000 you can enter a limit sell order at 5,005 and if the market moves higher and through the order level it gets executed automatically.

A broker may offer the following markets on a major index such as the FTSE 100:

- ✔ **Daily market:** For day trading

- ✔ **Weekly market:** For positions of up to a week

- ✔ **Monthly market:** For positions of up to a month

- ✔ **Quarterly market:** For positions of up to 2–3 months

- ✔ **Yearly market:** For multi-month positions

Dealing with the downsides

With spread betting your losses are theoretically unlimited. Therefore, using risk-control measures, such as the ones I discuss in this section, is certainly worthwhile. You pay a little extra for caps on your losses, but you need to do so to control your downside.

Stopping your losses

A *stop loss* is your automatic get-out plan if a trade doesn't work out. It immediately closes your position when the price moves against you by a certain amount. By closing the position at a loss, at least you're saved from incurring even bigger losses.

Imagine that you're trading the value of an index such as the FTSE. The FTSE can be volatile, sometimes moving hundreds of points within the space of a couple of hours. You think that the FTSE is going to rise, and so you buy when the index is 5,100 at £10 a point. Many spread-betting systems now automatically put on automatic stop losses based on one of two key variables: the minimum margin requirement (which I explain in the earlier 'Meeting the concept of margin' section) or how much money on account you have:

- ✔ **Scenario 1 – minimum margin requirement:** The minimum margin is 30 and the maximum computer-generated stop loss is 150 (the maximum in margin it holds for a £1 position). So the minimum margin required is $30 \times 10 = £300$, and because you're buying the FTSE, the stop loss is placed 24 points below your entry price (80 per cent of the margin is typical).

- ✔ **Scenario 2 – amount on account:** You put £100,000 in your account and run the exact same trade. In this case many spread-betting platforms take the maximum amount of margin required (150 of index points) and place the automatic stop loss 120 points below your entry price (again, the typical 80 per cent of the margin). If the market falls 120 points, your trade is stopped automatically and on this occasion you've lost £1,200.

One especially useful feature in spread betting is a *trailing stop*, a special type of stop loss order in which, instead of setting a specific price as the trigger that closes your position, you set a percentage level. This percentage always remains the same but follows (or *trails*) the price as the price moves. As long as the price doesn't fall below the specified percentage, the stop order doesn't get triggered.

Setting a trailing stop helps you to secure your gains as the market moves in your favour, giving you added flexibility because trailing stops automatically track your profitable positions so that you don't have to monitor your position continuously and move your stop manually. For example, say that you set your trailing stop to 15 per cent. For a stock that is selling for £100, the stop would be triggered if the price fell to £85, but if the stock price rises to £110, the new trigger is still 15 per cent below that price; now the sell order would be triggered if the price fell to £93.50.

You need to set the distance you want your trailing stop away. If the market then moves in your favour, the trailing stop moves in. Always ask yourself the following questions:

- ✔ How far can a price move against me before I'd change my view about the outlook for the asset I'm trading?
- ✔ How much can I sensibly afford to lose on this trade?

Move your stop loss as events change, but also be cautious about moving your stop further away when things start going against you!

Hedging your portfolio using spread bets

Assume for a moment that you're worried by a major downwards move in the big equity markets, following a big scare of some sort. Although you can dump all your shares and wait in the hope you'll be able to buy them back at cheaper prices, this strategy is pretty risky (what with all those trading costs, plus the fact that market timing is notoriously difficult and knowing its exact top or bottom is never easy).

Another alternative is to use spread bets to hedge your portfolio. Imagine that you hold £20,000 of FTSE 100 shares and the market falls from 6,500 to 6,200 points. The losses on your portfolio would be around 4.6 per cent (£920). However, if you'd placed a down bet on the index using a spread bet at £3 per point you'd recoup a profit of around £900 (£3 × 300 points), which almost offsets the losses within the main part of your portfolio.

To work out how much you need to bet to hedge your portfolio, take the value of your holdings (£20,000 in this instance) and divide by the level of the index at the time of the bet (6,500 points). The result is approximately £3 in this case. The hedge achieved isn't exact – you still lose a little bit – but that's better than losing £920.

Taking advantage of spread-betting benefits

The huge rise in popularity of spread betting – especially in the UK where a number of successful companies boast tens of thousands of loyal customers – is a direct consequence of its flexibility. The advantages of spread betting include:

- ✔ Tax-free profits.
- ✔ No commissions or stamp duty.
- ✔ Trading with smaller amounts of money, which can be great for beginner investors.
- ✔ Instant access to a huge range of markets.
- ✔ Ability to go short easily.
- ✔ Excellent technology and Internet support.
- ✔ Unique markets, such as on property, and binary bets, which are similar to fixed odds bets, in which you know exactly what you stand to gain or lose when you place the bet. In binary bets, you wager on whether the asset (or index) will close higher or lower than the current spot price by the end of the day.
- ✔ Leverage, which is useful if you know what you're doing!
- ✔ No stockbroker commission.

Remembering the disadvantages

Just in case you think that spread betting sounds too good to be true . . . you may be right! Spread betting is for certain investors only, and most people are advised to steer well clear of it. First and foremost spread betting is incredibly risky and for tactical, short-term investors who think they know the likely direction of a stock market on a day-to-day basis.

Most statistics coming out of major spread-betting companies suggest that the vast majority of spread bets lose investors money, which helps explain why companies such as IG Index have become so incredibly successful, boasting many tens of thousands of investors actively trading, many on a daily basis, wracking up dealing charges as they take bets on the direction of the financial markets.

The specific risks to look out for include:

- ✔ **Unlimited losses:** Therefore ensure you make use of stop losses and other risk-control measures (read the earlier section 'Dealing with the downsides').

- ✔ **Wide bid-offer spreads:** Spread-bet brokers make their money from the spread; the bid-offer prices quoted are often wider than if trading the cash product. (For details on why tighter spreads are better, refer to the earlier section 'Perusing some practical issues'.)

- ✔ **Credit offered:** If you have a good credit rating, spread betters offer credit accounts. Avoid like the plague!

Going Another Route: Contract for Difference

A mainstream alternative to spread bets is the humble *contract for difference* (CFD), which is similar to a spread bet in most ways but uses a slightly different structure. A CFD is an agreement between two parties to settle, at the close of the contract, the difference between the opening and closing prices of the contract, multiplied by the number of underlying shares specified in the contract. In essence, a CFD is a mutant cross between a mainstream options contract and a spread bet.

CFDs are traded in a similar way to ordinary shares. The prices quoted by many CFD providers are exactly the same as the underlying market price and you can trade any quantity, just as with an ordinary share.

To trade in a CFD you're usually charged a commission on the trade, and the total value of the transaction is the number of CFDs you buy or sell multiplied by the market price. But instead of paying the full value of a transaction you only need to pay a percentage of the initial trading position, called the *initial margin*. The key point is that this margin allows leverage, so that you can access a larger amount of shares than if buying or selling the shares themselves.

Following an example CFD long trade

Here's a straightforward CFD trading example. As with options and spread bets, you have the choice of making a long or short trade.

HSBC shares currently trade at 550–550.5. You think that HSBC will rise in price and so you place a trade to buy 10,000 shares as a CFD at 550.5. The total value of the contract is £55,050 but you need only to make an initial 10 per cent deposit (the initial margin) of £5,505. The commission on the trade is fairly low (around 0.2 per cent of that £5,505) and because you're buying a CFD, no stamp duty applies.

A week later you discover that your prediction is correct and the share price of HSBC rises to 555–555.5 pence. You decide to close your position by selling 10,000 HSBC CFDs at 555 pence. Your trade makes a 4.5 pence per share profit, which equates to £450 in total.

But to calculate the overall profit you need to take into account commission and financing charges on the deal. Financing charges are usually on a LIBOR plus basis, with interest worked out on a daily basis (***note:*** LIBOR is an inter-bank lending rate; for non-banks, the rate is higher by a certain number of base points), and so here financing is anything from £5 to £20 depending on interest rates (see the note on interest in the later section 'Considering interest').

Short (bearish) trades work in exactly the same way as long trades, but in the opposite direction, in that you make money when you borrow stock to sell for what you believe is a high price and then buy it back when the price falls.

Appreciating the advantages of CFDs

CFDs are incredibly popular with many mainstream investors, especially those who deal in smaller company shares and more exotic markets. CFDs make great sense *some* of the time:

- ✔ They're traded on margin so you can maximise your trading capital.

- ✔ They incur no stamp duty (saving 0.5 per cent compared to a traditional share purchase).

- ✔ They represent tax-efficient trading. If you have a holding of physical shares you can sell CFDs against this holding without crystallising a potentially taxable capital gain. Therefore, you can control the time at which you realise capital gains or losses and perhaps reduce your tax liability.

✔ They allow you to profit from falling or rising markets by trading long or short.

✔ They give you access to a great range of financial markets through a single account.

✔ They help limit and manage your risk using stop losses and limit orders as for spread bets (check out the 'Dealing with the downsides' and 'Working out your time frame and strategy' sections, respectively, earlier in this chapter). Make sure that the limit order is one that's executed at a better price than the prevailing market price; that is, for a long CFD trade when the stock drops to a certain level or for a short CFD trade when the stock rises to a certain level.

Using CFDs works well as part of a number of different trading strategies:

✔ **Short-term trading:** The ability to gear up your trading capital by trading on a margin combined with no stamp duty make CFDs a useful instrument for short-term trading.

✔ **Hedging:** You can use a CFD to protect your long-term holdings against variable market conditions. Opening a short CFD position in the shares may be cheaper than selling the physical shares in order to buy them back later.

✔ **Pairs trading:** If you believe that one company is undervalued compared to another company (for example, Barclays against Lloyds), you can use CFDs to go long on the cheaper stock while going short on the more expensive stock. I discuss pairs trading in detail in Chapter 3.

Knowing the risks

Of course, inevitable and major worries apply to using CFDs. As with all spread bets, CFDs are geared, leveraged financial instruments and that introduces a number of specific risks, including:

✔ Profits and losses can be magnified; unless you place a stop loss you can incur very large losses if your position moves against you.

✔ CFDs don't work for longer-term, buy-and-hold investors. Over time, the costs of holding a CFD increase and buying the underlying asset may have been more beneficial.

✔ You have no rights as an investor, including no voting rights.

✔ Overnight financing costs are real and compound over time. Long CFD positions are charged interest if they're held overnight; short CFD positions are paid interest.

Considering interest

The rate of interest charged or paid with a CFD varies between different brokers and is usually set at a per cent above or below the current LIBOR.

The interest on position is calculated daily, by applying the applicable interest rate to the daily closing value of the position. The daily closing value is the number of shares multiplied by the closing price. Each day's interest calculation is different unless no change occurs at all in the share price.

Part VI
The Part of Tens

the
part of
tens

Enjoy an additional Part of Tens chapter online at www.dummies.com/extras/
managingyourinvestmentportfoliouk

In this part . . .

✔ Understand the value of cash and acknowledge the risks associated with it to set yourself up for investment success.

✔ Get invaluable tips from professionals on how to preserve the value of your accumulated wealth.

✔ Learn to stay focused and disciplined when making important investment decisions in order to maximise returns.

✔ Look at ways in which potential investment funds are governed as a safeguarding measure for you and your capital.

Chapter 18

Ten Top Tips to Protect Your Stash

In This Chapter

▶ Protecting your wealth

▶ Understanding the value of good old cash and hedging

▶ Using a conservative structured investment

*T*his chapter helps you to preserve the value of your accumulated wealth, by passing on invaluable tips from hedge-fund professionals and showing you how to make best use of all the available financial instruments. So don't expect talk here about mad growth prospects or ten baggers that'll make you a fortune by multiplying your initial investment tenfold. You've worked long and hard to accumulate a bit of wealth – so follow these tips to keep it!

Welcoming Cash as Your Friend

Surprisingly, many investors involve themselves in a form of psychological self-deception, in which they start to think of cash as an almost entirely different asset class to, say, equities and bonds. For these people, cash seems to sit in a different universe, in cash-deposit accounts and within savings bonds, while the risky stuff is over in the 'alternative universe', filled with equities, bonds and racy commodities.

This far-too-simple division of the investment universe into cash versus the rest produces a dangerous tendency for even advanced investors to bet everything they have within the 'investment' half of their portfolio, going 100 per cent long bonds or equities with hardly a pound of cash in sight.

This approach is a big mistake. Cash is just another asset class, and at some points in the market and investment cycle it suddenly becomes attractive.

Cash has two very big advantages over riskier alternatives:

✔ Cash contains enormous *optionality value*, which simply means that a cash reserve gives you lots of options about what to do with the money. In particular, many investors look to increase their cash levels even as markets are increasing in value. This strategy seems perverse but is in fact incredibly sensible. All asset classes are susceptible to price bubbles and as the price of an asset becomes ever greater, the chance of a very big (downwards) correction increases dramatically. In these situations, increasing your cash levels as values grow gives you the chance to buy later in the cycle when prices start to fall (the bubble turns to bust).

✔ Cash is a great controller of risk because it's essentially risk free – as long as your bank doesn't go bust. For instance, if you're keen to gear up your returns from holding risky equities, you can still hold a large amount of cash (say, 10–50 per cent) as a way of controlling risk, but then gear up the remaining risky exposure using options or derivatives. The in-reserve cash allows you to control risk in your portfolio and focus on working out where to hike up your risk levels.

Cash isn't always your best friend; it's inherently risky when an economy is undergoing an inflationary episode. In these circumstances, stuffing your mattress with fivers may be the worst idea because all those crisp notes will devalue over a relatively short period of time if inflation starts shooting past 20 or even 30 per cent a year.

Hedging, Hedging, Hedging

Conviction in a great investment idea is all fine and dandy, but remember that risk and return go hand in hand. If you think that you have a wizzo way of making a large fortune by betting big on a concentrated investment, be aware that you may be (and in fact probably are) wrong. If you're mistaken and that big bet goes wrong, you can lose everything. So make sure that at the very least you consider hedging a major position.

Two particular forms of hedge stand out:

✔ **Taking an idiosyncratic risk (a generous term!):** That is, you take an individual decision to focus on a particular stock or bond because you think that a very special situation is about to unfold (such as a company becoming a target for some acquirer). In this circumstance, consider hedging away some of the downside risk by *shorting* (making money from a decline in the price) an equivalent stock in the same sector. Or maybe choose to sell some puts in your main position. (A *put* is a type of option that you have the right to sell at an agreed upon price by a certain date.)

✔ **Investing only a relatively small amount of money in your big position:** That is, you leverage up your potential for returns while keeping a large amount of income-producing cash as a hedge.

Also think about the systematic risks involved in taking a major long or bullish position. For example, if you believe that Tiny Minnow Oil Company is about to shoot up in price because of a new discovery in the deep Atlantic, but then all oil stocks crash, you lose money as a result of the larger sensitivity around the price of oil even though your idiosyncratic bet was spot on.

In these circumstances you may be better off buying some overall hedging exposure that protects you against a downturn in the economic cycle; that is, some S&P 500 or FTSE 100 puts that make you money as markets react to a slowdown in the economy.

Remembering that Bonds Can Be Risky

On average, leading government and top corporation bonds are far less risky than equities. An amusing concept of modern financial theory, however, is that bonds are risk free, especially government bonds; but nothing, not even cash, is entirely risk free. If your cash-rich bank crashes and the government refuses to protect you, you're in trouble. Yet the chances of that happening are very small, as is the risk of government bonds going wrong, but it's not impossible. The US Treasury is hugely unlikely to default on a 3-month bond due any day now – effectively it's risk free – but the chances of the US government defaulting on a 30-year bond must be more than zero. Who knows what the US is going to look like in 30 years' time?

Although the US government is regarded as a blue chip, low-risk government customer, other governments are deemed much riskier: think of the Greek government defaulting on its debts, and other countries perhaps being forced to 'restructure' their debts (a glorious euphemism for defaulting through polite negotiation). In addition, history is littered with previously mighty investment grade corporations turning into corporate basket cases with bonds trading at a fraction of their issue price – GM and Kodak spring to mind.

The market usually calculates the risk levels of government and corporate bonds fairly accurately into the price. If a bond yields not very much and looks and feels 'classy', it's probably a good, low-risk investment. If it yields a lorry load, it's probably much higher risk.

Bonds and inflation aren't an ideal pairing (unless they're inflation-linked bonds, of course). Conventional bonds for which the interest rate or coupon is fixed tend to underperform massively as inflation increases.

Valuing Your Dividends

You don't tend to hear clever hedge-fund managers and switched-on investment bank traders chattering excitedly about dividends, but you should because for most modern-day investing any capital returns don't matter enormously over the very long term. Leading investment academics know that over the last 100 years an investment in bonds or equities would probably have given you a very low annual percentage gain.

Recognising that Covered Calls Are for Everyone

Many sophisticated investors hold a core of boring blue chip ordinary shares. They talk about their Masters of the Universe Leveraged Calls on Sterling, but scratch beneath the surface and you find a stack of Royal Dutch Shell shares or Exxon stock. But scratch a little deeper and you may also discover that, although they have these core income-producing equity assets, they also sold away options on this dividend rich stock.

This approach is called a *covered calls strategy* and I discuss it in greater detail in Chapter 3: view it as receiving enhanced income from owning deathly dull shares. The strategy works, and you too can run it if you have the tools (knowledge and a portfolio heavy in mainstream, high-yielding, liquid FTSE 100 stocks) and the patience.

Employing Defensive Autocalls

Professionals often make extensive use of structured investments that use options to amplify any returns from holding risky stuff such as equities. Using options is potentially a very good way of making extra money in markets that don't seem to be going anywhere, except perhaps down!

Used correctly, *defensive autocalls* (in which you receive an annual call return even if the market falls that year) can be a brilliant way of profiting even if the markets you're tracking are falling in price. For all the details on structured investments and defensive autocalls, turn to Chapter 11.

Loving the Blue Chips

Blue chips – big, reliable companies with substantial market capitalisations – are rightly popular among advanced professional investors. They may not admit it, but they like the defensive nature and predictable dividends of these shares (check out the earlier section 'Valuing Your Dividends').

Most importantly, big blue chip equity shares are a great way of taking a position on a major macro-economic theme or trend. For instance, if you believe that the US economy is about to power out of a recession, a directional bet on US equities is likely to be your favoured strategy. At this point, you can invest in a product or fund that tracks the benchmark blue chip index, the S&P 500, or in a key component of this index, such as Exxon. Your bet is that as the economy picks up, oil prices increase, thus benefiting the big oil majors.

The key to this strategy is making sure that the big blue chip individual stocks and their accompanying blue chip indices are very liquid and easy to trade in. For more speculative investors the difference in trading prices (the bid offer spread between the buying and selling price) may be tiny (fractions of a per cent). That tight spread and ample liquidity allows the speculator to move in and out of a position at very low cost, in a matter of milliseconds.

Handling Currency Risk

If you concentrate all your investment activities in one country (such as the US) you probably don't worry too much about currency risk. Unfortunately, most of the rest of the world can't afford to be quite so carefree. Maybe you intend to retire somewhere else, or more likely have a range of international investments where the underlying asset is quoted in a different currency from your default portfolio choice.

This international diversification introduces the very real issue of currency risk, something that investors in countries with their own currency regimes, such as the UK, tend to fret about. The temptation to hedge that currency risk becomes overwhelming and many investors find themselves irrevocably drawn into expensive short-term hedging strategies. Research suggests, however, that although this approach can help over the short term (1 week to 6 months) it's next to useless over the very long term.

Avoiding Too Much Focus on Income

Everyone likes dividends, that's for sure, and most people have also been in love with income-producing bonds over the last decade. Capital gains are out of favour and income is king. In many ways this development is a positive one, but it does present a very real risk. History shows that eventually every consensus trade unwinds and, when it does, it tends to lose some people a great deal of money.

So by all means build up your alternative sources of income but be aware that income is itself just one strategy among many, and that an over-reliance on income-producing assets can eventually produce a bubble with irrational pricing . . . and the inevitable bust.

Protecting Yourself if You're a Risk-Taker

Bureaucratic form-filling often means that professional investors are forced massively to diversify their exposure to make sure that they have a good explanation in case anything goes wrong. As a private investor, however, you're unconstrained and answer only to yourself. And although you absolutely need to diversify and control your downside risks, you may very well decide to be unconstrained and go against the consensus. Well, hat's off to you. But you can still take steps to protect your riskier positions. Here's how:

- ✔ **Think long term:** Lots of strategies, asset classes and trades require a massive amount of patience and nerves of steel, qualities missing from most professional fund managers, but you can afford to take those risks, especially if you're looking to the very long term. If you take the long view, you're less likely to panic at the normal ups and downs and abandon the very position that could, over time, produce the gains you're looking for.

- ✔ **Think strategically:** Educate yourself as much as you can at both the macro and micro levels and use that knowledge to plan your investment approach. For instance, if you decide that your biggest fear is the risk of future inflation, heavily bias your portfolio towards inflation-friendly asset classes, such as index linked gilts and commodities.

- ✔ **Think independently:** Rather than follow the crowd, decide what positions make sense to you and act on those. You may choose not to invest in a perfectly rational, efficient mixture of, say, 50 asset classes, but focus instead on a dozen core investment ideas. If you do, don't be afraid that you're a maverick – many of the best hedge-fund managers made their greatest gains by concentrating massive bets on relatively unknown asset classes and then sitting tight while the market moved their way. But take this maverick approach with a portion rather than the bulk of your portfolio.

Chapter 19

Ten Hedge-Fund Style Techniques to Grow Your Wealth

. . . .

In This Chapter

▶ Focusing on your key strengths and insights

▶ Spending time to work out what works

▶ Avoiding the disasters of the investment world

. . . .

*I*n this chapter I lead you through ten techniques that can make you money. These investing ideas help keep you focused and disciplined when you're taking those important decisions.

These techniques, strategies and approaches are designed to maximise your returns. Don't use them to invest money that you can't afford to lose.

Making Bigger, More Focused Bets

The great investors – hedge-fund managers or not – accrued most of their money (and much of their fame) by taking very large, very focused bets:

  ✔ **Warren Buffett,** one of the twentieth century's most successful investors, continues to make a huge fortune by concentrating on buying into a small number of great businesses where he can clearly see what he regards as a competitive 'moat of advantage' – that is, an advantage a company has over other companies in its industry.

  ✔ **George Soros,** veteran hedge-fund manager, made one of his first great fortunes (allegedly £1 billion) from betting big against UK sterling back in the early 1990s.

  ✔ **John Paulson,** latter-day hedge-fund guru, made billions in 2008–2009 by investing in a range of shorts against mortgage-backed securities, many of which ballooned in value as US house prices collapsed.

The list goes on and on and demonstrates one key point – you can *preserve* much of your wealth by building a diversified portfolio, but many investors *create* most of their wealth by taking a series of very focused investment decisions, frequently using leveraged positions (see the next section).

Using Leverage Smartly

Confidence in your investment decisions is a great thing, but you make serious money when you're willing to gear up your potential return by taking some leverage.

Imagine that you have a portfolio of £1 million, with 90 per cent of it invested in low-risk stuff such as bonds (see Chapter 15 for more on these) or cash. If you're lucky, this lower-risk lump of assets may generate, say, 2 or 3 per cent per year in income. But with the remaining 10 per cent of your portfolio – worth £100,000 – you may find yourself willing to take on much greater levels of risk. In particular, you may invest that 10 per cent 'risk bucket' in a single bet on the direction of financial markets. Your core view can be, for instance, that the equity markets are due a massive correction and by the end of the year they may fall by as much as 20 per cent.

You can leverage your 10 per cent risk bucket on the upside by ten times by using various options-based products, so that in effect you're betting the equivalent of £1 million when taking into account the leverage on offer. Crucially, these options let you limit the downside on this risk bucket to that £100,000 stake – you can't lose more than 10 per cent. If you're right with your big bet your returns can be very substantial, with the possibility of making returns of £1 million or more . . . and yet you've risked only £100,000 of your portfolio. (Refer to Chapter 10 for more on using leverage.)

Of course, you have to understand the downside of leverage – when you lose, you lose everything, and so you can end up losing a massive amount if you use spread bets without a margin call. Leverage works both ways and encourages speculators to take massive gambles on key themes, with most of those bets probably failing. The key is to use leverage intelligently, in small pockets of your portfolio, while also managing your total risk budget across the portfolio. Chapter 10 gives you a few pointers on developing an intelligent leveraged strategy.

Shorting Poor Value

Many private investors looking to emulate the best of the professional investment community sometimes forget about the *short* side of investment opportunity, when the asset is falling in price. They're drawn to see only the upside, seemingly believing that the only way of making a big speculative profit is to make a capital gain from an increasing share price.

Yet the successful hedge-fund managers demonstrate that many of their successes are the result of making inspired bets on an asset falling in price. In these circumstances, they make money from shorting a stock.

As Chapter 3 explains, you can run a well-executed short in parallel with a long (buy) trade or on its own – with or without leverage. Shorting can deliver fantastic returns but you need to understand two very specific risks:

- ✔ **Shorting can go spectacularly wrong:** Unless your risk controls are firmly in place, you can lose an extraordinary amount of money.

- ✔ **Shorting well is a rare skill:** Looking continuously for the very worst of an opportunity is a difficult challenge and may well require even more research than that undertaken looking at an asset you expect to increase in value.

Investing Bottom Up

Most ordinary investors' idea of hedge-fund trading activity is heavily coloured by the antics of the *macro* trade; that is, top-down, big idea investing where a manager takes pint-sized punts on a currency going up or down or a government defaulting on its debts. But hedge funds didn't start this way. They began with a *bottom-up* approach, which involved a very detailed analysis of each and every particular opportunity.

As an investor, I suggest you do the same: start with a basic investment opportunity at the bottom-up level and then work up to a bigger speculative play. Smart investing is frequently about taking a top-down insight (say, that inflation will rocket upwards in the future) and then applying it to a bottom-up position based on an individual stock or bond.

Looking for New Sources of Beta

Beta sounds like a terrifically technical term, but it simply means that different investment markets, spaces and strategies produce different returns. Investors tend to focus on key areas of mainstream equities or government bonds but, as I describe in Chapter 1, many successful managers make extensive use of *alternative beta*, which in this book usually implies a liberal use of hedge funds – or at least the techniques and strategies they employ.

But you can also interpret this idea of alternative beta to mean investing in alternative assets, especially ones producing returns not closely correlated with those from equities or bonds. Ideally, you want to build a portfolio in which the equity component goes one way, the bond segment the other way and the alternative assets in their own, alternative direction (preferably up!).

Avoiding Fraudsters and Scams

If you decide to invest directly in hedge funds aimed at 'sophisticated' investors, be very careful about potential Bernie Madoffs still lurking out there. Very few shocking cases exist of mainstream fund managers running mutual funds or unit trusts ripping off their end customers, but in the world of hedge funds every year seems to bring news of some new scam. That greater risk is partly a consequence of looser regulatory controls – the authorities in the US and UK argue that smarter investors should know what they're doing when investing in more adventurous stuff.

Many hedge-fund managers and their promoters play on the mystique of the trade, talking about clever algorithms or incredible quantitative research that give them an extra edge. But this talk is all bluff and they aren't any smarter than you or I. So always ask managers to explain their strategy properly, see how their portfolios have worked in real-life situations and check how the fund is governed. Look specifically at the rules, practices and processes the fund managers follow to attain the fund's objectives.

Keeping Costs Low

In addition to running focused trades and using well-thought-through strategies, the key to long-term investment success is keeping costs to the absolute minimum. These costs come in many different shapes and sizes:

- **Trading costs:** Based on actual dealing, these are of course a hugely important factor.

- **Bid–offer spread cost:** Between the buying and selling price of a security this can easily amount to a few per cent (though most liquid investments shouldn't cost you more than 0.30 per cent).

- **Expressing a particular investment view:** For instance, in Chapter 16 I note that many hedge-fund managers trade in and out of exchange-traded funds, which incur running expenses when tracking a major index. These management fees can amount to as much as 1 per cent per year (although most charge less than 0.50 per cent).

✔ **Investing directly in hedge funds:** Usually done through a mutual fund or unit trust or via a stock market listed vehicle, these actively managed funds charge fees that can easily amount to 2 per cent per year as well as an additional 'performance fee' (the trigger for an extra payment can be as little as a few per cent a year).

Add in the fund fees, include the costs of running your tax wrapper (401k pension fund in the US or self-invested personal pension plan in the UK) and suddenly the total ownership cost is above 3–4 per cent per year.

Many commentators think that the total cost of ownership (including paying for any financial advice) shouldn't be more than 1.5–2 per cent per year. Anything higher can eat into more than one-third of your likely real returns – an impossible level to sustain. Crucially, the long-term effect of extracting 2–3 per cent per year in costs from your accumulating long-term savings can be disastrous, leaving you with a smaller retirement pot.

I advise you to target net costs of less than 1 per cent per year, with long-term real returns (before costs) of 6–8 per cent per year.

Understanding That Hedge-Fund Replication Can Work

Engaging hedge-fund managers can be an expensive exercise because they rack up annual charges and performance fees. So if you're determined to invest in hedge funds, consider a popular alternative in the institutional space called *hedge-fund replication*. This attractive idea says that people can use computers to figure out the strategies most hedge-fund managers pursue and copy them. The clever bit is that the replication is enacted through an index, which is in turn tracked by a tracking fund, possibly an exchange-traded fund (which I discuss in Chapter 16). In theory, this means that you get close to the same returns you'd get from investing in an actual hedge-fund strategy but at lower costs (typically less than 1 per cent per year and no performance fee).

Obviously you can't expect this hedge-fund replication to be a complete success, because you can't copy the very best managers without being them, but a well-thought-through and executed index strategy can certainly produce most of the return expected from a typical hedge-fund strategy. And the 1 per cent reduction in costs (possibly more when you allow for the non-existent performance fee) can be a real lifesaver in the long term.

Staying Away From Ideas That Look Too Popular

If it looks too good to be true, it probably is. Like most clichés, this one contains much truth. Time and again investors stare in awe at a chart showing past returns or back-tested models (illustrating how a particular strategy would have worked had it been employed in earlier time periods) and see an almost pristine upward-looking returns chart, with just a few small dips along the way. But investing in hedge funds or using sophisticated investing strategies is incredibly hard work and even the very best hedge-fund managers – virtually all multibillionaires – have many bad months and even bad years.

Check out Chapter 6 for more on this aspect and the key forces at work.

Being Careful about Fund of Funds

With so many strategies on offer, you may think that the default position of the amateur investor – with little time to spare on complex market analysis – should be simply to follow the best managers, trusting another manager to find those great hedge-fund managers. In other words, investing in a *fund of fund manager* who picks the very best managers in each particular space or strategy.

This idea sounds beguiling and is a marketer's dream. But two teeny-weeny problems exist, because fund of fund managers:

- **Have as much skill at crystal-ball gazing as you and I:** They struggle to pick tomorrow's winners and more than frequently end up pumping your money into a constant series of hedge-fund duffers.

- **Charge an additional layer of charges:** On top of the hedge-fund manager's 2 per cent annual fee and 20 per cent performance fee, they also have to cover their own expenses. In many cases these combined fees add up to an annual charge of 3 per cent or more. Such costs are simply impossible for most investors to bear – wealthy or otherwise.

Index

About the Author

David Stevenson is an investment columnist for the Financial Times's best selling weekend edition. His weekly Adventurous Investor column looks at everything from momentum based quants strategies through to investing in frontier markets like Cambodia. He's also a columnist for the Investors Chronicle in the UK and previously has written on investment for Citywire and the Independent.

An economist by training, David started at the Economist Intelligence Unit and then moved over to the BBC where he was chief financial investigative reporter for programmes as varied as The Money Programme and Panorama. He's also director of a successful corporate communications company called The Rocket Science Group.

Publisher's Acknowledgements

We're proud of this book; please send us your comments at http://dummies.custhelp.com. For other comments, please contact our Customer Care Department within the U.S. at 877-762-2974, outside the U.S. at (001) 317-572-3993, or fax 317-572-4002.

Some of the people who helped bring this book to market include the following:

Acquisitions, Editorial, and Vertical Websites

Project Editor: Erica Peters

Commissioning Editor: Claire Ruston

Assistant Editor: Ben Kemble

Development Editors: Tracy Barr, Andy Finch

Technical Reviewer: Sanjay Banerji

Proofreader: Kate O'Leary

Production Manager: Daniel Mersey

Publisher: Miles Kendall

Cover Photos: © iStockphoto.com/George Clerk

Composition Services

Project Coordinator: Kristie Rees

Layout and Graphics: Melanee Habig, Joyce Haughey, Ron Wise

Indexer: Steve Rath

Special Help

Brand Reviewer: Rev Mengle